History's Greatest
Conspiracies

History's Greatest Conspiracies

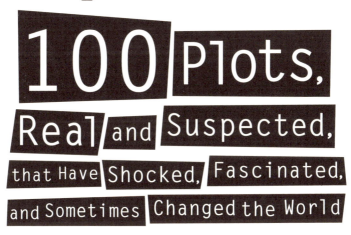

100 Plots, Real and Suspected, that Have Shocked, Fascinated, and Sometimes Changed the World

H. Paul Jeffers

FALL
RIVER
PRESS

Fall River Press
122 Fifth Avenue
New York, NY 10011

ISBN-13: 978-0-7607-7843-2
ISBN-10: 0-7607-7843-4

Printed and bound in the United States of America

5 7 9 11 13 15 14 12 10 8 6 4

For Al Leibholz

Plots, true or false, are necessary things.
To raise up commonwealths and ruin kings.
—John Dryden, 1680

And yet, the order of the acts has been schemed and plotted,
and nothing can avert the final curtain's fall.
—Boris Pasternak, Dr. Zhivago, *1958*

Contents

Introduction

A PLOT IS AFOOT

Throughout history, and almost certainly before anyone thought to write down the deeds and misdeeds of humanity, someone, somewhere, was skulking around in search of one, two, or more like-minded individuals to join in an exploit to change the status quo. Some did it out of idealism. Others acted in anger, frustration, jealousy, envy, greed, and revenge. More than a few took part because they were bored. Some were fools, dupes, or just crazy. And millions of people who were otherwise logical and reasonable frequently believed there was a conspiracy afoot when none existed.

Ranked in order of historical significance, boldness, complexity, and public fascination, these one hundred plots, real and imagined, include schemes that occurred from biblical times to today. They range from Adam and Eve trying to fool God and the arrest and trial of Jesus of Nazareth to murders, assassination plots, kidnappings, spectacular robberies, organized crime, espionage, political dirty tricks, and international terrorism.

Also listed are enduringly intriguing "conspiracy theories," from the Jack the Ripper murders as a scheme by the British Royal Family to the assassinations of John F. Kennedy and Dr. Martin Luther King, Jr.; "alien" corpses that many people believe were spirited away by the

U.S. government from a "flying saucer" crash in 1947 at Roswell, New Mexico; and sinister swarms of "black helicopters" engaged in a plot to create an evil "New World Order."

Selection and rankings are entirely mine.

"O conspiracy!" wrote William Shakespeare in *Julius Caesar*. And in *The Tempest*, "Open eyed conspiracy his time doth take."

The dictionary definition of a conspiracy is "a planning and acting together secretly, especially for an unlawful or harmful purpose." Used as a noun, a "conspiracy" is the group that participates in the plot. The word is derived from the Latin *conspirare*, which means "to breathe together." Those who do so are "conspirators." Criminal law generally holds that an individual is guilty of conspiracy if the individual agreed with one or more persons to engage in or cause a crime to be committed. Because the mere planning (conspiring) to engage in a criminal deed is in itself illegal, prosecution for conspiracy can proceed regardless of whether the plot was consummated. Frequently in criminal cases, especially those involving organized crime, proof of a violation of conspiracy laws has been the only way for the prosecution to obtain convictions. This has become possible due largely to the invention and perfection of electronic eavesdropping devices that enable law enforcement agencies to catch conspirators in the act.

Advances in technology have also produced periodic and persistent outbursts of public paranoia in which the conspirators are not criminals, but governments whose purposes are to keep earthlings from knowing that their planet has been visited, and is being surveyed by unearthly creatures; that powerful political figures are plotting a future in which the world and its people will be controlled through a global economic conspiracy; that diseases such as AIDS are man-made genocide devices; and that the U.S. space program is a gigantic fraud in which the landing of astronauts on the moon was a fabrication.

With the possible exception of murder, nothing has so captured the dark side of human imagination as has the notion that secret things were going on. And are still.

1.

SATAN AND ADAM AND EVE

According to the Bible's book of Genesis, the first conspiracy unfolded shortly after God placed in the Garden of Eden a man named Adam, and later a mate for Adam, named Eve.

Pleased with his handiwork and confident that he could entrust Earth to human beings, God blessed the couple and told them, "Be fruitful, and multiply, and replenish the earth, and subdue it; and have dominion over the fish of the sea, and over the fowl of the air, and over every living thing that moveth upon the earth."

The fruit of every tree in the garden was theirs for the eating, except one. Under no circumstances, God cautioned, were they to eat from the Tree of Knowledge. Do so, God warned, and they would surely die.

The Bible provides no description of this banned fruit, but the poet John Milton in his 1667 epic poem *Paradise Lost* introduced the idea that it was an apple. How it came to be eaten, first by Eve and then by Adam, is described in the Book of Genesis as the result of the arrival in the Garden of a "fallen angel" named Satan. Although Genesis provides no explanation of how Satan suddenly showed up in Eden, biblical accounts describe Satan as a beautiful angel who had believed he was the equal of God.

Feeling that he was entitled to be placed in charge of the new Earth, he led a conspiracy of other angels to challenge God. Defeated, he and his cohort of allies were cast down from Heaven into Hell. Depicting this titanic clash in *Paradise Lost*, Milton sketched a dramatic scenario in which Satan and his chief lieutenant, Beelzebub, hatched a plot to subvert God's plan for an earthly paradise by undermining his faith in his prized human beings, and thereby forcing God to recognize his error in not giving dominion over Earth to Satan.

Smoldering with resentment and eager to prove that God's trust in the new creatures was misbegotten, Satan left Hell and headed for Earth. Disguised as a handsome cherub, he fooled another angel, Uriel, who stood guard at the entrance to Eden.

Finding Eve wandering alone through the garden, Satan observed her gazing admiringly at the forbidden tree. Recognizing a promising opportunity, he spoke to her in the form of a serpent. If God had told her and Adam that they were free to eat of every tree in the garden, he wondered, why was she so hesitant about helping herself to the fruit of this particular tree?

While they could eat of the fruit of all the other trees of the garden, Eve answered, they would die if they so much as touched the Tree of Knowledge.

Satan replied in a knowing, confident, and teasing tone, "You shall not surely die."

God didn't want them to eat the fruit of this tree, he explained, because he understood that if they did, their eyes would be opened to knowledge.

Wisdom would make them God's equal.

According to Genesis, "When the woman saw that the tree was good for food, and that it was pleasant to the eyes, and a tree to be desired to make one wise, she took of the fruit thereof, and did eat."

Finding the fruit delicious, and herself still alive, Eve rushed to share her discovery with Adam. Evidently not recognizing the origin of the fruit that Eve encouraged him to try, he bit into the apple. Informed that it was from the forbidden tree, he discovered to his relief that the result was not the sudden death God had promised. He also realized that he and Eve were naked.

After making aprons of fig leaves, the Bible recorded, "They heard the voice of the Lord God walking in the garden in the cool of the day."

Acutely aware that they were probably in serious trouble, they conspired to avoid the consequences. They "hid themselves from the presence of the Lord God amongst the trees in the garden." No doubt trembling with fear, they heard God call to Adam: "Where art thou?"

As they emerged from hiding, Adam sheepishly explained, "I was afraid, because I was naked; and I hid myself."

God asked, "Who told you that you were naked? Have you eaten of the tree that I commanded that you shouldn't eat from?"

With history's first conspiracy unveiled, recriminations followed.

Adam blamed Eve.

She accused the serpent.

God pronounced all guilty and meted out punishment. Adam would have to work for a living. Eve would endure the pains of childbirth. The serpent was cursed. Satan was ordered back to Hell to await a final showdown that he would certainly lose.

Banished from the Garden of Eden, Adam and Eve left the paradise knowing that they had committed the first sin, and that God's punishment for their conspiracy would fall not only on them, but also upon all their descendants.

They also provided a lesson about conspiracies that countless generations of their heirs have failed to heed. It is not just the misdeed that matters; it is the attempt to cover it up.

2.

THE GREATEST CONSPIRACY
EVER KNOWN

Some may argue that the story of Adam and Eve should be viewed upon only as a parable, not a conspiracy in the true sense of the word. But a momentous plot that resulted in the crucifixion of a troublesome itinerant preacher named Jesus is not confined to New Testament Gospels of Matthew, Mark, Luke, and John. In a book called *Jewish Antiquities*, covering the history of the Jewish people from Creation to the outbreak of the Jewish Revolt (A.D. 66), first-century chronicler Flavius Josephus (A.D. 37–101) wrote that because of "the accusation of the leading men" of the city of Jerusalem, the Roman governor of Judea, Pontius Pilate, condemned Jesus to death by crucifixion.

While Josephus attributed no motive to the leaders, the four Gospels present a complex explanation for a plot that altered the course of history like no other. The writers described a convergence of the interests of the defenders of prevailing religious dogma, a governor's fear of alienating public opinion, mob mentality, a hunger of Jews for the arrival of a long-promised savior (Messiah), a personal betrayal, and the belief of the drama's central figure that he had been born the Son of God.

At the age of thirty and convinced that he had been given life on earth to preach of the coming of the Kingdom of Heaven, requiring him to suffer and die to redeem humanity from the original sin of disobedience to God that was inherited from Adam and Eve, Jesus left the town of Nazareth in the province of Galilee where he had grown up and worked as a carpenter to set out on his mission. After recruiting twelve followers, he traveled for three years preaching a religious doctrine that differed radically from that taught by the elders of Judaism in the Temple in Jerusalem. Speaking to a multitude gathered on the side of a mountain, he told them to obey the Ten Commandments, seek righteousness, love their neighbors, be pure of heart and merciful, and that the meek would inherit the earth.

He had not come to destroy the law, he said, but to fulfill it.

The Gospels record that the hierarchy of the Temple in Jerusalem received reports that Jesus was espousing these ideas and was attracting a larger and larger following. When Jesus arrived in Jerusalem, they became so alarmed that they "assembled together" in the palace of the high priest, Caiaphas, where they "consulted that they might take Jesus by subtlety and kill him."

A means for achieving this goal presented itself in the form of Judas Iscariot. One of the original twelve followers of Jesus, he asked what they would give him if he were to "deliver him unto you?"

Offered thirty pieces of silver to do this, wrote Matthew, Judas from that time "sought opportunity to betray him."

It occurred on the eve of the Passover holiday. Having led a group of armed Temple guards to a garden where Jesus was praying, Judas identified Jesus by kissing him.

Taken before Caiaphas and the high priests, scribes, and elders, Jesus was put on trial on suspicion of blasphemy. Caiaphas demanded, "I adjure you by the living God that you tell us whether you are the Christ, the Son of God."

Jesus answered, "You have said it. Nevertheless, I say unto you, hereafter shall you see the Son of man sitting on the right hand of power, and coming in the clouds of heaven."

Infuriated, Caiaphas declared Jesus a blasphemer. The priests and elders decreed the penalty of death. Because only the Roman procurator could order an execution, Jesus was taken before Pontius Pilate, with a demand by Temple authorities that he do so forthwith.

Keenly aware that some Jews were agitating for a revolt against Roman rule, and afraid of sparking an uprising if he refused to comply with a demand from the Temple leaders, Pilate was informed that Jesus was from Galilee. Seeking to deflect the problem from himself, he ordered Jesus taken before the Jewish ruler of that province, King Herod, who was in Jerusalem for the Passover. After questioning Jesus, and mocking him by ordering him draped in a royal cloak, Herod sent Jesus back to Pilate.

With a large crowd of people looking on, and remaining reluctant to impose death on a man who appeared to have broken no Roman law, Pilate saw another opportunity to get himself off the hook. According to a Passover tradition, the people were allowed to demand a pardon for any condemned prisoner they named. Pilate offered a choice between a notorious murderer and thief named Barabbas, who had been convicted of sedition, and Jesus.

To Pilate's dismay, the mob chose Barabbas—a decision likely encouraged by agents of the Temple officials.

After literally washing his hands of the matter, Pilate "delivered Jesus to their will."

According to the Gospels, the crucifixion came as no surprise to Jesus. His purpose, he had told his disciples, was to give his life "for the ransom of many."

In a best-selling 1967 book, *The Passover Plot*, Dr. Hugh J. Schonfield theorized that the events leading to the crucifixion had been a scheme planned by Jesus himself. His goal was to prove he was the Messiah by seeming to fulfill biblical prophesies concerning the life and fate of the Jewish savior.

In order to do this, Schonfield wrote, Jesus "dealt individually and singly with Judean individuals who were in a position to carry out the various parts of his design. His was the mastermind, and those to whom he gave his instructions neither worked together nor were acquainted with more than their specific function."

Schonfield continued, "A conspiracy had to be organized of which the victim was himself the deliberate secret instigator. It was a nightmarish conception and undertaking, the outcome of the frightening logic of a sick mind, or of a genius."

In this scenario, Jesus had planned all that happened leading to the crucifixion, including Judas's offer to turn him over to the Temple priests. His plan was to feign death on the cross through the administration of a drug to render him unconscious, be placed in a tomb, and then appear to have been resurrected, fulfilling a prophecy that the Messiah would rise from the dead after three days. But the scheme went awry when a Roman solder followed crucifixion tradition by thrusting a spear into Jesus' side, inflicting a mortal wound.

It is only on events following the burial of Jesus that New Testament accounts, Josephus, and Schonfield's book share common ground. All state that on the third day the tomb was found empty. Matthew, Mark, Luke, and John proclaimed that Jesus had been resurrected, and that he appeared to his followers. After directing them to travel the world to spread the "good news" that God had redeemed the world from sin, he ascended into Heaven with the promise that he would return to establish the kingdom of God on earth. Josephus recorded much the same. But Schonfield proposed that Jesus' group of conspirators removed his corpse from the tomb and claimed that he had risen from the dead.

Many years later, Josephus noted that to "the present day" the devotion of those who called themselves Christians "has not ceased."

It continues to this day.

As a result of the greatest conspiracy ever known, within three centuries Christianity had been decreed the Roman Empire's official religion. After two millennia, the faith would claim more adherents than any other in a world in which time is divided between the years before the birth of Jesus and those after.

Centuries have come and gone, noted an American minister, Dr. James Allan Francis, in a famous 1920s sermon on the life of Jesus, and "today he is the central figure of the human race and the leader of mankind's progress. All the armies that ever marched, all the navies that ever sailed, all the parliaments that ever sat, all the kings that ever reigned, put together, have not affected the life of man on this earth as much as that one solitary life."

3.

DECLARATION OF INDEPENDENCE

When a group of political plotters gathered in Philadelphia, Pennsylvania, on July 4, 1776, to affix their names to a document declaring that thirteen British colonies were henceforth the independent United States of America, the oldest of them summed up the meaning of the word "conspiracy." Revered seventy-year-old scientist, inventor, philosopher, publisher, editor, and statesman Benjamin Franklin warned, "We must all hang together, or surely we shall all hang separately."

Thirty-six years earlier at Harvard College, one of the earliest of these schemers had shown his colors in a debate by vowing that if rebellion against the king of England was the only way for Americans to gain their freedom, he was for it. Born in the town of Quincy on September 22, 1722, Samuel Adams was the son of a beer brewer. Although his father wanted him to take up the practice of law after college, he followed his mother's advice and became a counting house clerk. When an attempt at running his own business proved a failure, he became a tax collector. Continuing to exhibit interest in public affairs, along with a cousin, John Adams, he opposed taxes levied on Americans by the English Parliament. Taxation without the consent of the affected people, he declared, reduced the character of free people "to the state of tributary slaves."

Sam soon found himself serving on almost every committee and dominating whatever meeting he attended at which the dangerous subject of Republicanism was discussed. When the English Parliament imposed a tax that required an official stamp on all goods to signify that the tax had been paid, Sam helped organize a conspiracy of resistance called the Sons of Liberty. In the autumn of 1770 he urged the formation of a "committee of correspondence" to coordinate resistance throughout Massachusetts. Among the items eventually circulated was Adams's own "State of the Rights of the Colonists," a "List of Infringements and Violations of those Rights" written by Joseph Warren, and a "Letter of Correspondence" by Benjamin Church (later to be unmasked as an informer; always a danger when a conspiracy is afoot).

Three years later, similar committees of correspondence were flourishing in all but two of the colonies. Among the participants in Virginia were Thomas Jefferson, Patrick Henry, and Richard Henry Lee.

On December 16, 1773, on a signal from Adams, a plot to show defiance of a tax on tea by raiding a tea-carrying ship and dumping the crates into Boston Harbor was carried out by fellow conspirators disguised as Mohawk Indians. The result of "the Boston Tea Party" was punishment in the form of what would become known as the "the Coercive Acts" and stationing of British troops in Boston. The effect of this occupation was to broaden and deepen the chasm between Crown and colonies, and to engender a dramatic widening of the circle of conspirators for outright independence, by force of arms if necessary. Their activities included spying on the British troops. Consequently, on the night of April 18, 1775, as the red-coated soldiers marched from Boston on a mission to confiscate arms and ammunition believed stored in the village of Concord, two American spies, silversmith Paul Revere and physician William Dawes, rode ahead of the troops to sound the alarm. The result was an exchange of gunfire at Lexington, an intense battle at Concord, and a British retreat to Boston under withering sniper fire. A conspiracy that had been hatched by a small group of men had become a wide-open, bloody rebellion.

Meeting in Philadelphia the next year, a "Continental Congress" that had organized in 1775 issued a formal declaration of independence in which the delegates pledged their "lives, fortunes, and sacred honor" in the cause of liberty.

When Benjamin Franklin warned those who signed that if they failed, they would surely be hanged as traitors, the possibility was very real. Never in the history of the world had anyone dared to not only challenge the greatest military power on earth, while providing a list of grievances against a king, but to assert the "self-evident" truth that "all men are created equal, that they are endowed by their Creator with certain unalienable Rights, that among these are Life, Liberty, and the pursuit of happiness."

The only legitimate government, said the Declaration, was that which existed with the "consent of the governed." Otherwise, it was "the Right of the People to alter or abolish it."

The significance of the conspiracy to gain American independence that culminated in the Declaration of Independence in 1776, said enthusiastic signer Samuel Adams, was not only "whether we ourselves shall be free, but whether there shall be left to mankind an asylum on earth for civil and religious liberty."

Four score and five years later in a speech at Independence Hall on February 22, 1861, as the Union formed in 1776 faced possible dissolution and a civil war, president-elect Abraham Lincoln mused on the nation's revolutionary founding document. "It is not the mere matter of separation of the colonies from the motherland," he said, "but that sentiment in the Declaration of Independence which gave liberty not alone to the people of this country, but hope to the world, for all future time."

4.

JAPAN'S SNEAK ATTACK ON PEARL HARBOR

Demonstrating that a conspiracy can have unexpected consequences, a Japanese plan to launch a sneak attack on the naval and military forces of the United States centered at Pearl Harbor, Hawaii, on December 7, 1941, resulted not only in Japan's ultimate defeat, but in the emergence of the United States from isolationism to a nation that at the end of the twentieth century found itself the world's dominant military, economic, political, and cultural power.

The goal of Japan's expansionist militarist government was to nullify American power in the Pacific Ocean and clear the way for Japanese domination of Asia. Beginning by invading China in July 1937, the "Empire of the Rising Sun" envisioned rapid conquests of Indochina, Formosa, Hong Kong, Singapore, the Dutch East Indies, the Philippines, and Australia.

The only foreseeable hindrance to this dream of a Pacific "Co-Prosperity Sphere" that ruled from the heart of the "Empire of the Rising Sun" at Tokyo was the American Pacific Fleet. Japan's military rulers, eventually led by General Hideki Tojo, with the approval of Emperor Hirohito, decided to destroy it, and thereby America's ability to wage war, with a blow at Pearl Harbor.

Admiral Isoroku Yamamoto was elected to plan the assault. Taking command of Japan's Combined Fleet in August 1939, he brought to the task knowledge of the United States, having lived in America for several years. By March 1940, he had devised a bold plan to attack the U.S. Navy, Army, and Air Force facilities at Pearl Harbor, Oahu Island, Hawaii, on a Sunday morning, when the Hawaiian bases would be most vulnerable.

As this planning took place and the Japanese government engaged in the deception of "peace talks" with the U.S. government, wide-scale espionage commenced in Hawaii. It was directed by Japan's new Consul General, Nagao Kita, a trained intelligence officer. He set up a large network of spies to observe activities at Pearl Harbor and map targets.

This espionage activity did not pass unnoticed by the United States. Using a decoding machine called "Magic," American intelligence officers were reading Japan's military traffic, but rivalries involving independent elements of U.S. intelligence services resulted in a lack of communication between themselves and the War Department in Washington, D.C. Concurrently, Japanese diplomatic communications were being intercepted by decoders using a "Purple Machine" at the State Department.

These internal problems notwithstanding, the U.S. government knew that something was afoot in the Pacific, including the likelihood of a Japanese attack, although where it might occur remained a mystery. Despite a warning in January 1941 from Joseph C. Grew, the American ambassador in Tokyo, that he had learned of plans for a Japanese attack on Pearl Harbor, no one in Washington took Grew seriously. The prevailing view was that if the Japanese launched an attack, it would be against the Philippines.

By September 1941, Yamamoto's planning for the Pearl Harbor attack was finalized. In command of the striking force was Vice Admiral Chuichi Nagumo. After rendezvousing in the Kuriles, a flotilla of thirty ships, including six aircraft carriers with about 430 planes, were set to sail to a point about 200 miles north of Oahu, arriving no later than December 5. Joining in the assault would be an Advance Expeditionary Force, including five midget, two-man submarines that would be launched from larger submarines. Beginning at 6 AM, Sunday,

December 7, 1941, the attack would involve 360 aircraft launched in three waves.

Coinciding with the attack, Japanese diplomats Saburo Kurusu and Admiral Kichiburo Namura would deliver a long document breaking off peace talks. The document would be, in effect, a declaration of war. But as a result of a delay in receiving the message from Tokyo and a delay in arranging a meeting between the Japanese diplomats and Secretary of State Cordell Hull, the message was not delivered until after the attack at Pearl Harbor had begun.

Executing Yamamoto's plan, virtually unopposed Japanese bombers spent two hours and twenty minutes raining destruction on the bulk of the U.S. Pacific Fleet anchored in Pearl Harbor, along with U.S. Air Force planes at Hickam, Wheeler, Kaneohe, and Ford Island air bases. When the raid was over, 2,403 Americans were dead, 1,178 wounded, and eighteen ships and boats had been sunk or damaged, along with seventy-seven aircraft of all types.

Had the timing of Japan's war message gone as planned, the attack would have started after the declaration of hostilities. That it did not resulted in Japan being branded with the stigma of carrying out a sneak attack that President Franklin D. Roosevelt denounced in a speech to the Congress the next day as "dastardly," he said, Sunday, December 7, 1941, would be "a date that will live in infamy."

A frequently occurring revisionist-history account of events leading to the attack on Pearl Harbor proposes that President Roosevelt actually provoked it. Arguing that FDR knew about it in advance and covered up a failure to warn the commanders in Hawaii, this theory contends that Roosevelt needed the attack to justify U.S. entry into the Second World War in order to achieve his main purpose, the defeat of Nazi Germany. To open this "backdoor to war," FDR is alleged to have kept forces at Pearl Harbor in the dark about an attack he knew was coming. To do this, FDR withheld intelligence reports while carrying out a charade of negotiations with Japan.

It was reported that when Yamamoto learned of the success of the attack at Pearl Harbor, he did not celebrate. To those who hailed him for the accomplishment, he said, "I fear that we have awakened a sleeping giant." The price that he paid as the planner of the attack was extracted by the United States on April 18, 1943. With information that Yamamoto was touring Japanese forces in the Western Solomon Islands, American P-38 fighter planes based at Guadalcanal Island intercepted his plane and shot it down. Saluted as a hero and given the full honors of a military funeral in Japan, Yamamoto had escaped the fate of several other conspirators, including Tojo. They were hanged as war criminals.

5.

AL QAEDA

In 1987 a hearing was held by a U.S. Senate committee into allegations that the administration of President Ronald Reagan had traded missiles with Iran to obtain freedom for hostages, and then illegally diverted the money to support anti-communist rebels in Nicaragua. A central figure in what was known as the "Iran-Contra Scandal," White House aide and Marine Corps Lieutenant Colonel Oliver North, was asked by Democratic Senator Al Gore of Tennessee: "Did you not recently spend close to $60,000 for a home security system?"

North replied, "Yes, I did, sir."

Mockingly, Gore asked, "Isn't that just a little excessive?"

"No, sir," North grimly answered.

"No? And why not?"

"Because the lives of my family and I were threatened, sir."

Gore retorted, "Threatened? By whom?"

"By a terrorist, sir."

"Terrorist? What terrorist could possibly scare you that much?"

"His name is Osama bin Laden, sir."

As Gore tried to repeat the name, but was unable to pronounce it, spectators laughed.

Still in a dubious, taunting tone, Gore inquired, "Why are you so afraid of this man?"

"Because, sir," replied North, "he is the most evil person alive that I know of."

Few people in the United States at that time had heard of bin Laden, but after the Twin Towers of New York's World Trade Center lay in ruins, a portion of the Pentagon had been destroyed, and more than three thousand people were murdered on September 11, 2001, everyone in the world knew his name and the terrorist organization known as al Qaeda that he had founded. As mastermind of the plan to hijack airliners and crash them into symbols of American power, bin Laden suddenly became the world's most-wanted criminal. His organization, al Qaeda (the base), was revealed as the most significant and savage terrorist conspiracy in history.

Osama bin Laden was born in Saudi Arabia to a Yemeni family in 1957. His share of the inheritance from the estate of his father's multi-billion-dollar construction business was more than $300 million. Attracted to fight against the Soviet Union's occupation of Afghanistan (1979–1989), he founded the Maktab al Khidmat (MAK) to recruit thousands of Arabs to help expel the Soviets. Upon the defeat of the invaders, with assistance from the United States, bin Laden went back to Saudi Arabia, only to be expelled because of anti-government activities. When the same thing took place five years later in his new base of operations in the Sudan, he returned to Afghanistan with the blessing of the country's fundamentalist Islamic government (the Taliban). Announcing formation of an "Islamic World Front for the struggle against Jews and Crusaders [Christians]," bin Laden decreed it the duty of every Muslim to kill Americans and their allies everywhere.

Claiming justification of this call for a worldwide campaign in the Koran, bin Laden felt he had a religious duty to lead Muslim believers in a global struggle against heretics. The main enemy was "the Great Satan" (the United States), because of the presence of its troops in Arab lands. In issuing a "Declaration of War Against the Americans Occupying the Land of the Two Holy Places" (Mecca and Medina in Saudi Arabia), bin Laden saw an American plot to take over Muslim countries and assist Jews in the conquest of Palestine. Aiding

American "infidels" were the "heretics" of "pragmatic" (secular) Muslim regimes, such as Saudi Arabia.

Given sanctuary by the Taliban in Afghanistan, bin Laden established training camps and directed terrorist operations that included the murders of U.S. soldiers in Yemen who were on their way to participate in a humanitarian mission ("Operation Restore Hope") in Somalia in 1992; the bombing of a part of the World Trade Center in 1993; a plot to assassinate Egyptian President Hosni Mubarak in 1995; murders of nineteen U.S. soldiers in Saudi Arabia in 1996; a plan to blow up U.S. airliners over the Pacific that was thwarted; and bombings of U.S. embassies in Kenya and Tanzania in August 1998 that killed more than 300 people and injured 5,000 more. "If someone can kill an American soldier," declared bin Laden, "it is better than wasting time on other matters."

Only after the arrest of a bin Laden operative, Mohammed Sadiq Odeh, in 1998 at the airport in Karachi, Pakistan, were U.S. intelligence services provided an insight into the extent of the al Qaeda terror network, and into its training bases in Afghanistan. The result was the first U.S. attack on those facilities (August 20, 1998). That bin Laden and al Qaeda remained a threat was revealed by a suicide attack on the U.S.S. *Cole* in Yemen in 2000.

Yet it was not until the morning of September 11, 2001, that the American public was shown the extent of al Qaeda's evil.

That night, President George W. Bush addressed a stunned, confused, scared, and angry nation for the first time from the Oval Office in the White House in a role he never expected to undertake. Suddenly a wartime commander-in-chief, he declared that he would make no distinction between terrorists who carried out the first attack on the U.S. homeland since the War of 1812, and countries harboring them. "Terrorist acts can shake the foundation of our biggest buildings," he asserted, "but they cannot touch the foundation of America."

Three days later he stood beside a New York City firefighter on top of a crumpled fire truck amid the ruins of the World Trade Center. To rescuers who chanted "U.S.A. . . . . U.S.A." he used a bullhorn to reply, "I can hear you. The rest of the world hears you and the people who knocked down these buildings will hear from all of us soon."

U.S. retaliation was not immediate, but within months the Taliban had been driven from power in Afghanistan. With al Qaeda's training camps and caves destroyed, the greatest terrorist conspiracy the world had ever known was, in Bush's words, "on the run." Although Osama bin Laden remained at large when President Bush traveled to Capitol Hill on January 29, 2002, to deliver his first State of the Union address, Bush reported, "In four short months our nation has comforted the victims, begun to rebuild New York and the Pentagon, rallied a great coalition, captured, arrested, and rid the world of thousands of terrorists, destroyed Afghanistan's terrorist training camps, saved a people from starvation, and freed a country from brutal oppression."

Although al Qaeda continued to operate, its global network found itself under constant attack, its operations fragmented, and thousands of its agents captured or killed. Like Admiral Yamamoto in 1941, Osama bin Laden had discovered that in attacking the American homeland he had awakened a sleeping giant.

6.

LENIN AND THE BOLSHEVIKS

No organizer and leader of a political plot had a greater impact on the course of world history than the central figure in the creation of history's longest and most murderous conspiracy against individual liberty. In overthrowing a revolutionary government in Russia in October 1917, and establishing the Union of Soviet Socialist Republics, Vladimir Lenin initiated eight decades of a terrorism-based tyranny and forged a worldwide conspiracy that lasted eight decades.

Born in Simbrisk in Czarist Russia in 1870, Vladimir Ilyich Ulyanov gave up the study of law to embrace the idea of a workers' revolution and ultimate establishment of a utopia based on Communism as envisioned in writings of Karl Marx. Exiled to Siberia for five years because of his revolutionary agitation, he left Russia in 1900 to continue his activities in the West, using the name Lenin. Three years later in Brussels, Belgium, a meeting of revolutionaries known as the Russian Social Democratic Party divided on issues of party membership and tactics. Lenin's minority faction advocated a violent change of government in Russia that would be led by full-time Marxist revolutionaries, followed by the imposition of a party dictatorship. The majority preferred a more open membership and a post-revolution, democratic system of Marxism.

Following a tactical error by seven members of the majority in walking out of the meeting over the membership issue, Lenin's group gained control of the party and proclaimed themselves the majority (Bolsheviks). The "minority" (Mensheviks), he said, were not true revolutionaries. But two years later, it was neither of these Marxist groups that sparked an uprising against Czar Nicholas II. On Sunday, January 22, 1905, Father Georgi Gapon, a priest of the Russian Orthodox Church, led a peaceful march on the Winter Palace in St. Petersburg, only to be fired upon by troops. The result of this "Bloody Sunday" was a series of paralyzing strikes. The shaken czar granted citizens the right to elect members of the Duma, the lower house of the Russian parliament.

When a pardon was declared for all political exiles, Lenin rushed back to Russia and immediately called for a general revolt. Russians responded, but by the end of December 1905 the uprising was crushed. Again exiled, Lenin spent the next twelve years writing pamphlets and attending revolutionary meetings in England, Germany, Sweden, Finland, Switzerland, and Austria-Hungary. With the outbreak of war in 1914, as Russia joined England and France against Germany and Austria-Hungary, Lenin expressed a belief that if Russia were defeated, it would provoke another revolution. Discerning opportunity to weaken Russia by supporting Lenin and his party, Germany secretly provided them financial support.

When the revolution occurred in March 1915, forcing Nicholas to abdicate, the result was the creation of a democratic state, headed by Prince Georgi Lvov, with a Soviet (council) of Workers' and Soldiers' Deputies. Lenin was in Switzerland. As the Lvov government continued Russia's participation in the war, Lenin sought to return to Russia, but getting there required traveling across Germany. With the war going badly on all fronts in the spring of 1917, and hoping to foster further unrest in Russia that would force the Lvov government to end Russian participation in the fighting, the German government permitted Lenin to traverse the country by train, but under guard. Arriving in Petrograd on April 16, 1917, he called for the overthrow of the Lvov government and Russia's withdrawal from the war. When his hope for a Bolshevik revolution failed, a provisional government was organized under Alexander Kerensky, with Bolsheviks representing a minority of the membership in the first all-Russian Soviet Congress.

Branded a German agent, Lenin escaped to Finland. After describing how to organize a revolution and describing the means of organizing a government that would be a Communist dictatorship, in a paper titled "The State and Revolution," he told his followers, "History will not forgive us if we do not assume power now."

The route to power that he envisioned would not be another uprising in the streets, but a Bolshevik coup d'état. Back in Petrograd in October 1917, he called for immediate action. After an ally, Leon Trotsky, president of the Petrograd Soviet, won the allegiance of troops, members of the navy agreed to support the takeover. With little violence, the Bolsheviks seized the city on October 25, 1917 (memorialized as November 7 on a later-revised calendar). As Kerensky fled to the West, the Bolsheviks captured control of Moscow. When the Second All-Russian Congress of Soviets opened on November 8, 1917, Lenin was made chairman of a new Council of People's Commissars. Convinced that the Bolsheviks could remain in power only by withdrawing from the war, Lenin sued for a separate peace with Germany. He got it, but only after agreeing to give up vast territories, including Finland, Poland, Bessarabia, Ukraine, Latvia, Estonia, and Lithuania. With peace secured at a high price, he quickly set out to dispose of all opposition. To ensure that the Czar and his family could not escape and become a rallying-point for a counter-revolution, he ordered them executed. Non-Bolsheviks were driven from worker's councils and banned from political activity.

Following an attempt on his life, Lenin unleashed the world's first campaign of state terrorism. It was ruthlessly carried out by secret police (the Cheka). Formally titled "Extraordinary Commission for Combating Counter-Revolution, Sabotage, and Criminal Offenses by Officials," the Cheka was headed by Felix Dzerzhinsk and terrorized the people of the USSR through assassinations, abductions, beatings, and confinements to the "gulags" (prison camps). Its successors, the GPU, NKVD, OGPU, MVD, and KGB, would operate around the globe in a conspiracy to spread Soviet-style Communism through subversion, espionage, and murder as part of a Lenin-dictated "Communist International" (Comintern).

Lenin had come to power promising peace, land, and "power to the Soviets." What he imposed was state ownership of everything and a dictatorship that he described as "power, based directly upon force, and unrestricted by any laws."

Although Lenin was relentless in his determination to impose his vision of a Communist state on Russia, he encountered opposition from democrats, nationalists, czarists, and others in distant regions of a vast territory that spanned two continents. When these resistors coalesced to wage a civil war, Lenin formed the "Red Army" to suppress them. The dissidents took the name "Whites." Although they gained support from Western nations, including the United States, they lacked unity of purpose and effective organization. The Civil War ended in 1920 with Lenin's Bolsheviks firmly entrenched. Two years later, Russia was formally named the Union of Soviet Socialist Republics. It would exist for the next sixty-nine years, not as the proletarian utopia of Karl Marx's theories, but as the twentieth-century's longest lasting, most brutal, and most bloodstained dictatorship. When Lenin died in 1924 after a series of strokes, an even worse tyrant, Josef Stalin, succeeded him.

"The failure to strangle Bolshevism in its cradle," said Winston Churchill in the 1950s of the failure of the Whites in the Russian Civil War, "weighs heavily upon us today."

For the next four decades, the democracies of the West would engage in a struggle with the Soviet Union that Churchill dubbed the "Cold War." Enshrined in a massive tomb in the heart of Moscow throughout those years, Lenin had established a pattern for nearly a century of ruthless emulators. They included Stalin and a string of successors in Moscow; China's Mao Tse-tung; Tito of Yugoslavia; Hitler in Germany; lesser tyrants in Europe, Asia, Latin America, Africa, and the Middle East; and the brutal conspirator Saddam Hussein, who seized control of Iraq in a military coup in 1979 and made it a terrorist state possessing an arsenal of weapons of mass destruction with which to wage war against his Muslim neighbors, terrorize and slaughter his own people, and threaten the peace of the world.

7.

SOVIET THEFT OF THE ATOMIC BOMB

When President Harry S. Truman informed Josef Stalin at a conference of the Big Three Allies of World War II at Potsdam, Germany, in July 1945 that the United States had developed a "new weapon of unusual destructive force," Stalin impassively expressed a hope that it would be used quickly to bring an end to the war with Japan. Truman's announcement of the existence of the atomic bomb came as no surprise to the Soviet dictator. In the most historically significant espionage ring ever conceived, spies, intelligence agents, and traitors in the United States and Britain had kept the Soviet government informed about the development of the A-bomb from its earliest stage, known as the Manhattan Project, to the successful testing of the weapon at Los Alamos, New Mexico, just two days before the Potsdam Conference.

Leading the Soviet Union's global espionage network from a combination headquarters and prison, known as the Lubyanka, in Dzerzhinski Square (so named in honor of the USSR's first spymaster) in the center of Moscow, was Lavrenti Beria. As head of the Commissariat for Internal Affairs (NKVD) since 1938, he was also in charge of the USSR's worldwide espionage system. One of its agents in London, Yuri Modin, reported in 1941 that scientists in Great Britain and the United States were studying the possibility of developing an atomic bomb. Modin's source of information was John Cairncross.

Secretary to the chairman of the British committee on atomic energy, Cairncross was a graduate of Cambridge University and a member of Britain's Communist Party. He had been recruited as a Soviet spy along with other young sympathizers, including Harold (Kim) Philby, Guy Burgess, and Donald MacLean. As Beria's atomic espionage ring was being created, these men held positions of trust in Britain's government and found themselves able to pass along atomic and other secrets to Moscow. Motivated by Cairncross's information, Beria began organizing a system of espionage agents and well-placed Communists and Soviet sympathizers in the United States and Britain in order to breach the wall of secrecy around the A-bomb project. Among these collaborators was a German-born scientist, Klaus Fuchs. A refugee from Nazi Germany and a Communist, he found himself working on aspects of bomb experimentation in England. Sent to the United States in 1943 to participate in A-bomb development (Manhattan Project), he was assigned to a top-secret laboratory at Oak Ridge, Tennessee, known as "Site X." He then joined the U.S. atomic-bomb scientific team at Los Alamos, New Mexico. As an enthusiastic agent for Soviet Military Intelligence (GRU), Fuchs passed along data by means of couriers known only by code names. One of these agents was an American, Harry Gold. Using the pseudonym "Raymond," he received numerous packages of documents from Fuchs to be forwarded to Moscow.

A Russian-born chemist whose original name was Heinrich Goldokitsky, Harry Gold had been a Soviet spy since 1934. In addition to acting as a courier for Fuchs, he dealt in secrets with David Greenglass. A U.S. Army corporal assigned to Los Alamos, Greenglass gave Gold plans of the Los Alamos laboratory complex and a sketch of one of the two A-bombs developed at Los Alamos. A plutonium weapon known as "Fat Man," it would be the second A-bomb dropped on Japan, hitting Nagasaki on August 9, 1945, while President Truman was returning from Potsdam.

To the spymasters in Moscow, Greenglass was known by the code name "Caliber." He would claim that after he was assigned to Los

Alamos, he had been induced to become a Soviet spy by his sister, Ethel Rosenberg, and her husband, Julius. Children of Russian immigrants, they were born in the United States and raised in New York City. Julius was an electrical engineer; both were Communists. A leader of a Soviet spy cell consisting of engineers, Julius used his jobs in defense plants and military bases to steal whatever he felt would be useful to the USSR. One of Julius's friends was another Soviet spy, Morton Sobell. They had met as students at the City College of New York.

Although the Rosenbergs were not initially part of the USSR's atomic spy ring, their recruitment of David Greenglass and admission to spying by Klaus Fuchs would lead to the arrest of the Rosenbergs, a sensational trial, and their execution as spies that made their names synonymous with treason. Although their children and others have labored to prove that the Rosenbergs had been innocent victims of American Cold War hysteria of the 1950s, former Soviet Premier Nikita Khrushchev recalled, "I was part of Stalin's circle when he mentioned the Rosenbergs with warmth. I cannot specifically say what kind of help they gave us, but I heard from both Stalin and Molotov, then Minister of Foreign Affairs, that the Rosenbergs provided very significant help in accelerating the production of our atomic bomb."

In secret U.S. recordings of Soviet communications made during World War II and known by the code name Verona, the Rosenbergs were referred to by the names "Antenna" and "Liberal." While evidence that Ethel had been an active participant in the espionage can be questioned, one declassified Soviet cable mentioned her as "a devoted person" who "knew about her husband's work."

The consequence of Ethel's association with the Soviet Atomic Bomb spy plot was death in the electric chair at Sing Sing Prison, giving her the distinction of being the first woman to be executed by the U.S. government since the hanging of Mary Surrat in 1865 for her role in the assassination of Abraham Lincoln.

Others who assisted in the theft of atomic bomb secrets were luckier. Klaus Fuchs went to prison. Released in 1959, he settled in Communist East Germany and became head of the Central Institute for Nuclear Physics. Retiring in 1979, he lived the rest of his life as an honored hero of the USSR. The central figure of the "Cambridge

Spies," Kim Philby, escaped to Moscow and also died as a Communist icon. Guy Burgess and Donald MacLean also found refuge behind the Iron Curtain and died there. Harry Gold was sentenced to thirty years in prison. Paroled in 1965, he settled in Philadelphia, recipient of the USSR's Order of the Red Star. Greenglass was given a reduced sentence of fifteen years in return for testifying against his relatives. Captured in an attempt to flee to Mexico, Sobell was sentenced to life in prison, but was released in 1969.

In the same year in which the Rosenbergs were executed (1953), Lavrenti Beria was executed in Moscow. How he died remains a mystery. Nikita Khrushchev claimed to have shot Beria in the Kremlin to keep him from seizing power after the death of Stalin. But a Western spy in Moscow, Colonel Oleg Penkovsky, stated that Beria was executed by General Frol Kozlov in the basement of the Moscow Military District Headquarters after being condemned for treason by the Soviet Supreme Court.

Because of the work of these individuals in the complex Soviet conspiracy to steal the secrets of the atomic bomb, the USSR was able to detonate its own in 1949. Thus began a nuclear arms race between the U.S. and the Soviet Union, and a policy of "mutual assured destruction," that lasted until the collapse in 1989 of the greatest conspiracy against liberty in history, the Soviet Union.

8.

THE "FINAL SOLUTION" AND THE HOLOCAUST

Although the Holocaust sprang from the twisted mind of Adolf Hitler, and elimination of Jews from German society had been a policy of the Nazi government since it came to power in 1932, the main method of killing as the German army conquered most of Europe between September 1940 and mid-July 1941 was through firing squads (Einsatzgruppen). Concluding that this method was not only cumbersome, inefficient, and too slow, but also that the shootings demoralized the soldiers who were assigned the gruesome task, Vice Chancellor Hermann Goering ordered development of an overall plan for the "final solution of the Jewish question."

The recipient of this order was the head of the Reich Department of Security, Reinhard Tristan Heydrich. At thirty-seven years old, Heydrich was a protégé of Heinrich Himmler, the chief of the secret police (SS). The task that Goering presented was massive in scale. It would require uprooting every Jew in a territory stretching from the English Channel to the conquered lands of Eastern Europe, providing transportation, building concentration camps, and developing an efficient method of mass killing.

For the first time in history, murder was to be industrialized.

Recognizing that this would involve Germany's entire governmental structure, Heydrich planned a meeting of state ministries for December 9, 1941. Because of the Japanese attack on Pearl Harbor and Germany's declaration of war against the United States on December 8, the conference was postponed to January 20, 1942. The chosen site was a villa in the Berlin suburb of Wannsee (named for an adjacent lake) that had been used as a resort for SS officers. Among the nineteen officials invited to participate, eight held doctorate degrees. All were intimately familiar with the massacres of Jews that had already occurred. The secretary of the meeting was SS-Obersturmbannfuhrer Adolph Eichmann. An efficient bureaucrat, he provided a summation of the conference in the form of a "protocol." Only one of thirty numbered copies would survive. It provided not only documentation of the Wannsee Conference, but evidence against Eichmann after he was captured by Israeli agents and tried for war crimes.

Gathered in the elegantly furnished mansion overlooking the Wannsee, the conferees sipped cognac and feasted on fine food while discussing the challenges of moving millions of Jews in the largest forced migration in history. Eichmann opened the meeting with historical facts of Germany's handling of "the Jewish problem" to that date. Heydrich then noted that in shifting from an "emigration" policy to "evacuation," the number of Jews affected would total eleven million. While some would be used as laborers, he continued, the ultimate fate of all would be death. A failure to eradicate every Jew, he warned, was to risk "a new Jewish reconstruction."

Eichmann would later recall that the conference had two parts. During the first, he said at his trial, "everyone was quiet and listened to the various lectures, and then in the second part, everyone spoke out of turn and people would go around, butlers, adjutants, and would give out liquor. Well, I don't want to say that there was an atmosphere of drunkenness there. It was an official atmosphere, but nevertheless it was not one of those stiff, formal official affairs where everyone spoke in turn."

While Eichmann's protocol made no mention of a discussion of mass murder of Jews, he said at his trial, "Finally there was a discussion of the various types of possible solutions. These gentlemen were standing together, or sitting together, and were discussing the subject quite bluntly, quiet differently from the language that I had to use later in the record. During the conversation they minced no words about it at all. They spoke about methods of killing, about liquidation, about extermination."

While these conversations were being held at Wannsee, vans into which poison gas was pumped in a test to kill Jews had been operating at a camp at Chelmno for six weeks. At Belzec, a chamber that would use carbon monoxide was under construction. Experimentations with Zyklon-B gas pellets and use of a crematorium for disposing of corpses had been underway at the camp at Auschwitz since the fall of 1941. A gas chamber in a converted farmhouse at Birkenau was in the works, but not quite ready.

According to Eichmann, the Wannsee conference lasted an hour and a half. It closed with a plea by Heydrich for the "cooperation" of all the participants. Expressing "great satisfaction" with the meeting, Heydrich lingered and joined others in savoring cognac, although it was rare of him to drink publicly. More than anybody else, Eichmann recalled, Heydrich had "expected considerable stumbling blocks and difficulties" during the conference. But instead, Eichmann noted, Heydrich had found "an atmosphere not only of agreement on the part of the participants, but more than that, one could feel an agreement that had assumed a form which had not been expected."

In ninety minutes at Wannsee the fate of millions of Jews had been discussed and sealed. The result was a "final solution" that included new death camps at Auschwitz, Treblinka, Belzec, Sobibor, and Lublin. By the end of the war, six million Jews would be gassed, shot, starved to death, and killed in death marches.

As a reward for his contribution to the "final solution," Heydrich was named "Reichs Protector" of Bohemia and Moravia. But in May 1942, he was shot and mortally wounded by Czech resistance fighters. In retaliation, the SS descended on the village of Lidice, slaughtered all male inhabitants over the age of sixteen, and burned the town to the ground. Further revenge for Heydrich's assassination was extracted in Prague with the execution of 1,331 Czechs, including more than two hundred women.

Adolph Eichmann succeeded Heydrich in carrying out the final solution. Eichmann escaped from Germany at war's end, and believed he had found a safe haven in Argentina, until Israeli agents abducted him from a street near his home. He was taken to Jerusalem to answer for his war crimes.

9.

ASSASSINATION OF ABRAHAM LINCOLN

Having starred in William Shakespeare's *Julius Caesar*, John Wilkes Booth had often heard the line in act 2, "O conspiracy! Sham'st thou show thy dangerous brow by night, when evils are most free?"

In the spring of 1865, Booth was twenty-six years old and the youngest member of the most famous family of actors in America. Women admirers considered him "the handsomest man in the world." For his brilliant performances in *Romeo and Juliet*, *Othello*, *Macbeth*, and the play about Caesar's assassination, he had garnered the public's plaudits "as the youngest tragedian in the world."

Born in Maryland on May 10, 1838, the ninth of ten children of the famed actor Junius Booth, he grew up surrounded by slaves on his father's farm. In 1859 he watched approvingly as John Brown was hanged for leading an armed uprising in the hope that it would result in the abolition of slavery. Following the election of Abraham Lincoln, as the issue of slavery plunged the nation into Civil War, Booth's sympathies were with the Confederacy. Arrested in the spring of 1862 in St. Louis for making anti-Union remarks, Booth exclaimed, "So help me holy God, my soul, my life, and possessions are for the South."

In a letter to his brother-in-law in November 1884, he wrote, "This country was formed for the white, not the black man. And looking upon African slavery from the same standpoint, as held by the noble framers of our Constitution, I for one, have ever considered it, one of the greatest blessings (both for themselves and us) that God ever bestowed upon a favored nation."

At the time of this letter, Booth's passion for the Confederate cause, and his hatred for Lincoln, had taken the form of a scheme to kidnap the president. The plan was to take Lincoln to the Confederate capital of Richmond, Virginia, and hold him hostage to force the Union to release Southern prisoners of war. Enlisted into this conspiracy were Michael O'Laughlen, Samuel Arnold, Lewis Powell (aka Lewis Paine), David Herold, George Atzerodt, and John Surratt, son of Mary Surratt, a Washington, D.C., boarding-house owner. They were to capture Lincoln as he returned from a play at Campbell Hospital outside Washington on March 17, 1865. The plot was aborted when Lincoln changed his schedule.

Less than a month later (April 9), the Civil War ended with the surrender by General Robert E. Lee of his Army of Northern Virginia to Union General Ulysses S. Grant. On the night of April 11, Booth, Herold, and Powell were in a large crowd on the lawn of the White House as Lincoln spoke from a second-floor window. After asking the Union Army band to perform the Southern anthem "Dixie," Lincoln suggested that voting rights might be conferred on "the very intelligent" former slaves and on blacks who had served "our cause as soldiers."

Booth muttered furiously to Herold and Powell, "Now by God I'll put him through. That is the last speech he will ever make."

On the morning of Good Friday, April 14, 1865, Booth went to Ford's Theater, where he had often performed, to pick up mail. Informed that Lincoln and his wife were to be joined that evening by General Grant for a performance of a popular British farce, *My American Cousin*, he devised a bold plan in which the top leaders of the Union would be assassinated, leading to such a state of public panic and confusion that the Union would be in disarray and the Southern fight revived. At a meeting in a room in Mary Surratt's boarding house, Booth said that he would kill Lincoln and General Grant.

Atzerodt would murder Vice President Andrew Johnson at his hotel-residence (Kirkwood House). Lewis Powell, assisted by David Herold, would slay Secretary of State William Seward, who was confined to his home after suffering a broken arm in a fall from a carriage. The attacks were to be carried out at approximately the same moment: 10:15 PM. All were then to flee to a tavern that Mary Surratt owned, but leased, in Surrattsville, several miles away in Virginia.

When Lincoln arrived at Ford's Theater (a few minutes late), he entered the presidential box, not with Grant, who had declined Lincoln's invitation because he had another appointment that night, but with Major Henry Rathbone; the young officer's fiancée, Clara Harris; and Mrs. Lincoln. As they took their seats, the audience burst into applause, momentarily stopping the play. Meanwhile, Booth left his horse in a back alley in the care of a boy, Joseph Burrows, who was employed at the theater. Booth then went into a saloon next door.

Fortified with drink, and with a concealed derringer pistol and dagger, he entered the theater just past ten o'clock. He made his way up a narrow stairway leading to the presidential box, and found that Lincoln's bodyguard, John Parker of the Metropolitan Police, had left his post at the door. At about 10:15 PM, as the audience burst into laughter at a line of dialogue, he slipped into the box and fired one bullet point-blank behind Lincoln's left ear. Bounding to his feet, Rathbone felt the slash of Booth's dagger. It cut deeply into the officer's right arm.

As Booth leapt eleven feet from the box to the stage, his left foot became snagged in bunting. With his left leg shattered above the ankle, he shouted *Sic semper tyrannis!* (Latin for "As always with tyrants"). Watched by more than a thousand shocked and terrified people, he limped off stage, out a rear door into the alley where Burroughs held his horse's reins, and rode away.

Lincoln would lie unconscious in a too-small bed in a house across the street from Ford's Theater until his death at 7:22 AM, Saturday, April 15, 1865.

Meantime, the rest of the conspiracy was unfolding. Lewis Powell found himself struggling with Secretary of State Seward's son, Frederick. After clubbing Frederick with a revolver, Powell succeeded in stabbing his intended victim, though the attempt at assassination failed. Powell then escaped. Not far away, Atzerodt had gotten cold feet and made no attempt to enter Vice President Johnson's hotel. His accomplice, Herold, had also lost his nerve and fled.

After a brief rendezvous at Surratt's tavern, Booth and Herold rode to the Virginia home of Dr. Samuel Mudd. They arrived around four in the morning. They stayed only long enough for Mudd to set Booth's broken leg and apply a splint, then headed south and reached a farm near Port Royal, Virginia. When federal troops tracked them to that location early on the morning of April 26, the fugitives were hiding in a barn. Herold immediately surrendered, but Booth refused to give up. Although soldiers set fire to the barn, he remained inside. Despite orders that Booth was wanted alive, Sergeant Boston Corbett took a shot and killed him.

In a diary found on Booth's body, he had written, "For six months we had worked to capture [Lincoln]. But, our cause being almost lost, something decisive and great must be done."

Rounded up and convicted in a military tribunal, conspirators Herold, Atzerodt, Powell, and Mrs. Surratt were ordered hanged. They went to the gallows on July 7, 1865. Mrs. Surratt's son, John, escaped to Canada and then Europe, but was caught and tried in 1867 in a civil court. When the jury deadlocked, he went free. Dr. Mudd, O'Laughlen, and Arnold were sentenced to life, but were pardoned by President Andrew Johnson in 1869. An employee of Ford's Theater, Edward "Ned" Spangler, was convicted of helping Booth get out of the theater and was sentenced to six years in prison.

The many unanswered questions about the plot to kill Lincoln have given birth to several conspiracy theories. Why, for example, did Lincoln's bodyguard leave his post? Why wasn't Booth taken alive? Was Booth acting on orders from the Confederate government? Or had he been working for men in the U.S. government who feared that Lincoln would follow a policy of forgiveness toward the Southerners, rather than punish them for causing the nation four years of Civil War? Other conspiracy theorists have contended that Lincoln was the victim of international bankers, or the Roman Catholic Church, or Radical Republicans, or disgruntled Democrats. Secretary of War Edwin Stanton was suspected of scheming to kill Lincoln and the two men in line to succeed him as president in order to become the occupant of the White House. Beside Lincoln's bed at the moment of death, Stanton said, "Now he belongs to the ages." He was correct. Lincoln became and remains the most venerated martyr in American history.

John Wilkes Booth had hungered for fame. He is remembered now for hatching the most notorious murder plot since a group of Roman senators conspired to murder Julius Caesar. Because Booth had often performed in Shakespeare's play about Caesar's assassination, we can only wonder if, as Booth schemed to kill Lincoln, he pondered the words of Cassius in act 3:

> *"How many ages hence*
> *Shall this our lofty scene be acted o'er,*
> *In states unborn and accents yet unknown."*

10.

SOVIET MISSILES
IN CUBA

Nine years after Soviet Premier Nikita Khrushchev secretly installed long-range nuclear missiles in Cuba, and seven years after he was ousted from power by a group of Kremlin conspirators and exiled to a comfortable dacha provided to him outside Moscow, he published an autobiography. In the prologue to *Khrushchev Remembers*, he made two assertions. One was a lie. "The truth," he said, "has always been an inexhaustible source of strength for the [Communist] Party." The other was recognition of a reality that applies to all great historic conspiracies. "It will all come out in the end," he wrote. "Even the best-kept secrets will be brought out into the open."

A cunning survivor of decades of Communist plots, counter-plots, and complicated conspiracies, Nikita Sergeyevich Khrushchev burst upon the world stage in 1954 after winning a Kremlin power struggle with the head of the Soviet secret police, Lavrenti Beria, following the death of Josef Stalin. Sixty years old, fat, bald, gap-toothed, and with a deceptively comic demeanor that approached the buffoonish, Khrushchev was a committed Communist. He was a hardened and ruthless veteran of Moscow intrigues who would boast to the Soviet Union's capitalist enemies in the West, "We will bury you."

At a 1961 meeting with President John F. Kennedy in Vienna, Austria, in the aftermath of a disastrous attempt by the United States to depose the government of Cuban Communist dictator, Fidel Castro, in a bungled invasion of the island by Cuban exiles at the Bay of Pigs, Khrushchev decided that the new American president was weak. At a time of a crisis over the future of Berlin, which had been divided into Soviet and American and British zones since the end of the Second World War, the city had become a flashpoint of the Cold War. During the Vienna summit conference with Kennedy, Khrushchev recalled in his autobiography, "I could tell that he was interested in finding a peaceful solution to world problems and in avoiding conflict with the Soviet Union."

To demonstrate U.S. steadfastness on the Berlin issue, and to counter the impression of softness, Kennedy strengthened U.S. forces in the city. Khrushchev responded by cutting off all contact between East and West Berlin with the construction of a wall. Infantry and tank units were arrayed to defend it. When the Berlin Wall remained intact, Khrushchev's impression that he could bully Kennedy was reinforced. "I think it was a great victory for us," he recalled, "and it was won without firing a shot."

Emboldened by the outcome of the Berlin crisis, Khrushchev attempted to safeguard Fidel Castro's regime against another American-sponsored attack by installing Soviet missiles with nuclear warheads in Cuba, within striking range of the U.S. east coast. "In addition to protecting Cuba," Khrushchev wrote, "our missiles would have equalized what the West likes to call 'the balance of power.' The Americans had surrounded our country with military bases and threatened us with nuclear weapons and now they would learn just what it feels like to have enemy missiles pointing at you; we'd be doing nothing more than giving them a little of their own medicine. And it was high time America learned what it feels like to have their own land and her own people threatened."

Convinced of the shrewdness of his idea, Khrushchev presented it to Kremlin comrades at a secret meeting. He won enthusiastic approval. Keenly aware that Cuba was being closely monitored by super-secret, high-flying American U-2 spy planes, movements of materials to build the missile installations were explained as routine trading activities and peaceful assistance to an ally. Personnel to construct the bases and troops to protect them posed as tourists. Although the American government noted this increase in traffic between the USSR and Cuba in the summer of 1962, it was accepted as nothing more than an expected move to bolster the Castro regime. An exception to this interesting-but-nothing-to-be-alarmed-about attitude took the form of a warning to Kennedy on August 22, 1962, by John McCone, the director of the Central Intelligence Agency. He told the president, "The only construction I can put on the material going into Cuba is that the Russians are preparing to introduce offensive missiles."

On September 4, the White House issued a statement. It said that although there was "no evidence of any organized combat force of offensive ground-to-ground missiles, or of other significant offensive capability," it warned that the United States would not tolerate an attempt by the Soviet Union to "export its aggressive purposes."

A week later, the Soviet news agency Tass declared that any arms shipments to Cuba were "designed exclusively for defensive purposes." Kennedy replied a few days later. He said he would not allow "offensive weapons" in Cuba. But even as he spoke, Soviet ships were en route to the island with exactly that type of weaponry. On September 12, a Cuban newspaper, *Revolucion*, carried the headline "ROCKETS WILL BLAST THE UNITED STATES IF IT INVADES CUBA." The claim was dismissed in Washington as braggadocio. U-2 flights over Cuba found nothing to suggest that missile bases were being built, and no evidence of missiles. But on October 15, a U-2 flown by Major Rudolf Anderson, Jr. returned from an overflight of Cuba with photographs showing transporters for long-range missiles, erectors, and other equipment. The missiles were on the verge of becoming operational.

On Tuesday morning, October 16, 1962, President Kennedy's national security advisor, McGeorge Bundy, burst into Kennedy's bedroom and declared, "Mr. President, there is now hard photographic evidence that the Russians have offensive missiles in Cuba." With those words a crisis unfolded that would bring the world closer to a nuclear war than it had ever been.

Yet for the next six days, no one but Kennedy and a small group of advisers knew of the Soviet scheme to sneak missiles into Cuba and use them to blackmail the United States and its Cold War allies.

In a televised address from the Oval Office on October 22, 1962, Kennedy revealed Khrushchev's plot. He declared it "a deliberately provocative and unjustified change in the status quo." It would be met, he said, by an American "quarantine of all ships carrying offensive military equipment to Cuba." Any ship found carrying such material would be forced to turn back. Any nuclear weapon launched from Cuba would be considered an attack by the Soviet Union on the United States, requiring "a full retaliatory response."

As the world tottered on the brink of nuclear war, the "Cuban Missile Crisis" lasted two weeks. It ended when Khrushchev ordered the missiles withdrawn and the bases destroyed. He had learned, as he would write in his memoir, that even the best-kept secrets would be brought out into the open. His retreat, combined with other problems within the USSR in the following two years, resulted in yet another conspiracy in the Kremlin. Nikita Khrushchev was removed from power in a Kremlin coup in 1964.

11.

ASSASSINATION OF JOHN F. KENNEDY

Four decades after President John F. Kennedy was assassinated while in a motorcade in Dallas, Texas, theories abound that the thirty-fifth president of the United States was not the victim of a deranged lone rifleman with Communist sympathies named Lee Harvey Oswald who acted out of a personal motive, but that Kennedy was the target of a complex, sophisticated conspiracy.

The undisputed facts are that three shots were fired and that Kennedy was struck in the head and neck. At least two were fired from a sixth-floor window of the Texas School Book Depository, overlooking the motorcade route through Dealey Plaza. One of the bullets passed through the president and wounded a passenger in the limousine, Governor John Connally of Texas. Where the third bullet went could not be definitively ascertained. Kennedy was rushed to the nearest hospital, but was dead on arrival. In a search of the sixth floor of the book warehouse, an Italian-made rifle that had been recently fired was found.

Forty-five minutes after the events in Dealey Plaza, a Dallas police officer, J. D. Tippit, stopped a suspicious figure walking along a street some distance from the plaza. The man shot Tippit dead. The suspect in this shooting was captured in a nearby movie theater. He was identified as Lee Harvey Oswald.

An employee of the book depository who had taken a large package into the building and had been seen there at the time of the assassination, Oswald was a former U.S. Marine who had embraced Communism. He had renounced his American citizenship and moved to the Soviet Union in the 1950s. Married to a Russian, he'd returned to the United States and distributed pro-Castro literature. He also contacted the Soviet embassy in Mexico City seeking assistance in going to Cuba. He'd even bought a mail-order Italian-made rifle of the type found in the book warehouse.

Denying that he'd killed Kennedy, Oswald was arrested for the Tippit murder and held in a basement cell in the Dallas police headquarters. Scheduled for a court appearance, he was taken from his cell on November 24 and paraded before reporters, photographers, and television news cameras. As Oswald continued to claim innocence, a man lunged from the crowd and shot him dead. The shooter was identified as nightclub-owner Jack Ruby. He said he shot Oswald to avenge Kennedy's murder.

A conspiracy theory that arose within minutes of the Kennedy assassination was that the president had been ordered killed by right-wing radicals and fervid anti-Communists who faulted Kennedy for being too soft on the Russians and for entering into a nuclear test ban treaty with Moscow. This explanation was undermined by the revelations of Oswald's flirtation with Communism, his time in the Soviet Union, and his pro-Castro activities.

An investigation by a presidential commission of distinguished American leaders, headed by U.S. Chief Justice Earl Warren, heard testimony from 552 witnesses, studied reports by ten federal agencies, reviewed a 16-mm film of the motorcade made at the exact moment of the assassination, and reconstructed the sequence of events. The Warren Commission reported on September 24, 1964, that it had found no evidence that Oswald was part of a conspiracy. Nor was there any evidence that Jack Ruby had acted as part of a plot to silence Oswald.

With the ink barely dry on the multi-volume report, the findings were attacked, labeled a whitewash, and denounced as an attempt to conceal facts that would have revealed that Kennedy had been the victim of a complex, but unspecified conspiracy. Two years later, District Attorney Jim Garrison of New Orleans claimed to have evidence of such a plot centered in that city, but extending far and wide. This "conspiracy" became the basis for a 1991 film, *JFK*, directed by Oliver Stone.

Also in 1966, the first books to criticize the Warren Commission Report's findings appeared: *Rush to Judgment*, by Mark Lane; *Inquest*, by E.J. Epstein; and *Accessories After the Fact*, by Sylvia Meagher. Each pointed out inconsistencies in the commission's report. As a result, there arose among millions of people an unrelenting disbelief that an unassisted, deranged, leftist misfit could have killed the young, glamorous, and exciting president.

Among the various "conspiracy theories" that have been advanced:

- Kennedy's assassination was arranged by the KGB.
- It was a Mafia plot.
- Castro arranged it out of desire for revenge for the Bay of Pigs, the Missile Crisis, and CIA plots to assassinate him.
- Anti-Castro Cuban exiles did it because of resentment of Kennedy for not fully supporting the Bay of Pigs invasion and for "mishandling" the Cuban Missile Crisis.
- Right-wing businessmen plotted it.
- The CIA arranged it because it wished to prevent Kennedy from ending U.S. involvement in Vietnam.
- The assassination was ordered by FBI Director J. Edgar Hoover, who had been reined in by Kennedy's brother, Attorney General Robert F. Kennedy.

Most theories alleged that evidence of a vast conspiracy to kill Kennedy had been altered or destroyed: Oswald had been set up or duped. Oswald had a double. His rifle had been planted. Key witnesses who knew the truth had been murdered or died mysteriously. Kennedy's body had been altered and X rays faked to conceal evidence of shots from several locations. The coffin in which Kennedy's body had been placed in Dallas was not the coffin that was taken off Air Force One in Washington, D.C.

So persistent were such theories that in 1977 the House of Representatives established a Select Committee on Assassinations (HSCA). The committee reported that Lee Harvey Oswald fired three shots at President John F. Kennedy. The second and third shots fired struck the President. The third shot killed him. A review of acoustical evidence established "a high probability" that two gunmen had fired.

The committee believed, "on the basis of the evidence available to it," that Kennedy was "probably assassinated as a result of a conspiracy." But the committee was "unable to identify the other gunman or the extent of the conspiracy."

Excluded on the basis of the evidence available was a Soviet government plot, a scheme by the Cuban government, anti-Castro Cuban groups, a national syndicate of organized crime, the Secret Service, the Federal Bureau of Investigation, and the Central Intelligence Agency. The committee also reported that the Warren Commission performed with varying degrees of competency in the fulfillment of its duties, had conducted a thorough and professional investigation into the responsibility of Oswald for the assassination, but had failed to investigate adequately the possibility that there had been a conspiracy to assassinate the President.

Consequently, conspiracy theories concerning Kennedy's assassination have continued unabated.

12.

ASSASSINATION OF MARTIN LUTHER KING, JR.

When the Reverend Martin Luther King, Jr. stepped onto the balcony of his room at the Lorraine Motel in Memphis, Tennessee, on the evening of March 4, 1968, he was ready to add his support to the city's sanitation workers who had gone on strike for higher wages and better working conditions. As the nation's foremost leader in a struggle for civil rights for America's black population, he had led a movement whose purpose he defined as helping America "rise from the dark depths of prejudice and racism to the majestic heights of understanding and brotherhood."

At the "March on Washington" on August 28, 1963, King told a crowd of more than 250,000 on the Capitol Mall in front of the Lincoln Memorial: "I have a dream that one day on the red hills of Georgia the sons of slaves and the sons of former slaveholders will be able to sit down together at the table of brotherhood."

After receiving the Nobel Peace Prize in 1964, King conducted a voter registration drive in Alabama, culminating in a march from the town of Selma to Montgomery that was met by state troopers. The brutality of the police contributed to the passing of an historic civil rights bill. King then turned his attention to de facto segregation in housing and other economic grievances. Believing that the Vietnam War was unjust, and that it imposed an unfair burden on blacks, he spoke out against it.

Early in 1968, he launched a "Poor People's Campaign" that was designed to confront economic problems that had not been addressed by the new civil rights laws. It was to lend his name, voice, and prestige to garbage workers who'd gone on strike that he went to Memphis.

As he stepped out onto the balcony on the evening of April 4, he was shot and killed with a high-powered rifle with a telescopic sight from a building opposite the motel. The gun was abandoned at the scene. The FBI identified the fingerprints found on the weapon as those of James Earl Ray.

James Earl Ray was born on May 10, 1929, in Alton, Illinois, and he dropped out of high school in 1944. When he joined the army, he was quickly discharged for "ineptness and lack of adaptability to military service." His life as a small-time criminal began just as awkwardly in 1949 with the theft of a typewriter. In his haste to get away, he dropped his identification papers at the scene of the crime and was speedily collared. Ray was in and out of jails for the next eighteen years, and once broke out of a Missouri prison in 1967.

Learning that the FBI had named James Earl Ray as the chief suspect in the murder of King, Ray's astonished father, Gerald, exclaimed: "He couldn't have done it. He wasn't smart enough for that."

After fleeing to Europe, Ray was located at London's Heathrow Airport in June and sent back to the United States. In March 1969, he pleaded guilty because, he said, he wanted to avoid the electric chair. He was sentenced to 99 years. But three days later, he recanted his confession. He claimed that a man identified only as "Raoul" had given the rifle to him.

Insisting that he was innocent, Ray speculated that he had been merely a pawn in a conspiracy and government cover-up. In 1992, he published a book titled *Who Killed Martin Luther King, Jr.?* It contained an introduction by a King associate, the Rev. Jesse Jackson, who had been on the motel balcony when King was killed.

Jackson wrote, "I have always believed that the government was part of a conspiracy, either directly or indirectly, to assassinate Dr. Martin Luther King, Jr."

Other doubters pointed to Ray's record as a not-too-smart criminal. They claimed that to assassinate Dr. King was obviously far beyond Ray's capabilities. He must have had help, or been manipulated by conspirators to become the fall guy.

As if the saga of James Earl Ray was not dramatic enough, the nation was astonished by news reports in 1977 that Ray had again escaped from prison, this time from Tennessee. He was at large for three days.

When one of King's sons, Dexter, met with Ray in March of that year, he asked Ray, "Did you kill my father?"

Ray replied, "No, I didn't, no, no."

Dexter said, "I believe you, and my family believes you, and we will do everything in our power to see you prevail."

The question of whether King's murder was the result of a conspiracy was examined by a special subcommittee of the House of Representatives that also looked into the assassination of President John F. Kennedy. The committee concluded that Ray fired one fatal shot from the bathroom window at the rear of a rooming house opposite the Lorraine Motel. Noting that it was "highly probable" that Ray had stalked Dr. King in the weeks before the assassination, the report found his story about "Raoul" not worthy of belief.

While James Earl Ray "knowingly, intelligently, and voluntarily pleaded guilty to the first degree murder of Dr. King," said the report, the committee believed that on the basis of circumstantial evidence "there is a likelihood that James Earl Ray assassinated Dr. Martin Luther King as a result of a conspiracy."

But the committee stated that it did not believe any Federal, State, or local government agency had been involved in the assassination of Dr. King.

Although pleas were made by the King family and others that Ray be allowed to change his plea to not guilty and be granted a trial, neither were permitted. Meanwhile, Ray had been diagnosed with cirrhosis. Moved to Columbia Nashville Memorial Hospital, he fell into a coma and died of liver failure on April 23, 1998.

In a public statement the King family said they were "deeply saddened" by Ray's death. They also noted, "America will never have the benefit of Mr. Ray's trial, which would have produced new revelations about the assassination of Martin Luther King, Jr., as well as establish the facts concerning Mr. Ray's innocence."

As in the Lincoln and John F. Kennedy assassinations, a cloud of suspicion of a grand conspiracy persists. Like those conspiracy theories, it seems unlikely it will ever be dispelled.

13.

WHO KILLED BOBBY KENNEDY?

On the night that Dr. Martin Luther King, Jr. was murdered, U.S. Senator Robert F. Kennedy, whose brother John had been assassinated in 1963, reported the shocking news of King's death to a primarily black crowd in Indianapolis, Indiana. At what was to be a rally in support of Kennedy's bid for the Democratic Party's presidential nomination, Kennedy said, "In this difficult day, in this difficult time for the United States, it is perhaps well to ask what kind of a nation we are and what direction we want to move in."

Exactly two months later, June 4, 1968, Kennedy stood before jubilant supporters in the Embassy Ballroom of the Ambassador Hotel in Los Angeles. They were there to celebrate his victory on that day's primary to name a slate of delegates to the Democratic party's presidential nominating convention in Chicago in August. Because President Lyndon B. Johnson had chosen not to run for re-election, Kennedy had belatedly jumped into the contest for the nomination. The move pitted him against Senator Eugene McCarthy, whose criticism of the war in Vietnam had been credited in forcing Johnson to bow out. But Kennedy victories in Oregon and in California appeared to assure that Kennedy would emerge triumphant at the convention.

After a brief victory speech, and as the crowd chanted "Bobby . . . Bobby," Kennedy left the ballroom by way of the food service pantry. It was jammed with well-wishers. As he moved slowly through the crowd, three shots were fired. A bullet slammed into Kennedy's head behind the right ear. A second struck near his right armpit. A third hit about an inch and a half below the second. A few hours later, Kennedy's campaign advisor and aide Frank Mankiewicz announced that the senator had died.

As Kennedy slumped to the floor in the pantry, members of the crowd, including pro-football star Roosevelt "Rosie" Greer, had subdued a slender young man holding a .22 caliber revolver. Identified as Sirhan Bishara Sirhan, he was a twenty-five-year-old Palestinian. Born in Jerusalem in March 1944, he had come to the United States with his parents, Bishara and Mary, and a sister in 1946 as refugees. After living briefly in New York, they settled in Pasadena, California. When Bishara abandoned the family, Mary got a job as a teacher's aide. After Sirhan graduated from John Muir High School in 1963, where he learned to use a .22 caliber rifle as a member of a type of high school ROTC known as the California Cadets, he enrolled at Pasadena City College, but dropped out after two years. While working as a horse groom at the Santa Anita Racetrack, he hoped to become a jockey, but injuries from several falls from horses ended that dream.

During a search of Sirhan's room in Pasadena, police found several notebooks. Among the writings were: "RFK must die." "My determination to eliminate RFK has become more [and] more of an unshakeable obsession." "[He] must be sacrificed for the cause of the poor exploited people." "Robert F. Kennedy must be assassinated before June 5, 1968."

Investigators also discovered that Sirhan had attended at least two other Kennedy events. At one of these, said a witness, Sirhan had appeared "very intense and sinister." Another person placed Sirhan in the audience at a Kennedy speech on June 2.

Because it was not a federal offense to murder a presidential candidate, Sirhan was tried in a California state court. The evidence of his notebooks, and the fact that he'd been captured with a gun in his hand, resulted in a murder conviction and a death sentence. But after the U.S. Supreme Court ruled that the death penalty as employed by states was unconstitutional, Sirhan's sentence was changed to life in prison. Although he became eligible for parole in 1984, it was denied, as were periodic petitions for release.

While Sirhan remains in prison and continues to not only claim innocence, but also to have no memory of the shooting, he has gained the support of numerous individuals and groups who contend that he was the victim of a conspiracy. They assert that the assassination of Robert F. Kennedy was a plot of the U.S. government and was then covered up by the Los Angeles Police Department and the L.A. County District Attorney's office.

This conspiracy theory rests on questions surrounding Sirhan's position in front of Kennedy in the pantry, and thus his inability to have shot Kennedy from behind; the number of bullets fired and the bullet capacity of Sirhan's gun; the alleged disappearance of important physical evidence; a number of eyewitness accounts of another gunman in the pantry; a report of a woman in a polka-dot dress who had fled the hotel shouting, "We have killed him!"; a description of a blond man in a gray suit putting a gun in a holster and another of a dark-haired man in a black suit who fired two shots and ran from the pantry; and a claim that Sirhan Sirhan had been a subject in a CIA experiment in the use of hypnosis to program assassins like a similar scheme in a novel and motion picture, *The Manchurian Candidate*.

In a petition seeking a new trial for Sirhan, his attorney, Lawrence Teeter, claimed to have evidence that "virtually proves that powerful branches of the U.S. government were behind the murder." In support of this claim, a New York psychiatrist and hypnosis expert, Dr. Herbert Spiegal, said in an affidavit that Sirhan, "being an outstanding hypnotic subject, was probably programmed through hypnosis to shoot Senator Kennedy and to experience a genuine amnesia of the shooting." Concerning the objective of such a conspiracy, Teeter said, "There were good reasons to have wanted Robert Kennedy eliminated. He wanted to end the Vietnam War. He wanted to get to the bottom of his brother's assassination. He wanted to break the back of the Teamsters Union. He wanted to end the wild adventurism of the CIA."

Because the Robert F. Kennedy assassination was deemed an open-and-shut case, it was not investigated by the House Special Committee on Assassinations that in 1977 looked into the killings of President

Kennedy and Dr. Martin Luther King, Jr., concluding that both murders had probably been the work of conspirators.

Based on an assumption that if Kennedy had not been killed, he would have been elected president, a story circulated widely in which Sirhan was allegedly asked, "If you wanted to kill someone important, why didn't you shoot the president?" Sirhan replied with a smile, "But I did kill the president."

The official explanation remains as it was cited in 1968 by a police lieutenant who had investigated the murder: "Sirhan was a self-appointed assassin. He decided that Bobby Kennedy was no good because he was helping the Jews. And he was going to kill him."

14.

ASSASSINATION OF
ARCHDUKE FERDINAND

A conspiracy by Serbian Nationalists to assassinate the heir to the throne of the empire of Austria-Hungary, Archduke Franz Ferdinand, was the spark that ignited World War I. The leader of a group called Narodna Odbrana (Black Hand) was a veteran plotter of Balkan intrigues. Colonel Dragutin Dimitrijevic, also known by the code name "Apis," was Chief of Intelligence of the Serbian General Staff. When he learned that the archduke and his wife, Sophia, planned a visit to the Serbian capital, Sarajevo, he enlisted seven young revolutionaries to ambush Ferdinand's car on one of the city's main thoroughfares, Appel Quay, on the morning of June 28, 1914.

Their weapons, four Serbian army pistols and six bombs, were supplied from Serbian army arsenals. The men trained for the mission at a camp in Serbia and were smuggled into the city. They took up assigned places along the route that Ferdinand would travel from the railroad station in an open car to a reception at the city hall.

First in line was a nineteen-year-old former typesetter and committed anarchist, Nedjelko Cabrinovic. In the event he might fail and be captured, he had orders to commit suicide with a cyanide pill. Armed with a hand grenade, he mingled with the spectators and waited to hurl it until the archduke's car slowed to make a turn. But as the grenade hurtled toward the car, the chauffeur saw it and sped up. Raising an arm, Ferdinand deflected the grenade, causing it to bounce off the back of the car: it exploded in a following vehicle, seriously injuring two military aides.

In an attempt to make his escape, Cabrinovic jumped over a wall. Landing in a shallow stream, he gulped the cyanide pill, but it was too old to be effective. Hauled from the water, he was arrested.

Arriving at city hall, the archduke joked to the mayor, "So you welcome your guests with bombs!" Undaunted by the assassination attempt, and brushing off a plea from an Austrian general that he get out of the city quickly, he declared his intention to visit the wounded officers at a hospital. Because the driver of his car was unfamiliar with the route, he took a wrong turn into a street that was too narrow for the car to be turned around. It was a fateful error.

Purely by chance, another of the Black Hand's team of assassins, twenty-year-old Gavrilo Princip, found himself within shooting distance of the hated archduke. Stepping toward the car, he drew a pistol and fired two shots. Sophie was killed instantly. Ferdinand died minutes later.

Less than a month later, on July 28, 1924, Austria-Hungary declared war on Serbia. In a matter of weeks the European powers took sides, with Germany aligning with Austria-Hungary against England and France. A war that would last four years, with millions of men slaughtered, and that no one imagined would go into the history books as the first of two world wars, was underway.

Grabbed immediately after shooting Archduke Ferdinand, and beaten to the ground by police officers, Princip was a defiant prisoner. He refused to admit that he had been part of a conspiracy by the government of Serbia, and he said nothing about the role of the Black Hand. But his denials didn't matter.

Within days of the assassination, one of the plotters, Danilo Ilic, a former schoolteacher, had been arrested in a routine roundup of "usual suspects" and had given a confession. Hoping to be spared execution, he named all the conspirators. Those he'd implicated who were still in the city were rapidly apprehended.

Arrested nine days after the assassination, another former schoolteacher, Cvijetko Popovic, had been given a bomb. He'd taken up a position along the Appel Quay, but hadn't acted. Because he was under twenty, the age at which someone could be executed, he was sentenced to thirteen years in prison. Released in 1918 after the collapse of Austria-Hungary at the end of the war, Popovic went on to become Curator of the Ethnography Department of the Sarajevo Musuem.

Also betrayed by Ilic, seventeen-year-old Vaso Cubrinovic had also chosen not to toss a bomb on the Appel Quay. Convicted of treason, he was spared the death penalty and also gained freedom in 1918. He became a university professor and served as the Minister of Forests in the government of Yugoslavia. A country patched together after the war, Yugoslavia was a conglomeration of Balkan states, including Serbia, Herzegovina, Bosnia, and Montenegro, and was ruled by the Communist dictator, Marshal Tito.

Vaso's brother Nedjelko died of tuberculosis in prison in January 1916.

The last of the bombers stationed on the Appel Quay without taking action, eighteen-year-old Trifko Grabez, pleaded guilty and got twenty years. He also died in prison of TB.

Having escaped arrest, Mohammed Mehmesbasic fled to neighboring Montenegro and boasted about his role in the assassination. Serbia demanded that he be arrested and turned over, but he managed to slip out of custody. In 1917, he was implicated in another assassination plot and sentenced to fifteen years. Pardoned in 1919, he worked as a gardener and carpenter and died during World War II.

The mastermind of the assassination of Archduke Ferdinand, Colonel Dragutin "Apis" Dimitrijevic, was arrested in March 1917 in a Serbian government crackdown on the Black Hand. He was convicted of treason by a military tribunal that may have been rigged by men who had plotted Apis's downfall, and was shot at sunrise on June 24, 1917.

Ironically, the man who had betrayed the plotters, Danilo Ilic, was the only one to be hanged of the seven men who were in Sarajevo on that fateful morning. Ilic went to the gallows on February 3, 1915.

The lone Black Hand conspirator to actually succeed, Gavril Princip, stood trial for the murder and steadfastly denied that the Serbian Government was behind the assassination, or that he had any knowledge of the Black Hand. He told a court: "In trying to insinuate that someone else has instigated the assassination, one strays from the truth. The idea arose in our own minds, and we ourselves executed it. We have loved the people. I have nothing to say in my own defense."

He was found guilty. Whether he would be sentenced to death depended on whether he was twenty at the time of the assassination. The court gave him the benefit of the doubt and sentenced him to twenty years. He died in prison of tuberculosis in April 1918.

By then, the war that the murder of Archduke Ferdinand had ostensibly justified had been raging for four years.

15.

THE MAFIA

The world's oldest continuous criminal conspiracy, the Mafia was formed as a defensive organization after a Norman invasion of Sicily in the eleventh century. By the middle of the nineteenth century its "families," headed by "dons," used intimidation and murder to control all of the island's provinces. Members swore an oath of *omertà* (silence) that if broken was punishable by violent death.

Unable to expand its activities into Italy in the late nineteenth century because of the strength of another criminal society (the Camorra) that was centered in Naples, the Mafia took root in cities in the United States. As thousands of Sicilians and Italians emigrated, Mafia henchmen ran an extortion racket known as the Black Hand. Thugs such as Ignazio "Lupo the Wolf" Saietta preyed on their wealthy former countrymen, including opera singer Enrico Caruso, by threatening them and demanding money for "protection." But in the early 1930s, these older Mafia bosses, known as "Mustache Petes," were assassinated in plots concocted by a young and ambitious gangster named Salvatore Lucania. Better known as Charles "Lucky" Luciano, he had risen in the mob in partnership with a cold-blooded killer, Benjamin "Bugsy" Siegel, and a brilliant Jewish financial strategist, Meyer Lanksy.

Having eliminated the old dons, Luciano organized the New York City Mafia into five families and established a "commission" to coordinate activities of gangs in other cities and eliminate competition that could lead to gang warfare. The most notorious of these gangs was the Chicago mob. Run by the nation's most colorful gangster, Al "Scarface" Capone, it carried out the most famous mob rubout of all time, the St. Valentine's Day Massacre.

Although much of the underworld's earnings throughout the 1920s came from dealing in liquor that had been banned by the Eighteenth Amendment (Prohibition), the financial bedrock of the Mafia was control of gambling, loan-sharking, the protection racket, and prostitution. But the American people were generally unaware of the existence of this system until a New York City prosecutor, Thomas E. Dewey, revealed that "organized crime is a continuing menace to the safety of the community." Launching a "racket-busting" campaign that first targeted prostitution, he succeeded in sending Luciano to prison. Further probing of "the mob" uncovered a Mafia organization based in Brooklyn known as "Murder, Inc." It operated nationally to carry out gangland assassinations.

Although FBI director J. Edgar Hoover insisted that there was no such thing as the Mafia, the existence of a complex, national crime conspiracy was confirmed during a series of hearings in 1950 by the U.S. Senate Special Committee to Investigate Organized Crime in Interstate Commerce. The star witness of the televised probe was the New York mob boss, Frank Costello, although "Uncle Frank," as he was known in gangland, allowed cameras to show only his hands.

In a book about the investigation, Committee Chairman Estes Kefauver wrote: "Behind the local mobs which make up the national syndicate is a shadowy international criminal organization known as the Mafia, so fantastic that most Americans find it hard to believe that it really exists."

Further proof of a national crime syndicate burst into the headlines in 1957 when the New York State Police stumbled upon a meeting of the top Mafia figures from around the country in a small upstate New York town. This gathering, known as "the Apalachin Conference," resulted in many of the mob chieftains being arrested. Six years later, mob enforcer Joseph Valachi told another Senate committee that the mob name for the organization was "La Cosa Nostra" (Italian for "this thing of ours"), and went on to expose its inner workings, from taking the oath of *omertà* in 1930 to the mob's record of controlling gambling, narcotics, and prostitution, of its political payoffs, domination of labor unions, other rackets, and its control of gambling casinos in Las Vegas.

While Valachi was spilling the beans, the "boss of bosses" of the syndicate was the head of the most powerful of New York's five families. Sicilian-born Carlo Gambino had been an ally of Luciano and had reached the top echelons of the Mafia by murdering anyone who stood in his way. The capo (boss) of his own crew (gang) at age twenty-nine, he chose as an aide another up-and-comer, Paul Castellano. He became Gambino's relative by marriage when Carlo married Paul's sister in 1932. By 1969, the Gambino Crime Family had twenty-five crews with more than 850 members. Among them was a talented truck hijacker named John Gotti.

When Gambino died of a heart attack on October 15, 1976, Castellano inherited the family. Next in command as "underboss" was Neil Dellacroce. After he died, Gotti moved to seize control of the Gambino family by arranging Castellano's assassination. In one of the most daring rubouts in Mafia history, the murder took place at the height of New York's evening rush hour in front of a popular midtown steak house.

Unlike the reclusive Gambino and publicity-shy "Big Paul" Castellano, John Gotti was a flamboyant character who soon became the prime target of federal crime-busters. When several of their attempts to put him in prison failed, he became known as "the Teflon Don." Undaunted in pursuing Gotti, the feds got a break when one of Gotti's most trusted lieutenants, Sammy "the Bull" Gravano, turned against him and made a deal to trade his testimony for a lighter sentence. His story, combined with FBI tapes of Gotti ordering mob hits, resulted in Gotti's conviction on a host of charges that included five murders. Gotti was sentenced to life without parole.

Retired FBI agent J. Bruce Mouw, who helped convict Gotti, said of him: "John Gotti is a stone-cold killer. He is responsible for the deaths of scores of individuals. He's a very vicious and ruthless boss."

Still running the Gambino family from prison, Gotti named a committee that included his twenty-eight-year-old son, John Jr., to run the family. When the son pleaded guilty to federal racketeering charges, the family was in the care of John Gotti's brother, Peter. After John's death from cancer in a federal prison, the feds were soon in hot pursuit of Peter.

Although the conviction of Gotti and subsequent successful prosecutions of other crime bosses, and the rise of other competing ethnic gangs, resulted in a weakening of the Mafia/La Cosa Nostra, the world's oldest criminal conspiracy continues in business.

16.

THE KGB

The last of a string of Soviet secret police and espionage agencies, the KGB (Komitet Gosudarstvennoy Bezopasnosti) was for thirty-five years the instrument of Soviet espionage around the world and the apparatus of terror within the USSR.

Established in 1954 as a state committee following the death of Stalin, it was elevated to a Soviet ministry in 1979 and was second in size only to the Soviet military. Its roster in the 1980s was estimated at more than 400,000. It was augmented by hundreds of thousands of informers throughout Soviet society, at every level of the government, and among the Soviet armed forces.

To carry out global espionage, KGB agents posed as embassy and consular officials. According to United States counterintelligence agencies, between 1954 and 1989 the percentage of KGB agents at the Soviet embassy in Washington ranged between 40 and 60 percent of the diplomatic staff.

While every government since ancient times created a system of espionage and internal security, none lasted as long, nor operated as ruthlessly or on as vast a scale as the one created by the first dictator of the USSR, Vladimir I. Lenin. Within weeks after the Bolshevik Revolution, Lenin ordered the establishment of the Cheka (Extraordinary

Commission for Combating Counterrevolution and Sabotage). Headed by Felix Dzerzhinsky, it grew in size to more than a quarter of a million men and women. It ran scores of prisons and detention camps, and tortured and killed thousands of "enemies of the state." Many of them were executed without benefit of trial in the basement dungeons of Cheka headquarters, Lubyanka Prison, on a plaza in the center of Moscow. Eventually named Dzerzhinsky Square, it became a symbol of the terrorist state.

With the name of the secret police changed in 1922 to General Political Administration (GPU, later changed to OGPU), and with the creation of the People's Commissariat for Internal Affairs (NKVD), the terror continued. By 1925, the number of prisoners in six thousand jails surpassed 13 million. Under Lenin's successor, Josef Stalin, the role of the NKVD expanded tremendously. It became Stalin's principal weapon in eliminating anyone he deemed to be an enemy, both within the USSR and abroad. In 1940 the long arm of the KGB reached all the way to Mexico City to assassinate one of Stalin's old enemies, Leon Trotsky.

The KGB was also Stalin's vehicle for spreading Soviet Communism around the world, but especially in Great Britain and the United States. From 1938 to 1954, the head of the NKVD was Lavrenti Beria. When he plotted to grab power after Stalin's death, he was thwarted by a group of conspirators led by Nikita Khrushchev; Beria was then arrested, tried for treason, and executed. With him out of the way, the NKVD was given a new name—KGB. Described by Cold War historians as "the cutting edge" and the "linchpin" of the Soviet system, it was organized into nine "chief directorates." But it was the first that played the most significant role in the Cold War period. According to the U.S. Central Intelligence Agency, the KGB in the early 1980s was spending between three and four billion dollars a year to spread disinformation in the form of faked documents, including letters bearing the forged signature of President Ronald Reagan.

Responsible for foreign intelligence, analysis of intelligence data, counterintelligence, and "active measures," the KGB operated the largest espionage network in the history of the world. In addition to global espionage, recruitment of spies and counterspies, and assassinations ("wet jobs"), it established schools to train agents of Soviet satellite countries and sympathetic third world governments.

One of the KGB's greatest successes was revealed in 1960 by the U.S. ambassador to the United Nations, Henry Cabot Lodge. In the aftermath of the Soviet shooting down of a U.S. U-2 spy plane over the USSR, Lodge displayed a plaster wall plaque in the form of the Great Seal of the United States. It had hung for years on a wall behind Lodge's desk in the American embassy in Moscow. In it was a KGB-planted microphone and transmitter.

A result of the U-2 incident was an exchange of the plane's pilot, Gary Francis Powers, for Rudolf Abel. Arrested in New York in June 1957, Abel had been the KGB spymaster in North and Central America while posing as a photographer/artist. He'd performed so well as an agent that he was given the rank of colonel and in November 1990 his picture was put on a Soviet postage stamp.

The KGB also provided training on how to carry out terrorism. A facility at Pushinka, near Moscow, was set up solely for the instruction of Arab terrorists in assassination, hostage-taking, hijacking airplanes, and use of explosives.

According to Soviet defector and a former Under-Secretary-General of the United Nations, Arkady Shevchenko, in his 1985 book *Breaking with Moscow*, a KGB agent provided a chilling foreshadowing of the 1993 bombing of a garage at the World Trade Center with the intent of bringing down the buildings. Gazing through the window of Shevchenko's office in the U.N. Building at midtown skyscrapers, the KGB man said, "All those shining towers, they look so strong, so tall, but they're a house of cards. A few explosions in the right places and *do svidaniya* (goodbye)."

After the dissolution of the Soviet Union the opening of the KGB's secret files, and accounts of its activities by former KGB agents, have provided Cold War historians with a record of the numerous plots of the world's most sustained conspiracy against liberty.

Two former heads of the KGB rose to the pinnacle of power in Moscow. Yuri Andropov served as General Secretary of the Communist Party of the USSR (1982–84). The current president of the Russian Republic, Vladimir Putin, served in the foreign intelligence branch of the KGB from 1975 to 1990.

17.

DEATH OF STALIN

On Saturday, March 1, 1953, in a country house in a suburb of Moscow, seventy-three-year-old Soviet dictator Josef Stalin concluded a long night of eating and heavy drinking by unleashing a tirade of abuse against four terrified guests. The top echelon of the ruling Politburo, they were the head of the secret police, Lavrenti Beria; Georgi M. Malenkov; Nikolai Bulganin; and Nikita Khrushchev. Long after midnight, the survivor of the Bolshevik Revolution who had grabbed power and held it for more than three decades ordered the frightened four to get out and went to bed. When he did not appear at his usual time the next morning, a nervous guard entered the room and found the man whose Communist Party name meant "man of steel" lying semi-conscious on the floor by his bed, apparently having suffered a stroke.

Except for the unquestioned fact that Beria, Malenkov, Bulganin, and Khrushchev rushed to the scene, what happened in the following hours remains a mystery. According to one story, as Stalin lay sprawled on the floor Beria took a bottle from a medicine cabinet and poured its contents into Stalin's mouth. It may have been a tasteless blood thinner, Warfarin, which was also used as a rat poison. Another version depicted Stalin struggling to reach a small bottle of pills, only to have it kicked out of reach. No one summoned Stalin's doctors. The tyrant died four days later.

Although the officially announced cause of death was cerebral hemorrhage, few people who understand the history of the Stalin era have accepted it. A far more believable explanation was that the master of the Kremlin had at last become a victim of the kind of plotting of which he had been the mastermind during his reign of despotic terror over the Soviet people.

Not since the assassination of Julius Caesar by Roman senators who feared that he would become a dictator, had a conspiracy against the living symbol of governmental power changed the course of world events in such a profound way.

While the question remains unanswerable of whether Stalin's death was from natural causes or at the hands of conspirators, there is no doubt that before he gulped his final agonized breath a grab for power was already underway. According to Khrushchev, Beria was first to act.

Khrushchev wrote in his memoir, "Beria was radiant. He was regenerated and rejuvenated. To put it crudely, he had a housewarming over Stalin's corpse before it was even put in its coffin. Beria was sure that the moment he had long been waiting for had finally arrived. There was no power on earth that could hold him back now."

While Beria moved quickly to consolidate his position as Stalin's successor, he underestimated Khrushchev. Quietly biding his time, Khrushchev secretly discussed what to do about Beria with Malenkov, Bulganin, and other important Kremlin figures who were just as worried about Beria, but disappointingly timid about taking action. Not one was willing to move against the boss of the world's largest and most vicious secret police organization without assurances that others were committed to resorting to what Foreign Minister V. M. Molotov called "extreme measures."

Khrushchev moved to gain the support of the military, an element of Soviet power with ample reason to want Beria removed. Along with the general who had led the Red Army into Berlin in 1945, Marshal Georgi Zhukov, the plotters obtained the backing of ten marshals and generals. The next step was to lure Beria to a Kremlin meeting where he would be stripped of his offices, with the armed military officers stationed in an adjoining room. Fearing that Beria would come to the meeting armed with a pistol, Khrushchev carried a gun in his coat pocket.

With the press of a secret button, the armed generals were to burst in and arrest Beria. When they did so, Zhukov shouted to Beria, "Hands up!"

As Beria seemed to reach for a briefcase that was lying behind him on the windowsill, Khrushchev seized his arm to prevent him from producing a weapon. "We checked later and found that he had no gun," Khrushchev wrote in a chapter in his autobiography titled *Plotting Beria's Downfall.* "His quick movement had simply been a reflex action."

With Lavrenti Beria tried for various crimes and executed, Khrushchev began a three-year ascent to power that was to culminate in an address to the Twentieth Party Congress. In a speech that was kept secret for several years, he launched a "de-Stalinization" of the USSR by detailing Stalin's atrocities and attacking him for creating a "cult of personality."

Five years later, Khrushchev's next move in destroying Stalin was an order to remove his body from a place next to Lenin in a huge tomb in Red Square. Declaring it "inappropriate," he cited "serious violations by Stalin of Lenin's precepts, abuse of power, mass repressions against honorable Soviet people, and other activities in the period of the personality cult" that made it "impossible to leave the bier in the mausoleum of V. I. Lenin."

A few days later, the corpse was gone. Without ceremony and fanfare, it was interred about 300 feet from the mausoleum among graves of minor leaders of the Revolution. Near the Kremlin wall, it was obscured by trees. Not until 1970 was a small bust permitted on the grave.

By that time, Nikita Khrushchev had outmaneuvered Malenkov and Bulganin to become the undisputed successor to Stalin. Brash and bellicose on the world stage, and promising to bury capitalism, he believed, as he wrote in his autobiography, that its liquidation was "the crucial question in the development of society." This would occur, he said, "only under the complete domination of the [Soviet] system throughout the world." But in 1964, failure in Soviet agriculture, criticism of what was regarded in Moscow as an abject defeat in the 1962 Cuban Missile Crisis, and Khrushchev's entrance into a nuclear test ban treaty with the United States, prompted Kremlin conspirators to oust him.

18.

CAPTURE OF
ADOLPH EICHMANN

Almost immediately after Germany's surrender in World War II on May 8, 1945, members of the Jewish Brigade of the British Army formed an organization that they named "Nokmim," the Hebrew word for "avengers." Their purpose was to track down and kill Nazis who had slipped out of Germany or otherwise managed to avoid prosecution as war criminals in trials held in the German city of Nuremberg. High on their list was the man who had been recording secretary at the Wannsee Conference at which the "final solution of the Jewish problem" by genocide had been ratified. Adolph Eichmann would eventually be in charge of transportation of Jews to extermination camps. The problem facing the avengers was that their last record of anyone having seen him was in the final days of the war.

Eluding an Allied Forces roundup of known and suspected Nazis, and cutting himself off from family and friends, Eichmann remained in Europe until 1950. With the help of a group set up to assist fugitives in leaving the continent, he fled to Nazi-friendly Argentina. Confident that his trail was cold, feeling that he was safe, and with his name changed to Ricardo Clement, he sent for his wife and children two years later. But in the fall of 1957, a phone rang in the office of

Walter Eytan in the Foreign Ministry of the then decade-old State of Israel. The caller was Fritz Bauer, the public prosecutor of the province of Hesse, Germany. He informed Eytan that Eichmann was alive and well in Argentina. Eytan immediately contacted the head of the Israeli intelligence service, Mossad. Reviewing the Eichmann file, Isser Harel recognized that Eichmann's experience as "a past master of police methods" would make him "exceedingly dangerous quarry." There was the further problem for Mossad's Nazi hunters, Harel recalled, of "identifying their man beyond the slightest doubt." The proof of Eichmann's identity would be found in the form of a tattoo that all members of the Nazi secret police (SS) had branded under their left armpits.

An important break came when Mossad learned that one of Eichmann's sons had not only kept his name, but had bragged to a female friend of his father's role in killing millions of Jews. The son was located and followed by Mossad agents as he traveled to Eichmann's new haven on Garibaldi Street in the San Fernando section of Buenos Aires. With this exciting information, Harel launched one of the most complex and far-ranging conspiracies in world history.

The plan was to grab "Clement" at a bus stop and fly him out of Argentina on an Israeli plane that carried an Israeli delegation to Buenos Aires to participate in the 150th anniversary of Argentina's independence in May 1960. Harel arrived in the country to supervise the operation.

He recalled, "Nothing was left to chance." To ensure that there were no problems with documents, plane connections, visas, health certificates, and character references for the unit, a phony travel agency was set up in a European city. Mossad agents converged from all over the globe. On May 11, 1960, as Eichmann stepped from a bus and sauntered along Garibaldi Street toward his house to celebrate his wedding anniversary, he passed two Mossad agents who were pretending to have car trouble.

As Eichmann went by, one of the agents shouted, "Just a moment." When the agent pounced, Eichmann "let out a terrible yell, like a wild beast caught in a trap."

Eichmann was shoved into a car and driven away. "The whole operation," Harel noted in a book about the manhunt, *The House on Garibaldi Street*, "had taken less than ten minutes."

Although the agents easily confirmed that their quarry could be no one but Eichmann, they discovered that the SS tattoo had been surgically removed. Evidently resigned to his fate, Eichmann became docile and cooperative.

Harel wrote, "Gone was the SS officer who once had hundreds of men carry out his commands. Now he was frightened and nervous, at times pathetically eager to help."

While the Mossad agents could have easily killed him, the plan was to smuggle him out of Argentina to Israel in order to be put on trial. Drugged and disguised as an ill El-Al Airlines employee in uniform, he was placed on a plane for Tel Aviv.

When an astonished world learned of Eichmann's capture and that he had been taken to Israel, the government of Argentina protested to the Security Council of the United Nations. Israel's response was given by its foreign minister, Golda Meir. She said: "I am convinced that many in the world were anxious to bring Eichmann to trial, but the fact remains that for fifteen years nobody found him. But Jews, some of whom personally were the victims of his brutality, found no rest until they located him and brought him to Israel—the country to whose shores thousands of the survivors of the Eichmann horror have come home; to the country that existed in the hearts and minds of the six million, as on the way to the crematoria they chanted the great article of faith: *Ani ma'amin be'muna shelma beviat ha-Messiah* (I believe with perfect faith in the coming of the Messiah.)"

Protected within a cubicle surrounded by bulletproof glass in the courtroom and saying that he had been just "a cog in the machine" who acted "under orders," Eichmann pleaded for mercy. He was hanged in 1961.

19.

U-2 SPY PLANE

If espionage is defined as a conspiracy by one nation against another, the U-2 ranks as one of the most successful spy plots of all time.

Between July 4, 1956, and May 1, 1960, U-2 planes conducted unmolested photographic reconnaissance missions over the USSR. They provided the United States not only with data on the strength and location of Soviet military units, but on the status of Soviet development and deployment of intercontinental ballistic missiles.

This urgent American need to find out what the USSR was up to militarily was a result of the rejection by the Soviet leader, Nikita Khrushchev, of a dramatic plan called "Open Skies." As proposed by President Dwight D. Eisenhower at a summit conference in Geneva in July 1955, the United States was prepared to provide details of all its military plans to the USSR if the Soviets did the same. To be certain that no one was cheating, each country would conduct mutual surveillance overflights.

Suspecting an American trick, Khrushchev told Eisenhower, "You could hardly expect us to take this seriously."

A year later, the first U-2 took off from a secret U.S. base in Turkey. Needle-nosed, jet-powered, and with long thin wings and a snug one-man cockpit, it had tucked into its belly high-resolution cameras designed by Edwin Land, inventor of the Polaroid camera. Built by the Lockheed Corporation for the Central Intelligence Agency and code-named "Rainbow," each U-2 cost a million dollars to build. It flew at 70,000 feet. Higher than the altitude capacity of any Soviet aircraft, it was far beyond the reach of anti-aircraft guns and ground-to-air missiles.

Photos snapped by U-2s quickly revealed that the Soviets had not surpassed the United States in development and deployment of ICBMs and had not created a so-called "missile gap." But the pictures also showed that in a conventional ground war the Soviet Union could field ten times as many troops as the United States, eight times as many American tanks, and quadruple the number of U.S. aircraft. This information confirmed that if the Soviets launched an attack in Europe, the West's only recourse would be the use of tactical nuclear weapons. To deter any such Soviet adventurism, the U.S. would have to rely on a strategy of deterrence in which the Soviets would know that their major cities were targeted by American nuclear-tipped missiles.

Faced with this reality, the Soviets in turn felt they needed an arsenal of nuclear missiles that could hit U.S. cities. The result was an arms race and a policy on both sides that became known as "MAD" (mutual assured destruction).

When the USSR attempted to upset this balance of power by introducing offensive nuclear missiles ninety miles from the American mainland in 1962, the discovery of the bases was made by a U-2 piloted by Colonel Rudolf Anderson. The result was the Cuban Missile Crisis. Because the U-2s had to fly at lower altitudes over Cuba in order to get the best possible photos, one of the planes, also piloted by Colonel Anderson, was shot down by a Soviet-operated surface-to-air missile.

But the first loss of a U-2 had occurred two and half years earlier in the Soviet Union. Piloted by Francis Gary Powers, the U-2 crashed near the city of Sverdlovsk on a significant date on the calendar of the Communist world: May Day. When the USSR announced that it had brought down a U.S. aircraft, the CIA felt confident that the U-2 had been destroyed and that the pilot was dead, either as a result of the crash or because Powers would have followed orders not to be captured and taken a cyanide pill.

Washington explained that the plane had been on a routine weather mission from a base in Turkey and had gone astray. Only then did Nikita Khrushchev reveal that the plane was a U-2, its wreckage had been recovered, the pilot had been on a spy mission, and that Powers was in custody. To prove that the plane had been found, Khrushchev put its remains on display in Moscow's Gorky Park, along with pictures of Powers in captivity.

The timing could not have been worse. The U-2 had gone down on the eve of a summit meeting in Paris between Eisenhower and Khrushchev. It had been expected to be an amicable conference at which the leaders would agree on a policy of "peaceful coexistence." With only nine months remaining in his second term as president, Eisenhower hoped to cap his career as a general and statesman with a breakthrough in Soviet-American relations.

Arriving in Paris in a combative mood, and furiously denouncing the U.S. as "thieves and bandits," Khrushchev demanded that Eisenhower apologize. When Ike declined, Khrushchev stormed out of the summit.

Various theories were offered to explain how the supposedly invulnerable U-2 was lost. Powers stated only that he'd heard an explosion and had bailed out. Some speculated that the U-2 had been sabotaged. A Soviet pilot claimed to have been ordered to ram it. Others accepted the Soviet claim that the U-2 was brought down by a surface-to-air missile. The most likely theory is that Powers's U-2 had a mechanical problem, had lost altitude, and came within range of an SA-2 ground-to-air missile that exploded close to the plane.

In a show-trial held in Moscow, Powers was convicted of espionage and sentenced to three years in prison. Released after one year, nine months, and nine days, he was exchanged in a spy-swap for the Soviet agent Colonel Rudolf Abel. Powers was killed a few years later in the crash of a helicopter that he piloted as a traffic reporter for a radio station.

Continuing in use for half a century and with updated technology, the U-2 remained a vital part of American espionage activities throughout the Cold War, then in various crises after the collapse of the USSR. The unique aircraft was used in high-altitude weather research by the U.S. space program. It also served during the Gulf War (1990–1991). In 2003, U-2s were employed by United Nations inspectors in a search for weapons of mass destruction in Iraq.

20.

WATERGATE

The most significant political conspiracy in the United States since the assassination of President Abraham Lincoln began with what President Richard M. Nixon's press secretary, Ronald Ziegler, called "a two-bit burglary."

On June 17, 1972, five men were caught in an attempt to break into the offices of the Democratic National Committee in the Watergate Hotel in Washington, D.C. They had intended to plant electronic eavesdropping devices. Four of the men had connections to Cubans who had fled into exile in Florida after the overthrow of the government by Communist rebels led by Fidel Castro. Three had also been associated with the CIA. But the most interesting of them to the police was James W. McCord. A former agent for the CIA and FBI, he was coordinator of security for the Republican National Committee and the Committee to Re-elect the President, known as CREEP.

On September 15, a grand jury indicted the five for attempted burglary and attempted interception of telephone and other communications. Also charged were two men who had not taken part in the break-in, but had engaged in the planning. Ex-FBI agent and a former Treasury Department official and White House staff member G. Gordon Liddy was counsel to the Finance Committee of CREEP. White

71

House consultant and former CIA employee E. Howard Hunt was an author of espionage novels.

As the seven went on trial before Judge John J. Sirica, a special U.S. Senate committee, headed by Senator Sam Ervin, was conducting an investigation of campaign practices. At a press conference on March 15, Nixon denied that the White House had a role in the Watergate break-in. Yet he knew, as he wrote in his memoirs, "We already looked as if we had something to hide." On March 22, Nixon recalled, the situation was "increasingly volatile."

It became explosive the following day when James McCord sent Judge Sirica a letter that alleged a massive cover-up that was being run by presidential aides John Dean, H. R. Haldeman, John Ehrlichman, and others to conceal White House knowledge of the break-in plot. McCord also spoke with the chief counsel of the Erwin Committee, Samuel Dash. As newspapers picked up the story, Nixon wrote in his diary, "We have tended to sort of live in the idea that while the Watergate wasn't all that big as an issue in the country, that it was primarily a Washington–New York story, but now it is far more than that and with the media giving it an enormous assist, it will become worse, particularly as the defendants, if they do, begin to crack and put out various episodes of recollections which may or may not be true but which leave the terrible stigma of possible guilt on the part of the White House staff."

Summoned to testify by the Ervin committee, John Dean asserted that the break-in had been approved by Attorney General John Mitchell and that Nixon was directing the cover-up. But an equally devastating revelation came in the testimony of Alexander Butterfield about the existence of a secret tape-recording system. When a special prosecutor, Archibald Cox, sought to obtain all the tapes related to Watergate, Nixon ordered Attorney General Elliott Richardson to fire Cox. Richardson refused and was himself dismissed by Solicitor General Robert Bork. Leon Jaworksi replaced Cox as special prosecutor.

As a result of a public outcry over the Cox and Richardson firings (described in the press as "the Saturday Night Massacre"), the tapes were handed over to a grand jury that indicted several high-ranking White House officials. It named Nixon a "co-conspirator," but drew the line at indicting him.

Meanwhile, the Judiciary Committee of the House of Representatives had also been looking into Watergate. Convinced of Nixon's complicity, it adopted three articles of impeachment that charged Nixon with obstruction of justice.

Facing accusations that he had profited from financial shenanigans, Nixon told a press conference on November 18, 1973, that in his political career he had made mistakes, but he had "never profited from public service." He exclaimed, "People have got to know whether or not their President is a crook," and declared, "Well, I am not a crook."

With the Watergate conspiracy and cover-up unraveling like a cheap knitted sweater, and facing the likelihood that the House would vote for impeachment and that the Senate would vote to remove him from office, Richard Nixon became the only president to resign.

21.

DOWNFALL OF
NIKITA KHRUSHCHEV

Nikita Khrushchev's autobiography was published in the United States in 1970 after being smuggled out of the Soviet Union. In the prologue, Khrushchev wrote, "I now live like a hermit on the outskirts of Moscow. I have practically no communication with other people. I communicate only with those who guard me from others—and who guard others from me."

Between 1958 and 1964, as absolute ruler of the Union of Soviet Socialist Republics, and boss of the Communist Party, Khrushchev had been the scariest man on earth. Following the death of Stalin in 1953, he had employed the political cunning and ruthlessness that he'd learned as he rose in the ranks of the Party to eliminate or shove aside all rivals for power. In 1955 he'd startled the capitalist world by declaring, "We will bury you." At a summit meeting that year with President Eisenhower, he rejected a U.S. plan for "open skies" in which the U.S. and USSR would conduct mutual aerial surveillance of their militaries. In a speech to the Twentieth Party Congress in 1956 that was so explosive that it was kept secret for several years, he attacked Stalin's totalitarianism, denounced the "cult of personality," and launched a campaign of "de-Stalinization" in an attempt to revive the Leninist utopian ideal. Any hope in the non-Communist world that the Soviet Union might release its iron grip on countries of Eastern Europe that had been taken by the Red Army in World War II was dispelled in 1956 when Khrushchev ordered tanks into Hungary to suppress an uprising.

When conservative members of the Soviet political elite resisted Khrushchev's domestic changes, he reorganized the government and transferred key posts to allies and decentralized the Soviet system to give more power to regional governments. His goal was to surpass the United States in agricultural production through a scheme to develop the virgin lands and devote more money to farming. When his political foes tried to remove him from office in 1957 by a vote of the Politburo, he insisted he could only be replaced by a majority vote of the Central Committee of the Party. Because he controlled the committee, he remained in power. Those who had tried to remove him were no longer in a position to attempt to do so again, although none feared being sentenced to death, as they would have been under Stalin.

Khrushchev became even cockier in 1957 when the Soviets leapt into space with the launching of the first earth-orbiting satellite. Called Sputnik, it was no bigger than a basketball, but it both shook America's confidence in its technological superiority and raised the specter of Soviet intercontinental missiles tipped with nuclear warheads capable of reaching U.S. cities. While expressing a Soviet desire for "peaceful coexistence," Khrushchev was brash and rude in declaring his belief that Communism would triumph because it was "superior to the West in all things." Whether taking off a shoe and banging it on a table at the United Nations to show his displeasure during a speech by Britain's Prime Minister Harold MacMillan, embracing Fidel Castro and supporting Communism in Cuba, or challenging the right of West Berlin to exist independent of Communist East Germany, he was a very scary figure.

Convinced that Eisenhower's successor, John F. Kennedy, could be intimidated, Khrushchev sanctioned the construction of the Berlin Wall in 1961. In 1962 he gambled that he could shift the balance of world power by putting Soviet missiles in Cuba and that Kennedy would let him get away with it. It was the closest the world has ever come to nuclear war.

When the Soviet missiles were withdrawn, the end of the Cuban Missile Crisis was seen as a victory for the United States and a humiliation of the USSR. When Khrushchev agreed to a treaty to limit testing of nuclear weapons, hard-liners in the Kremlin saw it as another defeat at a time when most of the Soviet political elite was becoming increasingly angry with Khrushchev's agricultural reforms that were blamed for disastrous crop failures, resulting in an embarrassing need to import grain. Another embarrassment was a crackdown in 1963 on writers and artists who not only didn't conform to Communist ideology, but also criticized the Soviet system.

Evidently oblivious to these developments, or supremely confident in his ability to beat back all opposition, Khrushchev headed for a vacation in the Crimea in mid-October 1964. He'd barely settled when he received an urgent summons to return to Moscow. Upon arriving in the Kremlin, he was confronted by his trusted deputy Leonid Brezhnev, the esteemed Communist ideologist Mikhail Suslov, and other Party officials. Confronting him with his "failures," they accused him of the same crime of "cult of personality" for which he had blamed Stalin in 1956, and also of acting with "disregard to the state."

The next day, the Tass news agency said that the Communist Party of the Soviet Union's central committee had "accepted Mr. Khrushchev's request to be relieved of his duties and had elected Mr. Brezhnev as First Secretary; and that the Presidium of the Supreme Soviet, meeting on October 15 with President [Anastas] Mikoyan in the chair, had accepted Mr. Khrushchev's resignation as Chairman of the Council of Ministers and had appointed Mr. [Alexei] Kosygin to succeed him in that post." The official newspaper *Pravda* also reported that Khrushchev had resigned, but it went on to denounce him for "hare-brained schemes, half-baked conclusions, and hasty decisions and actions, divorced from reality." He was accused of "bragging and bluster" and "attraction to rule by fiat."

Without mentioning Khrushchev by name, *Pravda* then published an editorial on Oct. 17 which re-emphasized "the principle of collective leadership in the party," and declared that the C.P.S.U. remained "irreconcilably and consistently opposed to the ideology and practice of the personality cult"; stressed opposition to "subjectivism and drifting in the work of Communist construction"; and denounced "hare-brained scheming, immature conclusions, hasty decisions, actions divorced from reality, bragging, phrase-mongering, and commandism."

Western observers of this latest example of a Kremlin conspiracy noted that it had taken place without bloodshed and that Khrushchev had been permitted to "retire" to a government-supplied house outside Moscow. It was there over the next few years that he penned a memoir that omitted any reference to his downfall, except to complain about having to live like a hermit. When the book appeared in the West, he was forced to sign a letter saying that the publication was a fabrication and that he never sent his memoirs abroad. Three years after his death in 1971, the Soviet secret police (KGB) forced his son, Sergei, to sign a letter to the American publisher stating that the memoirs were a forgery.

Seven months before Khrushchev was ousted, the U.S. Central Intelligence Agency had noted in a memorandum ("The Coming Struggle for Power in the USSR") that because of the conspiratorial character of the leadership of the Soviet Union, it was impossible to predict with precision or certainty the outcome of the next succession crisis in the USSR. "While no one can name the man who will someday succeed Khrushchev, that man is probably at this moment sitting on the Presidium of the CPSU. And, while we cannot identify the policies that this successor will follow after his advent to power, the outline of these policies may already be at least faintly visible in the murk of current Soviet political controversy and in the changing form of Soviet society as a whole." Over the next quarter of a century there would be several successors to Khrushchev before Soviet society would change. When it did so in the 1980s under Mikhail Gorbachev, the future of the Soviet Union would again rest in the hands of a group of conspirators.

22.

IRAN-CONTRA

In an ultra-secret operation in the mid-1980s, top men in President Ronald Reagan's administration developed a plan to sell missiles to Iran in order to gain Iran's help in obtaining the release of Americans who were being held hostage by terrorists in Lebanon. The money from the missile sales was used to aid anti-Communist forces (Contras) in Nicaragua. But the intricate scheme raised problems for the plotters. As for gaining the freedom of the hostages, Reagan had pledged never to negotiate with terrorists. There was also an embargo on any trading with Iran. Aid to the Contras also violated a law (the Boland Amendment, passed by Congress over the objections of the Reagan administration) that prohibited any American government agency that was "involved in intelligence activities" from helping the Contras in their guerilla war with the Nicaraguan government, known as Sandinistas.

Like almost all conspiracies, Iran-Contra began as a plan of action with a single goal that was clearly defined and limited in scope: to free the hostages. But the possibility of achieving this by means of making an arms deal with Iran did not originate within the White House. The tantalizing prospect was presented in July 1985 by an official of Israel to Robert McFarlane, President Reagan's national security adviser.

The U.S. weapons would not go directly to Iran, but would be transported via Israel. The operation would be conducted in secrecy by the president's National Security Council (NSC), headed by McFarlane, assisted by Admiral John Poindexter and a young Marine officer, Lieutenant Oliver North.

Two weeks after the first planeload of arms arrived in Iran, a hostage was released in Lebanon. As the plan proceeded and other hostages were released, with the money from the arms sales approaching thirty million dollars, North wrote a memorandum to McFarlane proposing that some of the funds be secretly funneled to the Contras. Legal justification rested upon an interpretation of the Boland Amendment in which the conclusion was reached that it did not cover the NSC. To make all this legal, Reagan signed a presidential "finding" authorizing the CIA to handle the arms sales and the NSC to carry out the aid to the Contras. Both operations were to be kept secret, even from Congress. But in early November of 1986, the "arms for hostages deal" was disclosed in Lebanese newspapers.

As an outraged Congress rushed to investigate and the aid to the Contras became known, the American news media pounced on what headlines called the "Iran-Contra Scandal." Poindexter resigned and the spotlight turned to North. Immediately fired in an attempt at face-saving by the Reagan administration, the Marine officer received a summons to testify at a joint Senate-House investigating committee. When he appeared on the morning of July 7, 1987, in the Senate Caucus Room in the Russell Senate Office Building, on the chest of his olive-green Marine uniform was a rainbow of seven rows of medals signifying his battlefield heroism in Vietnam and elsewhere. As the nation eagerly tuned in to watch on television, one committee staffer predicted that the inquisitors would take "all the fruit salad off North's uniform."

Instead, Senators and Representatives found themselves beating a hasty retreat in the face of an outpouring of public sympathy for the clean-cut-looking Marine who had declared, "I think it is very important for the American people to understand that this is a dangerous world, that we live at risk, and that this nation is at risk in a dangerous world. And that they ought not to be led to believe, as a consequence of these hearings, that this nation cannot or should not conduct covert operations." Justifying the secrecy of the Iran-Contra operation, he said it was conducted "in such a way that our adversaries would not have knowledge of them." The plot also allowed the U.S. government to "deny American association with it, or the association of this government with those activities," he continued. "And that is not wrong."

Although North and Poindexter were convicted of withholding information from the Congress and for obstruction of justice, the verdicts were vacated on appeal because all their testimony before the joint committee had been made with a grant of immunity from prosecution based on it. Eventually, Reagan's successor, George H. W. Bush, granted presidential pardons to MacFarlane and other Iran-Contra figures, including Secretary of Defense Caspar Weinberger and Assistant Secretary of State Elliott Abrams. A 1994 report by an independent prosecutor found that Reagan and Vice President Bush had some knowledge of what their aides were doing and about the cover-up, but no evidence had been discovered to indicate that they'd committed a crime. In a speech from the Oval Office, President Reagan took responsibility for Iran-Contra, but he also said he did not believe he had actually traded arms for hostages.

23.

IRISH REPUBLICAN ARMY

After failing to assassinate Britain's Prime Minister Margaret Thatcher and members of her Cabinet by exploding a 100-pound bomb in the bathroom of her suite in the Grand Hotel as Britain's Conservative Party held its yearly conference in Brighton, England, on October 12, 1984, the Provisional Irish Republican Army issued a statement from Dublin, Ireland, that was a succinct and chilling definition of the power that rests in the heart of all conspiracies whose goal is gaining political power through violence. Addressed to Mrs. Thatcher and claiming responsibility for the attack, it said, "Today we were unlucky, but remember we only have to be lucky once. You will have to be lucky always. Give Ireland peace and there will be no war."

The group that tried to kill Thatcher traced its roots to a failed attempt to gain Ireland's independence from England in 1926. When this uprising, known as the "Easter Rebellion," was quelled, the most militant remnants of the Irish Republican Army (IRA) followed their leader, Michael Collins, to continue the violence as the "military wing" of a legal political party (Sinn Fein). Following creation of the Irish Free State in 1922, in which six predominately Protestant counties (Ulster) remained part of the United Kingdom, the IRA carried out bombings, raids, and street battles on both sides of the Irish border.

When a former IRA member, Eamon de Valera, took over the Free State government in 1932, popular support for the organization declined. It diminished further during World War II, when IRA anti-British vehemence took the form of sympathies with Nazi Germany. Outlawed by Ireland and Britain in 1949, the IRA became a secret organization and continued its campaign of violence through the 1950s in Belfast, Northern Ireland, along the border, and in London. Then came nearly a decade of inaction. But after a parade on August 12, 1969, by Protestants (known as the Orange Boys of Londonderry), through the Catholic area of the city known as "the Bogside," rioting resulted in the arrival of a British army of occupation.

Faced with this reality, the IRA split into factions. The "officials" hoped to attain a Socialist united Ireland by peaceful means. The "provisionals" began a reign of terrorism in the North and in England that included bombings, assassinations, kidnappings, punishment beatings, robberies, extortion, and attacks against train and subways stations and shopping areas. One of its most devastating actions occurred on "Bloody Friday," July 21, 1972, when twenty-six bombs in Belfast killed nine people and injured 130.

Allied with other terrorist groups in the Middle East, Germany, Italy, and Libya, and loosely allied with the Soviet Union's KGB, the IRA gained financial support in large part from Irish groups in the United States. Its most notorious act took place on August 27, 1979, with the assassination of Queen Elizabeth II's uncle and World War II hero Lord Louis Mountbatten. This was followed in 1981 by a foiled plot to kill Prince Charles and Princess Diana; the attempted assassination of Margaret Thatcher and her Cabinet; discovery in November 1987 of a shipment of weapons and surface-to-air missiles en route to the IRA from Libya; a mortar attack on the offices of Prime Minister John Major at Number Ten Downing Street in the center of London; a one-ton bomb set off in London's financial district that caused a billion dollars worth of damage on October 23, 1993; a bombing of London's popular tourist area called Canary Wharf in February 1996; and a bomb blast in Omagh, Northern Ireland, on August 15, 1998, that killed twenty-nine and wounded more than 200. Other, lesser acts of violence and terror took place in England and Ireland, and against British officials and organizations in Europe as well.

Since the creation in 1998 of a Northern Ireland Assembly, comprised of Catholics and Protestants, greater cooperation between Northern Ireland and the Irish Republic, and Sinn Fein participation in a Northern Irish government, various plans for a peaceful settlement of what the Irish and the British called "the troubles" or "the Irish problem" have depended upon the IRA's agreement to disarm themselves. As of 2003, they hadn't, leaving the issue of the peace of Ireland unresolved and the IRA still operating as one of the world's oldest conspiratorial groups.

24

THE HITLER-STALIN PACT OF 1939

When foreign ministers of Nazi Germany and the Union of Soviet Socialist Republics signed a non-aggression treaty in Moscow on August 23, 1939, the rest of the world gasped in astonishment. Seemingly like a bolt out of the blue, dictators who had despised one another, Adolf Hitler and Josef Stalin, had struck a bargain to "obligate themselves to desist from any act of violence, any aggressive action, and any attack on each other, individually or jointly with other Powers."

The agreement was especially shocking to diplomats of Great Britain and France. After a Nazi takeover of Czechoslovakia in 1938 (with the approval of Britain) and a promise by Hitler that he had no more territorial demands, the British and French had been engaged in negotiations with the Soviet Union for a mutual-defense alliance. Conducting the talks for the USSR was its Jewish foreign minister, Maxim Litvinov. What the negotiators did not know was that Stalin had decided to seek a mutual non-aggression treaty with Hitler.

This change of direction was based on Stalin's calculation that the Soviet Union was not militarily prepared to join in another war between Germany and its World War I foes. He was also distrustful of Britain and France. He suspected that if Hitler's army moved against

Russia, the British and French might choose to let Germany and the Soviet Union fight to the death. He also saw the prospect that a deal with Hitler could open the door to the Soviet Union gaining control of its western borders. A peace pact would also buy time for the Soviet Union to build up its military. But Stalin knew that in order to bargain with Hitler, he would have to replace his Jewish top diplomat. To replace Litvinov, Stalin chose Vyacheslav Molotov. Having survived by cunning and discretion through three decades of the intrigues of the Soviet system by allying himself with Stalin, he was the perfect choice to deal with Hitler's top diplomatic henchman, Joachim von Ribbentrop. Germany's chargé d'affaires in Moscow informed Berlin on May 3, 1939, that the new Commissar of Foreign Affairs was "one of Stalin's closest and most intimate advisors, and not a Jew."

Invited to Moscow, Ribbentrop arrived on August 23 and immediately sat down with Molotov to work out a deal. When it was reached and announced, it appeared to be exactly what had been expected—a straightforward pledge by Germany and the USSR not to attack one another and to settle disputes "through friendly exchange of opinions" or arbitration. The pact left the rest of the world feeling stunned that these dictators had declared themselves friends and allies. A cartoon by David Low in the *London Evening Standard* showed Hitler and Stalin bowing to each other over a corpse. Hitler asks, "The scum of Earth, I believe?" Stalin replies, "The bloody assassin of the workers, I presume?"

Unknown to the world was that Molotov and Ribbentrop had also agreed on a four-point secret protocol that was a death sentence for Poland. The country that stood between Germany and Russia was to be divided between them, and the Soviet Union would dominate the Baltic states of Estonia, Latvia and Lithuania. The immediate result of this conspiracy between Hitler and Stalin was Germany's invasion of Poland on September 1, 1939, the start of World War II, and the Soviet Union moving into eastern Poland and the Baltic states and remaining there at the end of the war.

This secret re-drawing of the map of eastern Europe in 1939 in what became known both as the "Ribbentrop-Molotov Pact" and the "Hitler-Stalin Pact," would eventually take the form of Soviet control of eastern Europe behind what Winston Churchill termed an "Iron Curtain" that would exist throughout the fifty years of the Cold War.

25.

THE REICHSTAG FIRE

A Nazi conspiracy to burn down Germany's parliament building, the Reichstag, on the night of February 27, 1933, and then blame the fire on Communists, was the most significant case of arson for a political purpose since British soldiers stormed through Washington, D.C., in the War of 1812 and torched the White House and the Capitol. The plot was part of a grander scheme by Hitler to grab control of a democratic government, the Weimar Republic, whose president was a revered but aged World War I hero, Paul von Hindenberg.

When the National Socialist (Nazi) Party won a large number of seats in the Reichstag, Hindenberg had reluctantly named Hitler as Chancellor. It was a post similar to that of prime minister, but Hitler intended to use its powers to legally establish himself as dictator. His first step in this scheme was to demand that Hindenberg approve the calling of a new election on March 5, 1933, in which Nazi thugs would ensure that the Nazi party would gain a majority of the seats in the Reichstag and be in a position to legally grant Hitler the dictatorship he coveted. To win the backing of German generals, Hitler promised that the army would not be supplanted by brown-shirted stormtroopers (SA) whose use of brute force had brought Hitler to power.

Another result of Hitler's maneuvering was the signing of an "emergency decree" by Hindenberg that gave the Nazis control of Germany's largest province (Prussia) and the German capital, Berlin. Hitler's second-in-command, Hermann Goering, was in charge of the police. His first act was to Nazify the force and unleash it against anyone he deemed an enemy, but especially Communists. He then ordered a raid on Communist Party headquarters in Berlin in which its membership lists were seized. Among the names was that of a twenty-four-year-old Marxist from Holland, Marinus van der Lebbe. Because he had been wandering around the city for more than a week calling for a Communist revolt and starting fires in government buildings to protest capitalism, he emerged as the perfect fall guy in a plot hatched by Goering and the Nazi Party's propagandist, Joseph Goebbels, to burn the Reichstag, and blame it on Communists.

Although the details of what happened on the night of February 27, 1933, are not known, it is recorded that van der Lebbe entered the Reichstag around nine o'clock and started several small fires. At the same time, Nazi arsonists made their way through a tunnel that connected Goering's offices with the parliament building and started additional fires. When Hitler raced to the conflagration from having dinner with Goebbels, he found Goering already at the scene and blaming the blaze on Communists. In the glow of the flames, Hitler blurted that the fire was "a beacon from heaven." He told a reporter, "You are now witnessing the beginning of a great epoch. This fire is the beginning."

Leaving the symbol of German democracy to burn and crumble into ruins, Hitler and Goebbels rushed to the offices of the Nazi newspaper, *Volkisher Beobacher*, and supervised its reporting that the fire had been started by Communists in a scheme to seize power. At a cabinet meeting on the morning of February 28, he obtained a decree "for the Protection of the people and State" that stated: "Restrictions on personal liberty, on the right of free expression of opinion, including freedom of the press; on the rights of assembly and association; and violations of the privacy of postal, telegraphic and telephonic communications and warrants for house searches, orders for confiscations as well as restrictions on property, are also permissible beyond the legal limits otherwise prescribed." Signed by Hindenberg that evening, the document made Hitler a dictator.

On March 3, 1933, Hermann Goering declared, "I don't have to worry about justice; my mission is only to destroy and exterminate, nothing more. Every bullet which leaves the barrel of a police pistol is now my bullet." He said that the forthcoming parliamentary election, which the Nazis were guaranteed to win, "will certainly be the last for the next ten years, probably for the next hundred years."

All that remained to complete the Reichstag fire conspiracy was to conduct a trial of the man who had been set up for blame. Marinus van der Lebbe was tried, convicted, and sentenced to death. He was beheaded on January 10, 1934.

26.

THE PLOT
TO KILL HITLER

On July 20, 1944, no one in the German army laid better claim to the status of war hero than Colonel Claus Schenk Graf von Stauffenberg. A career staff officer since 1926, he had served with distinction during the takeover of Czechoslovakia in 1938, the invasion of Poland in 1939, and the 1940 conquest of France. Assigned to the Tenth Panzer Division under Field Marshal Erwin Rommel's Afrika Corps in early 1943, he suffered the loss of his left eye, right hand, and two fingers of his left hand when Allied planes attacked a convoy and strafed his vehicle during the battle of the Kasserine Pass. Promoted to Colonel in June 1944, he was appointed Chief of Staff to the Commander of the Home Army (reserves), by General Friederich Fromm.

At this time, when Allied forces were expanding from D-Day beachheads in France and the high command was receiving increasingly disturbing reports about the army's involvement in mass executions of Jews and others in the countries of eastern Europe, a group of generals and important civilians agreed that the only way to save Germany from complete destruction was to remove Hitler from power, declare a new government, and seek an armistice. The basis for such a scheme was an already-existing plan. Called "Operation Valkyrie," it had been devised for the purpose of dealing with any anti-Nazi uprising that might occur.

Among the army officers who enlisted in the plot were Major General Henning von Tresckow, General Friedrich Olbricht, and First Lieutenant Fritz-Dietlof Graf von der Schulenberg of the army reserve. Aware of the conspiracy but not directly involved was Field Marshal Rommel, who was recuperating from wounds he'd suffered when his staff car was attacked on a road in France.

All of these men were aware that two attempts to kill Hitler had been made in March 1943. In the first, a bomb planted in Hitler's plane failed to explode. A second bombing was to be at an exhibition of captured Soviet equipment. The plan fizzled when the show was postponed. On March 11, 1944, a plan to shoot him at his Obsersalzberg mountain retreat had to be called off because the assassin, Hauptmann Ebehard von Breitenbuch, couldn't get close enough.

Because Stauffenberg was a genuine war hero with a spotless record as a staff officer, and was now in a position that frequently required him to attend Hitler's military strategy briefings, he was seen by the conspirators as the ideal individual to carry out the first stage of Operation Valkyrie by assassinating Hitler. How Stauffenberg was approached, and by whom, isn't certain. General Franz Halder said later that he had "recognized in Claus von Stauffenberg a born leader, one whose outlook on life was rooted in a sense of responsibility toward God, who was not prepared to be satisfied with theoretical explanations and discussions, but who was burning to act."

Hitler himself may have persuaded Stauffenberg. After observing Hitler during one of his meetings with his generals, Stauffenberg said, "Fate has offered us this opportunity, and I would not refuse it for anything in the world. I have examined myself before God and my conscience. It must be done because this man [Hitler] is evil personified."

Required to attend a meeting between Hitler and his generals at Hitler's Obsersalzberg hilltop fortress, the Berghof, on July 11, 1944, Stauffenberg carried a concealed time bomb in a briefcase, but for an unexplained reason was unable to carry out the assassination. A second plan (July 15) to kill Hitler, the head of the SS (Heinrich Himmler) and Air Marshal Hermann Goering, at Hitler's headquarters near Rastenburg in East Prussia, known as Wolf's Lair, was called off by senior conspirators in Berlin when they learned that Himmler and Goering would not be meeting with Hitler on the fifteenth.

Five days later, Stauffenberg returned to Wolf's Lair with an accomplice, Lieutenant Werner von Haeften, for another meeting. Their plan was for Stauffenberg to place a briefcase containing a time bomb under the conference table, and then be summoned from the building to take a phone call placed by Haeften. After the explosion, they were to fly back to Berlin in time for the launching of the coup. Unfortunately, the blast didn't kill Hitler. Injured and stunned, he stumbled from the wrecked building and recovered to take charge of rounding up the plotters and anyone merely suspected of belonging to the conspiracy.

At 12:20 AM the next day (July 21, 1944), Stauffenberg, Haeften, General Olbricht, and another plotter, Merz von Quimheim, were executed by firing squad.

27.

BODYGUARD OF LIES

When Soviet Premier Josef Stalin turned to British Prime Minister Winston Churchill during the 1943 conference with President Franklin D. Roosevelt at Tehran, Iran, he inquired as to how the British and Americans intended to keep the Germans from discovering the site of their planned invasion of Europe. Churchill replied, "It will be the greatest hoax in history."

The largest, most complex, daring, dangerous, and successful military conspiracy ever devised, the operation was not only conceived by Churchill, it also got its code name from him. "In wartime," he was fond of saying, "truth is so precious that she should always be attended by a bodyguard of lies."

Planning and carrying out "Operation Bodyguard" was assigned to the "Committee of Twenty." Consisting of British and American army intelligence officers, it was coordinated by the "London Controlling Section." They faced a double challenge. German army intelligence services, and Hitler himself, had to be convinced that Allied troops massing in the south of England opposite the French beaches at Normandy were a diversionary force. They also had to be tricked into believing that the actual invasion force would cross the narrowest point of the English Channel in the vicinity of the Pas de Calais.

This required not only the creation of a fake army in the north, designated First U.S. Army Group (FUSAG), but manufacturing of an illusion that it was large, engaged in training, and in constant communication with General Eisenhower's headquarters in London. To be sure that the Germans were informed of FUSAG's activity through their listening stations in France, bogus messages were transmitted from FUSAG's imaginary headquarters by radio. Expecting that German surveillance aircraft would be sent to overfly the region, buildings and tents were erected and military vehicles were sent out to ply the roads. Equipment such as trucks and tanks were made of inflatable rubber and shifted regularly from one spot to another while a real truck or tank laid down tracks. But the most persuasive of the FUSAG deceptions was naming as its commander the general whom the Germans expected to lead the invasion, George S. Patton. Fake radio messages were also sent from Scotland about a plan to invade Norway.

Essential to the credibility of this grand deception was keeping Hitler and his intelligence service from receiving contradictory reports from their spies in Britain. In this, the Allies had the benefit of possessing the key to reading Germany's military communications. An intricate code machine called "Enigma," it had been stolen before the war and deciphered by a small group of mathematicians and code breakers. (In a top-secret operation called "Ultra" they created the first computer.) As a result of this breakthrough, the Allies were able to read messages to and from Hitler and his generals, sometimes before the Germans even received them.

Because "Ultra" provided Allied intelligence with the names and addresses of every German spy in England and other countries, the agents were rounded up. "Turned" into double-agents, they became an integral part of the "Bodyguard" deception by sending Allied-supplied data that "confirmed" the existence of FUSAG as the real invasion force and that the massing of troops in the south of England for a landing at Normandy was a diversionary force. Consequently, when the Allied troops flooded ashore on June 6, 1944 (D-Day), the German tank and infantry units stationed around Calais remained in place, waiting for a FUSAG that never came.

One of the most bizarre deceptions of "Bodyguard" was memorialized in a 1956 feature movie called *The Man Who Never Was.* The body of a British solider who had drowned was put into the Mediterranean Sea off the coast of Spain. When it drifted ashore, it was found to have documents that indicated plans for another Allied invasion in the region of the Balkans, along with faked identity papers that if checked by German intelligence could be verified.

The idea of an invasion of southern Europe was also instilled in the German army's high command by using a former British actor. A virtual double for General Bernard Montgomery, he made himself conspicuous by inspecting British installations at Gibraltar, lending further credence in Germany to an impending invasion that didn't occur.

The "Bodyguard" deceptions succeeded, according to journalist/historian Ernest Volkman in his book *Espionage: The Greatest Spy Operations of the 20th Century*, for the same reason all other similar deceptions succeed: the willingness of the victim to be deceived. "In the case of the Germans," he noted, "they were victimized by their devotion to military logic, the prism through which they filtered what little [military] intelligence they had. It amounted to a classic case of a preconception firmly held, with no attempt to consider any alternatives."

28

ASSASSINATION OF SOUTH VIETNAMESE PRESIDENT DIEM

When bulletins flashed from South Vietnam on November 1, 1963, that the country's president, Ngo Dinh Diem, and his brother and closest advisor, Ngo Dinh Nhu, had been murdered during a military takeover of the government, the news was accepted by many Americans as one more baffling event in a seemingly endless war with the Communist Viet Cong, supported by Communist North Vietnam. The assassinations followed a series of protests by Buddhist leaders against policies enacted by the Catholic-controlled government of President Diem. When several monks committed suicide in public by setting themselves on fire, Nhu's controversial wife inflamed the crisis by dismissing them as the publicity stunts of pro-Communist Buddhists and calling them "Buddhist bonfires."

In May, these religious tensions erupted into violence when the Vietnamese police and military forces killed twelve Buddhist demonstrators while suppressing a demonstration in the city of Hue. This was followed on August 21 by raids, ordered by Nhu, on Buddhist pagodas throughout the country. The attacks were necessary, the government explained, because the Buddhists were collaborating with the Viet Cong and North Vietnamese. When the raids resulted in a worldwide backlash, Nhu tried to shift the blame to several key South Vietnamese generals. Their reaction was a plot to overthrow the Diem government. But in contemplating a takeover, they faced the problem of the United States. The question was whether a coup would provide President John F. Kennedy, a Roman Catholic, with an excuse to withdraw American support from the new government and pull the United States out of Vietnam.

What the coup planners could not know was that for Kennedy, support for Diem, who was viewed as a Roman Catholic dictator in a predominantly Buddhist nation, had become an acute embarrassment for the first Catholic president of the United States. Consequently, when the U.S. ambassador in Saigon, Henry Cabot Lodge, picked up whispers of a plot against Diem, it was welcome news at the White House. With Kennedy's blessing, Lodge immediately opened secret negotiations with the dissident generals. During these talks, Lodge communicated secretly with Kennedy, leaving the State Department, the Pentagon, and General Paul D. Harkins, the commanding American General in Vietnam who was against withdrawing support from Diem, in the dark. The problem facing Kennedy if he openly supported a coup was uncertainty about what might happen if it failed. He informed Lodge that although the United States didn't wish to "stimulate" a coup, it had no desire to prevent one. What mattered most to the United States was that whatever happened, the American government would be able to deny any part in it.

Believing that secret meetings with Lodge were in effect the American government's blessing on a coup, South Vietnamese generals, led by Major General Duong Van Minh, moved to seize control of the government. As fighting raged, President Diem telephoned Lodge and demanded, "I want to know what is the attitude of the U.S.?"

Lodge replied, "I do not feel well enough informed to be able to tell you. I have heard the shooting, but am not acquainted with all the facts." But he knew enough to tell Diem, "I have a report that those in charge of the current activity offer you and your brother safe conduct out of the country if you will resign." He then said, "If I can do anything for your physical safety, please call me."

By the time the rebels captured the presidential palace, Diem and Nhu had fled to the suburb of Cholon. Making contact with the generals, they were promised safe passage from the country. They accepted the pledge. Believing that they were on their way to exile, they entered an armored personnel carrier. Moments later, on orders of the generals, they were murdered.

Although Kennedy had no way of knowing that U.S. connivance in Diem's removal would result in the murder of Diem and Nhu, by indirectly helping to overthrow Diem, the United States had in effect taken over South Vietnam and the conduct of the war. Although much has been said and written in hindsight to the effect that Kennedy had been considering withdrawing from Vietnam, he not only continued the American commitment, but was in the process of expanding it when he was assassinated three weeks after Diem's murder.

A few months later, Kennedy's successor, Lyndon B. Johnson, who had opposed U.S. complicity in the plot to remove Diem, found an almost religious explanation for Kennedy's assassination. He told a friend it had been "retribution" for the death of Diem.

29.

THE BRINK'S ROBBERY

A bold stick-up caper pulled off with breathtaking audacity on the evening of January 17, 1950, in Boston, Massachusetts, "the Brink's job" was immediately labeled "the crime of the century" by the nation's newspapers. Spoken of with awe and admiration by cops as well as crooks, it was quickly enshrined in the annals of American criminal folklore in countless magazine articles, books, and movies. The robbery was carried out so efficiently and successfully that FBI director J. Edgar Hoover speculated it had to be the work of a Communist conspiracy. But the biggest hold-up to that time, which netted the gang $2,775,395.12, of which $1,218,211.29 was in cash, actually was the brainchild of previously small-time thief Anthony "Tony" Pino.

Fresh out of prison in 1944, Pino set his sights on making the greatest score of his life at the expense of the Brink's Armored Car Company. Convinced that pulling the heist by knocking off one of its famously guarded trucks was not only too dangerous, but not a promising-enough payoff even if it did succeed, Pino chose to go for the big bucks by raiding the company's main counting facility and depository where the armored trucks delivered the sacks of money they had collected from businesses and banks. After observing the Brink's operation, he was amazed to find that the country's most respected and trusted security firm had become shockingly sloppy in protecting its own property.

Determined to rob a new depository that Brink's opened in December 1948 at 165 Prince Street, Pino began recruiting accomplices. Experienced and professional criminals, the gang members were Joseph "Specs" O'Keefe, Stanley Gusciora, Joseph Ginnis, Adolph "Jazz" Maffie, Henry Baker, Michael Vincent Geagan, Jimmy Faherty, Thomas Richardson, Vincent Costa, and Joseph Sylvester Banfield. During months spent casing the target, they were able to sneak in several times, map the layout of the building, remove lock cylinders from five doors, have keys made, replace the cylinders, obtain delivery schedules, and observe the handling of the money sacks. Their transportation to and from the heist was a stolen Ford pickup truck.

At approximately 7:00 PM on January 17, 1950, the gang met in the Roxbury section of Boston. Banfield was the driver and alone in the front of the truck. Pino, O'Keefe, Faherty, Baker, Maffie, Gusciora, Geagan, and Richardson rode in the back. On the way from Roxbury Pino distributed Navy-type peacoats and chauffeur's caps. Each man was given a pistol, a pair of gloves, and a Halloween mask. O'Keefe wore crepe-soled shoes and the others had rubber overshoes. As the truck approached the Brink's offices, lights on the Prince Street side of the building were out. After continuing up the street to the end of the playground that adjoined the Brink's building, the truck stopped. All but Pino and Banfield stepped out and waited for an all-clear signal from Costa in the truck. After receiving it, the armed seven walked to the entrance, donned their masks, and entered with a copied key. Other keys enabled them to proceed to the second floor to catch five of Brink's employees by surprise. With them securely bound and gagged, the gang began looting the premises.

Before fleeing with the bags of loot, the seven attempted to open a metal box containing the payroll of the General Electric Company, but they'd brought no tools. With the loot piled in the truck, they sped away. As they did so, Brink's employees freed themselves and reported the crime. Banfield drove the truck to the house of Maffie's parents in Roxbury. The loot was then quickly unloaded, and Banfield sped away to hide the truck. By this time, the Boston police were already drawing up a list of most-likely suspects.

Before removing the loot from the house on January 18, 1950, the gang attempted to identify incriminating items. Extensive efforts were made to detect pencil markings and other notations on the currency that the criminals thought might be traceable. Fearing that new bills might be linked with the crime, McGinnis suggested a process for "aging" the new money "in a hurry." On the night of January 18, 1950, O'Keefe and Gusciora received $100,000 each from the robbery loot. They put the entire $200,000 in the trunk of O'Keefe's automobile. Subsequently, O'Keefe left his car and the $200,000 in a garage on Blue Hill Avenue in Boston. During the period immediately following the Brink's robbery, the heat was on O'Keefe and Gusciora. Both were taken into custody during the latter part of January 1950. O'Keefe got word to McGinnis to recover his car and the $200,000.

Out on bail a few weeks later, O'Keefe arranged to retrieve his share of the loot. It was given to him in a suitcase that was transferred to his car from another car occupied by McGinnis and Banfield. Later, when O'Keefe counted the money, he found that the suitcase contained $98,000. He had been short-changed $2,000. With no place to keep such a large sum of money, he chose to give it to Maffie for safekeeping. Except for $5,000 that he'd previously taken, O'Keefe would never see his share. Bitter about this and other matters (including an attempt to kill him), and while in jail in Pennsylvania for an unrelated crime, O'Keefe would eventually be pressured to confess to the FBI. He explained that talking was his way of "taking care of them all."

On January 11, 1956, the United States Attorney at Boston authorized Special Agents of the FBI to file complaints charging the eleven gang members with conspiracy to commit theft of Government property, robbery of Government property, bank robbery by force and violence and by intimidation, and assault on Brink's employees. McGinnis was named in two other complaints involving the receiving and concealing of the loot. FBI Agents arrested Baker, Costa, Geagan, Maffie, McGinnis, and Pino on January 12, 1956. Three of the remaining five had been previously accounted for. O'Keefe and Gusciora were in prison on other charges, Banfield was dead, and Faherty and Richardson had fled to avoid apprehension. Put on the FBI's list of "Ten Most Wanted Fugitives," they were arrested on May 16, 1956, in an FBI raid on an apartment in which they were hiding in Dorchester, Massachusetts.

O'Keefe was the principal witness when the case came to trial. On October 5, 1956, a jury deliberated for three and a half hours and convicted everyone. All were given life sentences. But nearly seven years after the robbery, more than $2,775,000, including $1,218,211.29 in cash, was still unaccounted for. While small amounts were eventually recovered, the tantalizing question of the whereabouts of more than $1,150,000 remained unanswered.

30.

THE GREAT TRAIN ROBBERY

Although train robbing had been invented by a gang of desperadoes led by Frank and Jesse James in the late 1800s, the most spectacular plundering of a train by a gang happened in England on August 8, 1963. The target was the Glasgow-to-London mail train, near the town of Cheddington in rural Buckinghamshire. The loot totaled 2.3 million pounds (the equivalent of nearly seven million American dollars), almost all of it in one-, five-, and ten-pound bank notes.

Mastermind of the heist was Bruce Reynolds. An antiques dealer, he lived the high life and drove the same kind of Aston-Martin preferred by the fictional British intelligence officer James Bond. Inspired by the exploits of the James brothers and other American train robbers, he assembled a gang of fifteen crooks. Among them were small-time burglar, fraud artist, and ex-boxer "Buster" Edwards; burly Gordon Goody whose muscular arms were adorned with tattoos; Charlie Wilson, a well-known face in Scotland Yard's collection of mug shots; John Wheater, a lawyer whose reputation and respectability were employed to rent a nearby hideout called Leatherslade Farm; Wheater's friend Brian Field; Roy James, who would drive one of two Land Rovers and a truck for the getaway; and a friend of Reynolds, Ronnie Biggs. The youngest of the gang, Biggs's value to the plot was his connection to a retired train driver with information on mail train schedules.

After gathering data on movements of cash and valuables by Royal Mail trains in and out of London, Reynolds looked for a location to pull a robbery that was close enough to London so that changes in the daily routines of the members of the gang would not attract the attention of the police. The site also had to be both secluded and near roads that were used by heavy trucks. Because Leatherslade Farm was near a Royal Air Force base at Haughton, and close to a bridge spanning the railway between the villages of Cheddington and Linslade, it was the ideal spot. To bring the train to a halt, a control light would be covered and a battery of fake lights would be substituted to flash a warning signal to halt the train near Bridego Bridge. When it stopped, the operators would be forced by the gang, who'd be dressed like railway workers, to uncouple the car with the money and then move the rest of the train forward.

As the scheme unfolded according to plan at 3:30 in the morning of August 8, the fireman of the train, David Whitby, stepped down from the locomotive, realized what was happening, and said to one of the gang, "It's all right mate, I'm on your side." But when engineer Jack Mills resisted, he was hit on the head with a pistol. Bleeding and groggy, he was forced to move the train forward, leaving the Post Office Sorting Coach to be looted without resistance from its staff. Working quickly, the robbers carried away 120 money sacks. Because the Land Rovers and truck were filled, other bags had to be abandoned. As the gang departed, Whitby, Mills, and the mail car workers were warned to "do nothing for half an hour."

That proved to be a mistake. It told Scotland Yard detectives that the gang planned to "hole up" somewhere within thirty minutes driving time. With the search area limited, they soon found what they were looking for. At Leatherslade Farm they found not only getaway vehicles, but empty mail sacks, money wrappers, sleeping bags, eating utensils, a food bowl for a cat, a salt box, a wrapper from a first aid kit, and a Monopoly game. All of these yielded fingerprints.

With identities of the robbers verified, Detective Chief Superintendent Thomas Marcus Butler of Scotland Yard commenced a dragnet that quickly scooped up five of them. "Wanted" posters of nine others and sleuthing resulted in nine arrests and convictions. Among those picked up was Ronald Biggs, but he and gang member Charles Wilson escaped from prison and fled the country. Wilson was located in Canada and returned to England, but Biggs had skipped to Rio de Janeiro where he was safe from Butler's grasp because Brazilian law did not permit his extradition. Also on the loose was the mastermind of what was now known as the "Great Train Robbery." Bruce Reynolds had slipped through the dragnet, traveling to Mexico, Canada, the United States, Germany, and the South of France until the need for money forced him back to England. When Butler surprised him in the seaside town of Torquay on November 8, 1968, the Scotland Yarder said, "Hello, Bruce. It's been a long time." Reynolds replied, "C'est la vie." He then went off with Butler and received a sentence of ten years.

That left only Biggs at large. A cheeky crook in his Brazilian safe haven, he sold his story to a London newspaper with the boastful title "The World's Most Wanted Man." He remained out of reach until he unwisely returned to England in May 2001. Arrested immediately, he was sent back to prison to complete his twenty-five year sentence.

Less than one-seventh of the loot was recovered.

31.

ASSASSINATION OF JULIUS CAESAR

Until John Wilkes Booth crept into the presidential box of Ford's Theater in Washington, D.C., shot a fatal bullet into Abraham Lincoln's brain, and jumped to the stage shouting the Latin phrase *"Sic semper tyrannis,"* history's most significant assassination had been carried out by a group of Roman senators led by Brutus. These senators feared their republic was in danger of becoming a dictatorship, not by means of force, but by popular demand that political power be put in the hands of Rome's greatest general, Julius Caesar.

"From this time," wrote a contemporary historian about a conspiracy that was hatched by a group of Senators led by Brutus, Cassius, Casca, and others, "they tried the inclinations of all their acquaintances that they could trust, and communicated the secret to them, and took into the design not only their familiar friends, but as many as they believed bold and brave and unafraid of death. And, though they neither gave nor took any oath of secrecy, nor used any other sacred rite to assure their fidelity to each other, they all kept their design close."

Knowing that Caesar would be attending a meeting of the senate on a day in mid-March called the "Ides," they agreed "to make use of that opportunity; for then they might appear all together without suspicion; and, besides, they hoped that all the noblest and leading men of the commonwealth, being then assembled as soon as the great deed was done, would immediately stand forward and assert the common liberty."

The place at which they chose to act was a portico of the senate. Called "Pompey's porch," it held a statue of the Roman hero Pompey. The conspirators agreed to meet at the home of Cassius and proceed to Pompey's porch with knives concealed in their togas. Their plan was to strike while senators and citizens voicing complaints and appeals surrounded Caesar. But when he arrived, he announced that he would not follow the custom that day because he was feeling ill. Popilius Laenas, who was not one of the conspirators, but had wished Brutus "good success," came up to Caesar and "conversed a great while with him." Fearing that Laenas was warning Caesar, the assassins, "looking upon one another, agreed from their countenances" that they had to act. As they drew their daggers, they saw Laenas kiss Caesar's hand and step away, "showing plainly that all his discourse was about some particular business relating to himself." As they crowded around Caesar's chair, he turned for a moment to face Pompey's statue, then rose and entered the senate as the members stood to welcome him.

As soon as he was seated, the conspirators again crowded about him. As one of them, Tillius Cimber, spoke on behalf of a brother who'd been banished, Cimber grabbed Caesar's robe with both hands. Lunging forward, Casca drew his dagger and inflicted a small wound. Seizing the handle of the knife, Caesar shouted, "Villain Casca, what do you?"

Struck by a great many hands, and looking around about him to see if he could force his way out, Caesar saw Brutus with his dagger drawn, let go of Casca's hand, and covered his head with his robe. As the others eagerly pressed towards him, so many daggers were hacking at him that the assassins cut one another. With all of them smeared with Caesar's blood, Brutus called for the terrified senators to stay put, but they "ran away in great disorder, and there was a great confusion and press at the door," though none pursued or sought to capture the assassins.

The conspirators' greatest fear now was that Caesar's friend and ally, Mark Antony, would rally the people against them. Instead, Antony asked only that he be permitted to speak at Caesar's funeral. Confident that he presented no threat, the assassins agreed. It was a serious mistake. While Antony's oration attributed the murder of Caesar to "honorable men" who had feared that Caesar was "ambitious," it was such a clever and irony-filled indictment of those who had conspired to kill Caesar that it signaled the start of a civil war. It eventually resulted in the very dictatorship that the assassins had hoped to prevent, from Augustus to a succession of tyrants and madmen, including Tiberius, Caligula, and Nero.

32.

WEATHERMAN UNDERGROUND

The Weatherman Underground, a revolutionary organization with a socialist/communist ideology that was conceived in the 1960s by mostly financially well-off, white, college-age malcontents, blasted its way into the headlines during the tumult of that overheated decade's civil rights protests, demonstrations against the Vietnam War, and fierce animosity toward capitalist society in general and the American government in particular.

A breakaway faction of Students for a Democratic Society (founded in 1962), the Weathermen advocated and carried out violence that included rioting, attacks on police forces, bombings of the U.S. Capitol and New York Police Department headquarters, and assaults on various U.S. political and financial symbols. The group boasted, "We are your mother's worst nightmare."

Having become disenchanted with what they saw as the SDS's lack of revolutionary fervor, Weatherman members took the group's name from a Bob Dylan lyric. ("You don't need a weatherman to know which way the wind blows.") Words of the group's marching song were adapted from the Beatles' "Yellow Submarine." ("We all live in the Weatherman machine, the Weatherman machine, the Weatherman machine . . . ")

Viewing racism and the Vietnam War as symptoms of American political and societal corruption, the Weathermen believed that the cure was in their destruction. An attack on capitalism could be as simple as shoplifting. The nation's moral structure and the fabric of American society could be undermined through a "free speech movement" in which words were bullets and the slang term for fornication seemed to be used in every sentence. Police were "pigs." All government officials were "war criminals." America was spelled "Amerika." U.S. enemies (the Viet Cong, USSR, and Cuba's Fidel Castro) were automatically Weatherman friends and allies. Heroes to the organization were Communist revolutionaries, including Communist China's Mao Tse-tung, Vietnam's Ho Chi Minh, and Cuba's Fidel Castro and Che Guevara. Among violent groups to which they pledged "solidarity" were the Black Panthers and an assortment of anti-war organizations.

The group's debut on the national scene took place on October 8, 1969, in Chicago. In a four-day anti-war riot called "Days of Rage," Weathermen used clubs and chains in attacks on stores and cars in the city's business district. Six of its members were wounded and sixty-eight arrested. But this spectacular entry into the headlines earned the group no popular support. Feeling a need to reorganize, they met for the last time as a group in December 1969 in Flint, Michigan. One member recalled, "People gave confession on how they had not fought hard enough, how they lacked courage. And the leadership gave speeches on practicing strategic sabotage." At the conference, they decided to break up into autonomous "cells." They declared their objective was "making war on the state." Among the first to go underground for this purpose were three of the top leaders, Mark Rudd, Bernardine Dohrn, and William Ayers.

A historian of the 1960s, Milton Viorst, noted in his book *Fire in the Streets* that the Weathermen "saw themselves as a merciless army of avengers" whose isolation "only seemed to convince them that they were the truest of the revolutionaries."

One of the Weatherman cells made headlines in March 1970 thanks to the explosion of a bomb factory. The blast in the basement of a townhouse on West Eleventh Street in New York's Greenwich Village killed three cell leaders: Ted Gold, Diana Oughton, and Terry Robbins. Two members, Kathy Boudin and Cathy Wilkerson, dashed out of the house naked, escaped, and went underground. Boudin would reappear in 1980 in a botched attempt to rob a Brinks car in suburban New York. Bernardine Dohrn and Ayers (now her husband) remained fugitives for more than a decade.

Ayers offered this justification for the Weatherman Underground's reign of terror: "We had a grand idea that we thought was important, and we were willing to spend a very important part of our lives reaching for it."

"They believed they were the vanguard of a great revolution," wrote Milton Viorst of the Weathermen. "Instead, their role in history was to mark the end of a movement."

33.

TEAPOT DOME SCANDAL

For half a century before the Watergate scandal, the synonym for governmental corruption had been "Teapot Dome." That something might be fishy in the administration of President Warren G. Harding surfaced on April 14, 1922, when *The Wall Street Journal* ran a story about a secret deal in which the Secretary of the Interior, Albert Fall, had leased a naval petroleum reserve in Wyoming to a private oil company without competitive bidding. The day after the newspaper's story, Wyoming's Democratic U.S. Senator, John Kendrick, introduced a resolution to investigate the matter. After Republican Senator Robert La Follette arranged for the Senate Committee on Public Lands to carry out the probe, he discovered that his office had been ransacked. As a result, the committee's leadership allowed its most junior minority member, Montana Democrat Thomas Walsh, to commence what was expected to be a complex, tedious, and probably futile inquiry into a government policy concerning U.S. government oil reserves dating back to a law passed by Congress in 1909.

Implemented by the administrations of Presidents William Howard Taft and Woodrow Wilson, it had remained in effect throughout World War I. To guarantee that oil-powered ships of the U.S. Navy would never run out of fuel, the Congress required the government to establish three oil reserves. Two were in California, one at Elk Hills and the second in Buena Vista. The third, near Casper, Wyoming, was named Teapot Dome because of a rock outcropping that looked like a teapot. When geologists and petroleum experts noted that the oil deposits were susceptible to being drained away by oil wells on adjacent non-government land, the Congress empowered the Secretary of the Navy to do what he deemed necessary to protect the reserves. He had two choices. He could arrange for drilling of government wells at the edges of reserves to prevent drainage, or he could lease the reserves to oil companies with guarantees that sufficient amounts went to the navy. Taft's Secretary of the Navy and his successors chose to keep the oil under government control.

This policy was changed in the Harding administration. At the urging of Secretary of the Interior Albert Fall, control of the reserves was transferred by presidential executive order from the navy to Fall's department on the basis that it had the responsibility to oversee development of the nation's natural resources. With control of the Teapot Dome, Elk Hills, and Buena Vista reserves in his hands, Fall began secret negotiations with the head of one of the country's largest oil firms, Harry Sinclair, to grant Sinclair's company, Mammoth Oil, rights to work the Teapot Dome reserve without the bother of bidding for them in an open contest. In exchange for this favor, Sinclair would give Fall $68,000 and arrange for Fall to obtain no-interest "loans." Fall made a similar deal for oil rights at Elk Hills and Buena Vista with a second oil mogul, Edward L. Doheny, of Pan American Petroleum Company.

When details of the conspiracy broke out and the investigation opened, Congress directed President Harding to cancel the leases. While the power of the legislature to do this appeared to be a violation of the Constitution's "separation of powers" clause, the U.S. Supreme Court settled the issue. It ruled that the leases were void because they were fraudulent and that Harding's transfer of the reserves from the navy had been illegal.

Although Albert Fall paid dearly for his greed (convicted of bribery, he went to prison), Sinclair and Doheny were acquitted of bribery and conspiracy charges, though Sinclair was found guilty of contempt of court and contempt of the Senate and received a sentence of six and a half months. Found to have played no part in the scandal, President Harding left on a "voyage of understanding" through western states. Stricken on July 17, 1923, by what doctors diagnosed as indigestion resulting from tainted crabmeat, he developed pneumonia and died on August 23.

Although physicians speculated that he'd succumbed to a blood clot that went from his lungs to his brain, rumors spread that he had either died of a "broken heart" because of "Teapot Dome," committed suicide, or may have been murdered by unspecified conspirators. While the scandal had little effect on the Republican Party, and Harding's successor, Calvin Coolidge, was elected president in his own right in 1924, and while "Teapot Dome" as a synonym for political corruption would be replaced by "Watergate," the scandal's significance continues to this day in a Supreme Court ruling during the Teapot Dome scandal that gave Congress the power to compel testimony during investigations of the executive branch.

34.

ATTACK ON
POPE JOHN PAUL II

On May 13, 1981, two years and seven months after Cardinal Karol Jozef Wojtyla of Crakow, Poland, was crowned pope of the Roman Catholic Church and took the name John Paul II, thousands of the faithful joined tourists who came from all over the world to enjoy the glories of springtime in Rome and crowd into St. Peter's Square to cheer him. He blessed them while riding in an open vehicle humorously called the "Popemobile."

As it made a right turn in the pathway through the adoring throng, three shots rang out. The man in white who was venerated as the Vicar of Christ on Earth suddenly slumped to the side and collapsed. As the Popemobile sped the bleeding pontiff away, a young man clasping a smoking 9mm pistol was wrestled to the ground.

Identified as Mahmet Ali Agca, he was a twenty-two-year-old Turk who had recently escaped from a prison in Turkey while standing trial for the murder of the editor of a left-wing Turkish newspaper. How he'd escaped and reached Rome was a mystery. Authorities were sure he'd needed help in getting away and obtaining money and a passport.

During questioning as to his motive in attacking the pope, Agca replied, "To me he was the incarnation of capitalism." After insisting that he had acted alone, Agca changed his story and claimed to be a member of the Popular Front for the Liberation of Palestine. This was promptly denied by the PFLP. He then shocked the world by asserting that he'd been recruited to kill the pope by the Bulgarian secret service on orders from the Soviet Union's spy agency, the KGB. This story made sense because Moscow's rulers certainly had ample reason to fear John Paul II.

Karol Jozef Wojtyla was born in Wadowice, Poland, on May 18, 1920. He grew up wanting to be an actor. But when Nazi Germany occupied his homeland in 1939, he gave up drama school to work in a quarry and chemical factory. Three years later, he felt the call to enter the priesthood and studied in a clandestine seminary, but found time to participate in a secret "Rhapsodic Theater." Joining an underground Christian group, he helped Jews escape the doom of Nazi death camps.

When the Nazi tyranny was replaced by the Soviet Union's Red Army, Wojtyla completed his religious studies and was ordained a priest on November 1, 1946. After two years of further theological study in Rome, he returned to Poland as vicar of several parishes in Crakow and chaplain to university students. Consecrated auxiliary bishop, he served in that capacity until Pope Paul VI made him archbishop in 1964. Named a cardinal in 1967, he took part in the selection of Paul VI's successor, only to be summoned to the Vatican when the new pope, John Paul, unexpectedly died (under mysterious circumstances). When the College of Cardinals met to elect the third pope in less than a year, they startled the world on October 16, 1978, by breaking a long tradition of naming an Italian and picking the cardinal from Crakow.

Honoring his predecessor by taking the name John Paul II, the youngest pontiff in history quickly became a key figure at a pivotal moment in a more-than-thirty-year Cold War between the Free World and the Soviet Union. Speaking out against the Soviet Union's subjugation of Eastern Europe, he voiced support of the rise of a Polish labor union movement, Solidarity, led by a Gdansk shipyard worker, Lech Walesa. When John Paul II traveled to Poland to celebrate an outdoor mass for hundreds of thousands of Poles, they cheered his message of freedom and human rights.

Although the Soviet Union and officials in Bulgaria denied any connection with a plot to assassinate John Paul II, a document discovered following the collapse of the USSR showed that the Kremlin was so worried about him that on November 13, 1979, ten members of the Central Committee of the Communist Party of the Soviet Union signed a secret document that directed the Foreign Ministry to collect and publish any material that might be used to discredit the pope. They also ordered a KGB study of "ultimate actions" that might be taken against him. Among the signers of these documents was Mikhail Gorbachev.

That Moscow might have put out an order for the assassination of the pope was not hard to believe. Gorbachev would later explain: "Don't forget that in 1979 the Cold War had reached its culmination; and, on both sides, the logic of thought and action was guided by this fact. In that context, the Pope's activity, geared to the struggle against totalitarian regimes, could only seem dangerous and hostile to the Soviet leaders."

While Agca was convicted of the attempt on the pope's life, three Bulgarians who had been held on suspicion of taking part in the plot were released for lack of evidence. Much to the surprise of the Turkish government in June 2000, the Italian government pardoned Agca and sent him back to Turkey to serve the remainder of his term for murdering the editor and for several other outstanding charges.

Whether Agca was acting on orders that had come from Moscow by way of Bulgaria may never be known. Italian Judge Rosario Priore, who conducted an official inquest in 1998 (the third), griped that his inquiries had been thwarted by the combined efforts of the "secret services in several different countries." But he also told reporters that he had "found substantial evidence to support the thesis."

Any hope of finding an answer to the question of a Bulgarian connection in the files of the country's National Intelligence Service went up in smoke in a mysterious fire. Claiming that agency archives contained neither "direct nor indirect" evidence, the head of the secret service, Dimo Gyaurov, asserted, "I don't think Bulgarians were involved."

During history's first papal visit to Bulgaria on May 24, 2002, perhaps for the sake of Vatican post–Cold War diplomacy, and in the papal spirit that moved John Paul II to meet Agca and forgive him, the pope declared, "I have never believed in the so-called Bulgarian connection because of my great esteem and respect for the Bulgarian people."

What is certain about Pope John Paul II having posed a threat to the Soviet Union is that by inserting himself into the contest between the West and the USSR, he contributed in a major way to the collapse of communist domination of Eastern Europe and the ultimate disappearance of the Soviet Union.

The Soviet Union's last premier, Mikhail Gorbachev, said "Everything that happened in Eastern Europe in these last few years would have been impossible without the presence of this pope."

35.

OKLAHOMA CITY
FEDERAL BUILDING BOMBING

In the hours immediately following the truck-bombing of the Alfred P. Murrah Federal Building in Oklahoma City that killed 168 people, including 19 children, and left hundreds wounded on the morning of April 19, 1995, theories concerning a foreign conspiracy spread across the United States like an Oklahoma prairie wildfire. Some people attributed the blast to retaliation on the part of agents of Iraqi dictator Saddam Hussein for his defeat in the 1991 Gulf War. Others detected the bloody work of Arab terrorists as a payback for American support of Israel. Speculating on a domestic cause, members of the pro-life movement saw an attack on the federal court system by anti-abortionists. Gun-control advocates associated the attack with anti-government militias. Everyone agreed that it could not have been planned and carried out with such efficiency by one person. Only a few noted that the date of the worst terrorist attack on U.S. soil (to that time) was the second anniversary of a fatal assault by federal agents against the compound of a group called the Branch Davidians at Waco, Texas in 1993.

Less than two hours after the bombing, Timothy McVeigh was stopped near Billings, Oklahoma, for a traffic violation. A gun was discovered in his car. While he was in custody, investigators of the bombing released sketches of two suspects who were named John Doe No. 1 and 2. Because McVeigh resembled No. 1, he was charged and taken to a federal prison in El Reno, Oklahoma. An investigation into McVeigh's background revealed that he was a veteran of the Gulf War who had blamed the United States for conducting an "unjust war."

When the investigation turned up friends of McVeigh's, Terry and James Nichols, they turned themselves in to authorities in Kansas. Protesting innocence, they were held as material witnesses. Neither brother resembled John Doe No. 2.

What is known is that McVeigh had begun planning the bombing in September 1994 as a means of expressing his disenchantment with the U.S. government and anger about Waco. Over the following months he'd assembled explosive materials; surveyed his target in the company of another friend, Michael Fortier; and rented a car that he left in Oklahoma City while Terry Nichols drove him back to Kansas. On April 17, 1995, he rented a twenty-foot Ryder truck using the name Robert D. King. Employees of the rental firm believed another man had accompanied him. It was their testimony that provided descriptions and sketches of John Doe No. 1 and 2.

But on June 14, federal investigators revealed that the sketch of No. 2 was erroneous and that the second man seen at the truck rental was an innocent Army private stationed at nearby Fort Riley, Kansas. Despite this admission of error concerning John Doe No. 2, along with other FBI mistakes and refusal to hand over thousands of documents to McVeigh's lawyers, suspicions of a far wider conspiracy had taken root on April 19, 1995, and remain alive to this day.

While McVeigh was charged with the bombing, the Nichols brothers were held on an unrelated explosives charge in Michigan. Terry Nichols was subsequently charged with murder and conspiracy in the Oklahoma City bombing. Michael Fortier struck a deal in which he would be a witness against McVeigh. Although he had cooperated, he was sentenced to twelve years in prison for having failed to warn anyone of the plot to bomb the Murrah Building.

For refusing to answer lingering questions about the plot, Terry Nichols was given a life sentence. In May 2004, he was convicted of murder and currently awaits sentencing. McVeigh was sentenced to death. Following a decision of the U.S. Supreme Court not to hear McVeigh's contention that his trial had been tainted by jury misconduct, McVeigh declared that he would make no further appeals and was prepared to die. He also ignored an opportunity to appeal for clemency from President Clinton.

On April 26, 2001, Fox News released a letter from McVeigh in which he said that before planning to bomb the Murrah Building, he had considered assassinating Attorney General Janet Reno for her actions authorizing the siege of the Branch Davidians; Federal Judge Walter Ridge, who'd presided over the trial that arose from the Waco tragedy; and an FBI agent involved in the shootout that ended with the destruction by fire of the Davidians' compound. During the fifty-one-day standoff, McVeigh had joined a vigil outside the compound. He told a reporter for the weekly *Oklahoma Gazette*, "These families died a slow, torturous death as they were gassed and burned alive at the hands of the FBI."

Of this experience, his attorney in the Oklahoma City bombing case, Stephen Jones, told jurors in his opening statement, "Tim McVeigh believed that the federal government executed seventy-six people at Waco, including thirty women and twenty-five children. That was his political belief. He was not alone in that opinion."

Evidently still believing that murdering 168 people, including children, was justifiable, McVeigh was executed on June 11, 2001. His death has not dispelled the belief of many Americans that he'd needed and had help, and that his conspirators remain at large.

36.

ST. VALENTINE'S DAY MASSACRE

Headline writers immediately named it the St. Valentine's Day Massacre. But three quarters of a century after the most infamous mass rubout in the annals of American criminal history, no one can say with certainty who ordered the slaughter of six members of Bugs Moran's gang of Chicago bootleggers.

At 10:30 AM on February 14, 1929, the six mobsters were gathered inside the SMC Cartage Company garage at 2122 North Clark Street to take delivery of a consignment of illegal booze. As they waited for Moran, a Cadillac pulled up and three policemen and two men wearing civilian clothes jumped out. Barging into the garage, they ordered Moran's men and a mechanic, John May, to line up against the back wall with their hands on their heads. A moment later, the two civilians yanked machine guns from under their overcoats and opened fire. After making sure the six were dead, the two gunmen handed their weapons to the uniformed trio and preceded them out of the garage as if they had been arrested.

One of the first witnesses to arrive at the scene was John Miller, a photographer for the *Chicago American*. Miller reported: "Sprawled grotesquely at the base of the bullet-riddled stone wall were six distorted bodies. A seventh lay slumped over a wooden chair."

A police officer recognized Frank Gusenberg. An ex-con, Gusenberg was the chief gunner for the Moran gang. Also identified were Al Weinshank, a Moran booze runner; Al Davis, a West Side mobster; James Clark, Bugs Moran's brother-in-law; gangster Adam Heyer; mechanic May; and Reinhardt "Doc" Schwimmer, a gangland hanger-on, optometrist, and friend of Moran. Only Gusenberg was alive. When asked who had shot him, he blurted, "No one shot me." He died soon after without naming the gunmen.

With no hard evidence to indicate who had been behind the killings, suspicions turned to Bugs Moran's gangland rival, Al Capone. But the country's most famous criminal had an alibi. He was vacationing in Florida. When reporters asked him about the slayings, he replied, "Only Moran kills like that." Moran's answer to the same question was, "Only Capone kills like that."

The consensus of students of the massacre is that it was developed and carried out by Jack "Machine Gun" McGurn, a Capone henchman and Moran-enemy who had previously tried to kill Moran. It's believed that Capone knew it was in the works, gave it his blessing, and went to Florida to make himself conspicuous as an innocent vacationer. McGurn's accomplices were two seasoned Capone gang gunmen, Albert Anselmi and John Scalise; an out-of-towner, Fred "Killer" Burke; and an outsider.

The plan was to lure Moran and members of his gang into a deadly trap by dangling before Moran the delicious prospect of obtaining shipments of Canadian liquor. After a quantity of the booze was delivered in order to convince Moran that the deal was on the up-and-up, a date was set (February 14, 1929) and Moran named the SMC garage as the place.

When the day came, McGurn had lookouts posted to signal Moran's arrival. When a man who looked like Moran entered the garage, the fake cops arrived to do their work. But what they did not know until later was that the man who'd entered the garage wasn't Moran. He arrived in North Clark Street just in time to see policemen entering the garage and sped away.

Also in North Clark Street at the time was teenager George Brichet. Having seen the five men enter the garage, he was able to identify a police mug shot of McGurn. Despite this, McGurn was able to avoid prison. After prosecutors failed to bring him to trial in the time that Illinois law required, the case was dropped and McGurn went free. Instead of being embraced by Capone, he found himself put "on ice."

The result of the Valentine's Day Massacre for Capone was an order from President Herbert Hoover to federal prohibition enforcement agencies to put Capone out of business. He was eventually convicted of tax evasion. With the end of Prohibition in 1933, McGurn became virtually forgotten by the public. But on the night before Valentine's Day 1936, he was shot and killed in a Chicago bowling alley. Before fleeing the scene, the unknown assassins shoved a valentine in McGurn's left hand that read:

> *You've lost your job,*
> *You've lost your dough,*
> *Your jewels and handsome houses.*
> *But things could be worse, you know*
> *You haven't lost your trousers.*

37.

BIRMINGHAM CHURCH BOMBING

When an estimated fifteen sticks of dynamite exploded in the basement of the Sixteenth Street Baptist Church in Birmingham, Alabama, on Sunday morning, September 15, 1963, youngsters Denise McNair, Carole Robertson, Cynthia Wesley, and Addie Mae Collins had been getting ready for the church's annual Youth Day. All four girls were killed. More than 400 people were in the church, including 80 children. Dozens were injured.

While there had been so many bombings in Birmingham over a period of eight years that the city got the name "Bombingham," this was first to result in deaths. The motivation for this blast appeared to be the result of an order by a federal court on September 4 that city schools be integrated, followed by a call from Alabama Governor George Wallace to defy the order. In the four weeks since the court decree, two bombs had gone off, but with no fatalities. To enforce the desegregation, President John F. Kennedy had federalized parts of the Alabama National Guard.

When angry blacks reacted to the church bombing by rioting, civil authorities responded forcefully. That same day, police killed two other black youths. "As darkness closed over the city," noted a report by *United Press International*, "shots crackled periodically in the Negro sections. Stones smashed into cars driven by whites." The executive secretary of the National Association for the Advancement of Colored People (NAACP), Roy Wilkins, warned Kennedy that unless the federal government offered more than "picayune and piecemeal aid against this type of bestiality" outraged blacks would "employ such methods as our desperation may dictate in defense of the lives of our people." A message from Dr. Martin Luther King, Jr., told the president that unless "immediate federal steps are taken," Birmingham and the state of Alabama would be the scene of "the worst racial holocaust this nation has ever seen." Visibly shaken and tearful, Mayor Albert Boutwell declared, "It is just sickening that a few individuals could commit such a horrible atrocity."

Investigators immediately turned their attention to the probability that the bombing was a conspiracy involving members of the Ku Klux Klan. High on the list of suspects was forty-two-year-old Klan member Bobby Frank Cherry along with three other men. Although no evidence was produced to implicate him, he remained the focus of suspicion even after he moved his family to Texas in the early 1970s. The others of great interest were Klansmen Robert Chambliss, Herman Cash, and Thomas Blanton, Jr. But two years after the bombing, FBI Director J. Edgar Hoover came to the conclusion that even if arrests could be made, the climate of racial animosity in Alabama was so intense that gaining convictions would be impossible.

Although the federal government officially closed its case in 1968, a state investigation by former Alabama Attorney General Bill Baxley opened in the 1970s. It resulted in Chambliss's conviction for murder in 1977. He died in prison in 1985. When Herman Cash died nine years later without being charged, Blanton and Cherry were the only remaining suspects. But without sufficient evidence to justify their arrests, the case again went into limbo. It stayed suspended for twelve more years.

A break that came in 1995 was not the result of a dogged investigation by the state or federal government, but as a consequence of a feud between Cherry and five members of his family. They and some of Cherry's suddenly antagonistic acquaintances reported that he had boasted about having been involved in the bombing. A granddaughter,

Teresa Stacy, reported, "He said he helped blow up a bunch of niggers back in Birmingham." His ex-wife, Willadean Brogdon, told investigators, "He said that he lit the fuse."

On the basis of testimony by these witnesses and secretly recorded tapes, Cherry and his co-conspirator, Blanton, were indicted, tried, and convicted on eight murder charges (two for each of the girls). One count was for intentional murder. The other, "universal malice," involved the placing of a bomb in a location at which any number of people could have been killed.

The infamous conspiracy that became known as "The Birmingham Church Bombing" continued nearly forty years. Its purpose was to oppose racial integration. But its effect was to not only increase enlistment of whites in the equality movement, but also to spur enactment of the federal Civil Rights Act of 1964.

38.

KU KLUX KLAN

The oldest terrorist organization in the United States, the Ku Klux Klan has had three lives. The first began after the Civil War in Pulaski, Tennessee. Formed by ex-Confederate General Nathan Bedford Forest to ensure the supremacy of the white race and Christianity, it spread rapidly in the South with the goal of terrorizing blacks and denying them political and civil rights. When much of this was achieved through state laws that segregated the races, and after being outlawed in 1871, it went out of existence and remained so through World War I.

The Klan rekindled in the early 1920s in large measure because of economic conditions. Also, as a result of glorification of the original Klan as valiant defenders of the white race in D. W. Griffith's epic film *The Birth of a Nation*, it took root in many northern states where poor whites and middle-class Americans resided. They embraced the idea that their difficulties were caused by a combination of blacks who flooded up from the south and the economic power of Jews. In this version, the Klan enjoyed such potent political power that its membership proved decisive in many state and national elections. But as KKK influence was at its peak, it quickly declined after its leader in Indiana, "Grand Dragon" David Stephenson, was convicted of murder and rape.

Symbols adopted by the Klan included white robes and identity-concealing hoods, the burning of crosses, various emblems in the shape of a cross, and names and titles for officers, such as Knight (inspired by the Crusades of the Middle Ages), "Grand Dragon," and "Grand Wizard." The name of the group was attributed to the Greek word for circle *(kuklos)* and to the sound of a rifle being cocked.

Klan rituals were steeped in Christian symbolism. In opening and closing prayers at meetings, members recited, "The living Christ is the Klansman's criterion of character."

Moribund during World War II, the KKK resurfaced in the South in the 1950s in reaction to a U.S. Supreme Court decision that struck down racial segregation in public schools and the resulting birth of the civil rights movement. Throughout the 1960s, the Klan was responsible for numerous acts of violence. These acts included bombings, lynching of blacks, and the murders of civil rights workers.

Following the Civil Rights Act of 1964 and federally enforced admission of blacks to public schools and colleges, along with a slow acceptance among whites in both the south and north of the futility of further resistance, the Klan fragmented into three groups: the Imperial Klans of America, American Knights of the Ku Klux Klan, and Knights of the White Kamelia. As the Klan was declining, other groups with similar goals and employing terrorist tactics came into existence, including the Aryan Nations, the National Alliance, and the Silent Brotherhood.

39.

THE MANSON FAMILY

More than thirty years after members of the Manson family murdered eleven on the orders of their deranged leader Charles Manson, no creator of a conspiracy who was not acting on behalf of a government has been at the same time so repulsive and yet so continually fascinating as "Charlie."

From the moment police arrived at a house on Cielo Drive in the hills overlooking Los Angeles on August 9, 1969, and discovered that blood had been used to scrawl the word "Pig" on the front door, "Death to Pigs" and "Helter Skelter" on other walls, and then found the bodies of actress Sharon Tate and three others in the house and on the grounds, the murders resulted in a wave of fear that swept from Hollywood, across the nation, and around the world. The horror multiplied the next day with the news of the murders of wealthy businessman Leno LaBianca and his wife, Rosemary, in their Los Angeles home. The slaughters brought to an end what the *Reuters* news agency writer Michael Miller called in a 1999 article the " 'Hippie era' of good vibes, peace and love."

A bearded, wild-eyed, self-styled guru whose followers believed him to be Jesus Christ, or the "fifth angel" (the others were the Beatles), Manson ordered the killings in a bizarre belief that they would incite blacks to attack whites. He named his plan "Helter Skelter" after a Beatles song. Manson actually killed no one himself. Those who did his bloody bidding were Susan Atkins, Patricia Krenwinkel, Leslie Van Houten, Charles "Tex" Watson, Sandra Good, and Lynette "Squeaky" Fromme. The conspiracy was revealed when Atkins told her prison cellmate of her participation in the murders, that Manson was Christ and her lover, and that he had promised to lead her to a hole in Death Valley where there was a secret civilization. She explained that Manson had wanted the family "to do a crime that would shock the world, that the world would have to stand up and take notice." The confession led to arrests of Manson and the family at a ranch that was often used as a setting for Western movies.

After a tumultuous nine-month trial in 1971 during which Manson carved a Nazi swastika into his forehead and the "Manson women" often chanted, Manson, Atkins, Van Houten, and Krenwinkel were convicted of the Tate and LaBianca murders and sentenced to death, only to be spared and their penalties reduced to life in prison when California abolished capital punishment. During the trial, Atkins told jurors the murders were committed "to instill fear into the establishment." Also convicted were Manson followers Robert Beausoleil, Charles Watson, Bruce Davis, and Steve Grogan, for the murders of Manson enemies Gary Hinman and Donald "Shorty" Shea. Four years later, "Squeaky" Fromme was convicted of attempting to assassinate President Gerald Ford. Sandra Good was convicted in 1976 for conspiring to send threatening letters to government leaders.

Repeatedly denied parole, Manson found himself the center of attention for members of Manson cults, the recipient of more letters than anyone in the history of American prisons, the subject of numerous Internet websites, and pictured on posters and T-shirts, as well as the topic of books, articles, television documentaries, films, and college courses.

40.

BOMBING OF
THE KING DAVID HOTEL

When a member of the British Labor Party checked into the King David Hotel on March 6, 1946, the lobby was the setting of a scene that would have had a writer of movie thrillers reaching for a pencil and notebook. He found the King David bristling with "private detectives, Zionist agents, Arab sheikhs, special correspondents, and the rest, all sitting around about discreetly overhearing each other."

During World War II, the plush hotel had hosted refugee potentates, including the Emperor of Abyssinia, Haile Selassie, ex-King Peter of Yugoslavia, and ex-King George III of Greece. Exiled monarch Alfonso III had arrived in 1931 soon after the hotel opened. In 1946 the hotel was the residence of Britain's High Commissioner for Palestine, the headquarters of the high command of the army, and the center of Britain's intelligence service in the Holy Land.

As part of these activities, a British raiding party barged into the offices of the Jewish Agency. Long known as "Jewish headquarters," it was the place where Jewish revolutionaries, known as the Irgun, plotted attacks on the British. It was also believed to contain a treasure trove of information on Irgun activities, both from the past and in planning stages. After the raid, the Irgun's leader, Menachem Begin (a future prime minister of Israel) said the "booty" that the British carried away was "considerable." It resulted not only in panic, but also an "eye for an eye" plot by the Irgun in which the target was to be British headquarters in the King David Hotel.

The first code name for the plan was the Hebrew word *Malonchik*, meaning "little hotel." As the planning went on, it was shortened to "Chick." Begin recalled, "We were well aware that this was the largest of our operations to date and that it might turn out to be unique in the history of partisan wars of liberation." He said later, "It is no simple matter to penetrate the very heart of the military government, to deliver a blow within the fortified headquarters of a military regime. I doubt if this operation had any precedent in history."

Five hundred pounds of explosives were to be packed into large milk cans, along with a synchronized timer and a triggering device that would detonate if a can were to be opened. To prevent that, a note would be put on each can: "Mines. Do not touch." The cans would be taken to the Regence Café in the basement of the government wing of the hotel by robed men disguised as Arab hotel employees. Since the café would be crowded at lunchtime, the planners chose to attack at eleven o'clock. Fifteen minutes before, a female Irgun "telephonist" would call the hotel with a notification that bombs had been planted and a warning that everyone "evacuate the whole building." Calls would also be placed to the *Palestine Post* and to the adjacent French consulate.

The date was set: July 22. Minutes before the detonations, firecrackers would be set off outside for the purpose of scaring away people who might be heading for the hotel. At the same time, another group, the Stern Gang, would bomb British offices in the David Brothers Building in an action code-named "Operation Your Slave and Redeemer." But at the last minute, this operation was called off. According to Begin's account of the execution of Chick, because of "consultations" about the cancellation of the David Brothers Building action, "the time of the attack was delayed by one hour and began at twelve o'clock instead of eleven."

All went according to plan. Fifteen overwhelmed Arab employees—cooks and waiters—were locked in a side room. But as the milk-can bombs were being put in place, two British soldiers appeared with guns drawn. Bullets flew. At the same time, Irgunists outside the hotel clashed with military patrols. While plans for surprise went up in gun smoke, the bombs' timing mechanisms were started, "Do Not Touch" signs were posted, and the men in the hotel escaped through the smoke from the diversionary firecrackers. At ten past noon, the telephonist placed her calls to the *Post* and the French consulate. When she informed a British officer in the hotel that everyone should evacuate, he retorted, "We are not here to take orders from the Jews. We give them orders."

The bombs exploded at 12:37 PM. Jerusalem shook from the force of the blast. A mixture of TNT and gelignite going off in the confined basement brought down six floors of concrete, stone, and steel. A reporter for the British Broadcasting Corporation told shocked listeners in Great Britain and around the world by shortwave radio that the entire wing of the King David Hotel was cut off "as with a knife." Ninety-one British, Arabs, and Jews were killed. Scores more were injured.

For months after the King David Hotel bombing, a full-scale war raged between Jews and the British army. The day after Britain withdrew its forces in May 1947, Israel declared itself an independent nation.

41.

YASSER ARAFAT AND THE PALESTINE LIBERATION ORGANIZATION

Founded in Cairo, Egypt, in 1963, during a meeting between the leaders of thirteen Arab nations, the Palestine Liberation Organization (PLO) claimed all Palestinians "natural members" and said that they had a duty to mobilize "so that they would be able to assume responsibility in the liberation of their country" from control by Israel. This basic document was later amended to include a call for the all-out destruction of Israel. A phased program authorized taking any "liberation step" to advance the PLO strategy for the establishment of a Palestinian state, and "completing the liberation of all Palestinian soil." The PLO emblem contained a map of the region without a trace of an Israeli state. In 1969, the PLO elected Yasser Arafat as chairman.

Under his leadership and direction, the PLO and its military wing, Al Fatah, and other terror groups carried out a terrorist campaign in accordance with a clause of the PLO charter that called for "commando action" (terrorism) as "the nucleus of the Palestinian popular liberation war." Meanwhile, Arafat created myths about himself as having been born in Palestine, though he had actually been born in

Cairo, Egypt. He adopted the same name (Arafat) as that of a famous Arab hero. Part of this deliberate cultivation of his image as Palestinian leader was never being seen without a neat black-and-white-checked kaffiyeh flowing from his head and across the right shoulder of an olive drab uniform. Arafat the Warrior addressed the United Nations General Assembly with a pistol strapped to his side. One of his biographers described him as "a natural publicist" who had an obsessive desire to be the leader of the pack, to get his way, and to justify any means to the desired end. In his mind and in the person he showed to the world, he became the unchallenged Palestinian leader.

Under Arafat, elements of the PLO known as Black September, the Popular Front for the Liberation of Palestine, Popular Democratic Front for the Liberation of Palestine General Command, and Al Fatah (headed by Yasser Arafat) became the world's most feared and effective terrorist organizations. Among their most infamous actions were the murders of eleven Israeli athletes at the 1972 Olympic Games in Munich, Germany; the slaughter of twenty-one schoolchildren at Ma'alot in Israel in 1974; an attack on a tourist bus on the Haifa–Tel Aviv road that killed thirty-five people and wounded eighty-five in 1978; numerous airplane hijackings; and the seizure in 1985 of the cruise ship *Achille Lauro* in the Mediterranean Sea in which a wheelchair-bound Jewish-American passenger was thrown overboard.

Based in Jordan until the Jordanian government in September 1972 kicked it out, the PLO set up shop in Lebanon, only to be ousted by the Israeli army in 1982. Largely due to worldwide revulsion over the *Achille Lauro* episode, Arafat decided to improve the image of the PLO by acknowledging Israel's right to exist and renouncing terrorism as a tactic. But as Arafat pursued a policy of negotiations, his Al Fatah terrorist group continued its activities. Following agreements with Israel made at Oslo, Norway, in which the PLO was to be replaced by the Palestine National Authority, with Arafat as its chairman, terrorism remained a tactic of Al Fatah and other groups. Following each attack by one of these organizations, Arafat was quick to issue a condemnation. This resulted in a false perception that Arafat was genuinely interested in peace, and that it could be achieved only through him. The tactic was so effective that he took part in negotiations with prime ministers of Israel and two U.S. presidents, Jimmy

Carter and Bill Clinton, at Camp David, followed by elaborate cere-monies in which documents were signed that seemed to open the way to peace and an end to terrorism. In each instance, the hopes were scuttled by terror groups under Arafat's control.

Only when President George W. Bush denounced Arafat as chief motivator of terrorism and refused to deal directly with him was Arafat replaced as the Palestinian negotiator. But as a so-called "Road Map to Peace" seemed to offer a way out of more than half a century of Arab–Israeli conflict, Palestinian terrorist groups (Hamas, Al Fatah, and the Al Aqsa Brigade) began a new wave of terrorism that had the implicit, if not direct, approval of the mastermind of political and terrorist conspiracy, Yasser Arafat.

42.

ACHILLE LAURO
HIJACKING

A cunning and brutal plot led by Palestinian terrorist Abu Abbas to take over a cruise ship in the Mediterranean Sea and hold it and its mostly elderly passengers hostage until the government of Israel released 50 members of the Palestine Liberation Front (PLF) from prison became a shocking story of cold-blooded murder at sea. For eighteen years afterwards, the conspiracy's mastermind remained at large, receiving the protection of several Arab countries, including Iraq, where he was embraced and celebrated as a hero.

The man who took the name Abu Abbas was born Muhammad Zaidan in 1948 in the Yarmouk Palestinian refugee camp in Syria after his family fled from their home in Tura, near Haifa, following the creation of the state of Israel. After earning a degree in Arab literature at Damascus University, he joined the Marxist Popular Front for the Liberation of Palestine (PFLP) in 1967 and took part in guerilla attacks against Israel. Dissatisfied with the PFLP's focus on a political resolution of the Arab–Israeli struggle, rather than an armed struggle, he broke with the PFLP in 1976. Forming the Palestine Liberation Front (PLF), he forged a loose alliance with Yasser Arafat. Its first action (1981) was a failed attempt to infiltrate Israel by launching two motorized hang gliders from southern Lebanon to attack an oil refinery near Haifa. A second mission later that year, using a hot air balloon, was also aborted. In 1984, he became a member of the PLO Executive Committee.

With Arafat's compliance, Abbas began planning to sneak aboard a cruise ship in the Mediterranean and seize control of it with the purpose of taking the passengers and crew hostage in order to blackmail Israel into freeing PLF prisoners. In Egyptian waters on October 7, 1985, he and several heavily armed accomplices took over the Italian *Achille Lauro*. It carried more than 400 passengers. Among nineteen Americans were Leon Klinghoffer and his wife of thirty-six years, Marilyn. Having suffered two strokes, the retired Jewish New York businessman was confined to a wheelchair. After communicating the demand that Israel release the PLF prisoners, Abbas decided to demonstrate his seriousness by ordering that Klinghoffer be killed and his body dumped overboard with his wheelchair. Abbas later offered a cynical explanation for this barbaric act, claiming that the crippled Klinghoffer had "created troubles" and provoked his own murder by inciting the other passengers.

Despite a plea from President Ronald Reagan that no port allow the *Achille Lauro* to dock, the Egyptian government struck a deal with Arafat in which the terrorists would surrender to Egyptian authorities at Port Said, but with a guarantee that they would not be prosecuted. They were to be put on an Egyptian airliner to be flown to the PLO's headquarters in Tunisia. When Reagan learned of this plan, and that an American had been murdered, he ordered U.S. Navy planes to intercept the Egyptian plane and force it down in Italian territory. But when it was on the ground in Sicily, the Italians buckled under an Arafat threat of "uncontrollable reactions" if the men were handed over to the United States. They refused to allow the Americans to arrest Abbas and the others. Denying a U.S. request that they be extradited, the Italians let Abbas flee to Yugoslavia, then tried and convicted him in absentia and sentenced him to life in prison.

Having escaped American clutches, Abbas found sanctuary in Tunisia, Libya, and finally Gaza. In 1990 he directed an abortive attack on a Tel Aviv beach by terrorists using a speedboat. Offered a safe haven by Iraqi President Saddam Hussein in 1994, Abbas lived openly in Baghdad and continued as a member of Arafat's PLO Executive Committee. When Arafat abruptly changed tactics and "renounced" terrorism (in part because of worldwide reaction to the *Achille Lauro* atrocity), Abbas presented himself to reporters in the role of Palestinian hero. "It is true that a large percentage of the Western world hopes that I am imprisoned or dead," he said. "But all my people, the Palestinians and the Arabs, wish me long life and freedom."

Abbas's ability to carry on terrorism while sheltered by Saddam Hussein came to an abrupt end in April 2003. Acting on intelligence gleaned during the liberation of Iraq, American Special Forces raided a three-building compound on the outskirts of Baghdad and took him into custody. When news of his capture flashed around the world, a Palestinian Authority Cabinet member, Saeb Erakat, declared that in seizing Abbas, the United States had violated an interim agreement made at Oslo, Norway, between Israel, Palestinians, the U.S., and other nations that no member of the PLO could be arrested and brought to court for any action that had occurred prior to September 13, 1993.

Although Abbas had been sentenced to life in prison by Italy, and his legal status in the U.S. justice system was in doubt, he remained in American custody. The U.S. Central Command in Iraq said in a statement, "One of our key objectives is to search for, capture and drive out terrorists who have found safe haven in Iraq. The capture of Abu Abbas in Iraq removes a portion of the terror network supported by Iraq and represents yet another victory in the global war on terrorism."

43.

NAZI
SUBMARINE SPIES

Before the United States entered the Second World War on December 7, 1941, Germany's military intelligence service (Abwehr) was ordered to carry out a daring plan that apparently had been dreamed up by Adolf Hitler. The idea was to send saboteurs to the United States by way of submarines to blow up factories and damage other facilities on the east coast that provided war materials to England. To execute the scheme, the head of Abwehr, Vice Admiral William Canaris, picked naval officer Lieutenant Walter Kappe, who had spent several years in the U.S. and had been active in the German-American groups seeking to propagandize and win adherents for Nazism among German immigrants in New York City.

Early in 1942, Kappe recruited twelve men who had similar familiarity with the United States. Their training for the mission, at a sabotage school near Berlin, included chemistry, making and using incendiaries, explosives, timing devices, secret writing, and identity concealment. This was followed by visits to aluminum and magnesium plants, railroad shops, canals, locks, and other facilities to familiarize themselves with the vital points and vulnerabilities of the types of targets they were to attack in the United States. Maps were provided that located principal aluminum and magnesium plants, important canals, locks, waterways, bridges, and railroads.

On May 26, 1942, four of the saboteurs boarded a submarine at Lorient, France. Their leader was George John Dasch. The others were Ernest Peter Burger, Heinrich Harm Heinck, and Richard Quirin. Shortly after midnight eighteen days later (June 13, 1942), they landed on a beach near Amagansett, Long Island, in the state of New York. A few hours earlier, a second group led by Edward John Kerling and including Werner Thiel, Herman Otto Neubauer, and Herbert Hans Haupt, landed at Ponte Vedra Beach, Florida, south of Jacksonville.

At this point, the Hitler plan that had proceeded as flawlessly as the plot of a spy novel began to take on aspects of comedy. Minutes after the Long Island invaders had buried their equipment and uniforms, an unarmed Coast Guard beach patroller spotted them. When the Germans offered him a bribe to forget that they'd met, he pocketed their money and went directly to his headquarters to report them. By then, however, the saboteurs were on a train to New York City. The next evening, June 14, Dasch phoned the New York office of the FBI. Using the name "Pastorius," he said that he had recently arrived from Germany and would call FBI Headquarters in Washington, D.C., the following week. He did so on Friday, June 19, from his hotel room, and waited calmly for FBI agents to come and arrest him.

Based on his information, the FBI picked up his three accomplices the next day in New York. Of the Florida group, Kerling and Thiel were arrested in New York on June 23, followed by Neubauer and Haupt in Chicago on June 27. All were tried before a Military Commission, comprised of seven U.S. Army officers appointed by President Roosevelt. (The only such body in modern American history, this commission provided a legal precedent for setting up military tribunals, if the administration of President George W. Bush chose to do so, to deal with persons detained in the United States, Afghanistan, Iraq, and other places and accused of terrorism anywhere in the world.)

All eight of the submarine saboteurs were found guilty and sentenced to death, but on an appeal for clemency by Attorney General Frances Biddle and FBI Director J. Edgar Hoover, President Roosevelt commuted the sentences of Dasch and Burger to thirty years and a life sentence respectively. The remaining six were executed on August 8, 1942. In April 1948, President Truman granted executive clemency to Dasch and Burger. Deported to the American Zone of Germany, they were freed.

Evidently undiscouraged by the abject failure of the Long Island and Florida saboteurs, Germany's espionage masterminds tried again in late 1944. Sent to spy rather than conduct sabotage, William Curtis Colepaugh and Erich Gimpel were landed on the coast of Maine. They were rounded up by the FBI before accomplishing any part of their mission.

Noting that postwar debriefings of German personnel and examination of Nazi records confirmed that no other attempt was made to land agents by submarine, the FBI justifiably boasts that although many allegations of plots were investigated by the Bureau during World War II, "not one instance was found of enemy-inspired sabotage."

44.

MURDERS OF THREE CIVIL RIGHTS WORKERS IN MISSISSIPPI

Near the hamlet of Philadelphia, Mississippi, on June 21, 1964, a car carrying a young black man and two white youths was pulled over by Neshoba County Deputy Sheriff Cecil Price. The black occupant identified himself as James Earl Chaney, a Mississippi resident. Michael "Mickey" Schwerner and Andrew Goodman were northerners who had come south to take part in a "Freedom Summer." They were headed toward the town of Meridian to join civil rights activists in urging blacks to register to vote. Informed that they were being detained on a traffic violation and escorted to jail, they were briefly locked up and released with a warning not to repeat the infraction. They continued toward their destination, but were stopped again, this time by twenty-two gun-toting members of the Ku Klux Klan.

When the young men did not arrive in Meridian, leaders of Freedom Summer feared the worst. With no confidence that the local police and sheriff's department could be relied on to investigate the disappearance of the youths, they conveyed suspicions of foul play to the Justice Department in Washington, D.C. Informed of the situation, President Lyndon Johnson ordered the FBI to launch a probe. Reports of the mysterious vanishings quickly became the dominant story in the nation's newspapers and radio and television newscasts, accompanied by reminders of the bombing by members of the Ku Klux Klan of a black church in Birmingham, Alabama, in which four black children had been killed in September 1963.

Although FBI agents, and everyone else in the country who had been shocked and outraged by the disappearance of the young civil rights crusaders believed that the KKK was involved, the federal investigators were unable to prove that Chaney, Schwerner, and Goodman had been murdered. When the break in the search came forty-four days after the men disappeared, it was through an informer's tip that the civil rights workers had been shot and their bodies buried in a fifteen-foot earthen dam at Philadelphia, Mississippi. The corpses were recovered on August 4.

The next development occurred on October 13 with the arrest of eighteen men. Because murder prosecutions in which the federal government has no jurisdiction are the responsibility of the state in which the crime was committed, the case was turned over to Mississippi authorities. But state prosecutors cited "lack of evidence" and declined to pursue it. This meant that if anyone were ever to be held accountable, it would be on a federal charge of conspiracy to violate the victims' civil rights. Arrested on that basis, two Klansmen, James Jordan and Horace Doyle Barnette, pleaded guilty to the killings. In their confessions they named Edgar Ray "Preacher" Killen; Neshoba County Sheriff Lawrence Rainey; Deputy Price; and Samuel Bowers, then the Imperial Wizard of Mississippi's Ku Klux Klan, as the ones who gave the order to kill Schwerner.

Jordan and Barnette told investigators that after the killings, "Preacher" Killen had told them, "We have a place to bury them, and a man to run the dozer to cover them up." But Killen had an alibi for the time of the murders. He'd been preaching at two funerals. At his trial, the jury deadlocked. But in a 1983 secret interview with the Mississippi Department of Archives and History, Bowers alleged that Killen was the instigator.

Federal juries convicted a total of seven men of conspiracy involving the KKK and Neshoba County's law enforcement. Other prosecutions ended in mistrials and acquittals, including that of Sheriff Rainey. Although Samuel Bowers was acquitted, he later stated that he had done everything he could to frustrate the investigation. On a tape made by the Department of Archives, the contents of which were discovered by reporter Jerry Mitchell in 1998 and published in the newspaper *Clarion Ledger*, Bowers boasted: "I was up there doing everything I could to keep those people from talking and everything else." He stated that he was "quite delighted to be convicted and have the main instigator of the entire affair walk out of the courtroom a free man." He added, "Everybody, including the trial judge and the prosecutors and everybody else, knows what happened." (Bowers was sentenced to life in prison in 1998 for the murder in 1996 of civil rights leader Vernon Dahmer.) Both Killen and Sheriff Rainey maintained that they'd had nothing to do with the killings, that Bowers lied, and that the FBI had been "paying all the witnesses to lie." While Killen denied having been a Klan member, Rainey admitted attending some of the Klan gatherings. "They had open meetings," he said, "but that was all [I had to with the Klan]."

In 2000, Mississippi's Attorney General Mike Moore announced that the state had asked the FBI to turn over its files on the case, along with trial transcripts. Declaring an intention to reopen the case, Moore said, "It's a chance for us to do justice for the families of those three young men. It's a mean-spirited murder case, maybe one of the most mean-spirited murder cases that I've ever seen."

Yet, had it not been for the use of federal law, the murders of James Earl Chaney, Michael Schwerner, and Andrew Goodman probably would have gone unsolved.

45.

ATTEMPTS TO ASSASSINATE CHARLES DE GAULLE

On August 22, 1962, Charles de Gaulle and his wife left the Elysee Palace, the home and office of the president of France, and settled into the rear seat of a sleek black limousine for a short drive to the military airport on Villacoublay, south of Paris. After the speeding French-made Cetroen and an identical car carrying a small group of bodyguards crossed a bridge a few miles from the airfield, the vehicles were raked by machine-gun fire. Although windows were shattered, no one was hit. Arriving at the airport, de Gaulle stepped from the car and said, "They were not very good shots."

Noting in an editorial two days later that "President de Gaulle lives dangerously," the *New York Times* observed, "This was not the first attempt [to kill de Gaulle] and, unhappily, it is not likely to be the last."

What the newspaper and de Gaulle didn't know was that the attack with guns had been the back-up plan conceived by embittered former solders of the Secret Army Organization (OAS). The group had planned to kill him by blowing up the bridge. Nor did anyone know that five weeks earlier the plotters had sent a sniper with a high-powered rifle to a building in Paris overlooking the annual ceremony at which de Gaulle commemorated the liberation of prisoners in the Bastille in 1789 that launched the French Revolution. The assassination attempt on July 15 had been thwarted because the gunman was unable to get an unobstructed sight on de Gaulle.

Striding majestically through European military and political history for much of the twentieth century with a haughty confidence that the people of France admired, but often frustrated their allies during and after WWII, Charles de Gaulle was the grandest self-proclaimed leader and popular French hero since the rise and reigns of Napoleon Bonaparte. When Nazi Germany overran France and forced a humiliating surrender in the grim, early months of the Second World War, de Gaulle broadcast on radio to his countrymen from England and urged France to fight in every way possible as "Free French Forces." With the ardent support of British Prime Minister Winston Churchill, but with only tepid agreement by President Franklin D. Roosevelt, the tall, self-confident, and frequently obstinate general headed a government in exile called the French Committee of National Liberation (later the Provisional Government of the French Republic) as the recognized leader of "Free French" in territories of what had been the French Empire and the "Resistance" inside France. Although he was not allowed to land with the D-Day invasion forces at Normandy on June 6, 1944, he returned to France eight days later. In recognition of his role during the war, and the political reality that he would certainly head a postwar government in France, he was given the honor of leading French forces into liberated Paris on August 25, 1944.

With France having suffered a humiliating military defeat by Communist insurgents in Indochina (Vietnam) in 1954, and threatened with civil war over the future of its North African colony of Algeria, the National Assembly urgently called on de Gaulle to return to government as premier with almost dictatorial powers. The result was the Fifth Republic, with de Gaulle as president. Determined to put an end to the continuing troubles in Algeria, he reversed a policy aimed at integrating the colony with France and spoke of independence. When this was seen as a betrayal of French-Algerians and members of the French military, there was open revolt that de Gaulle answered by invoking emergency powers to suppress the uprisings.

The rebel OAS was led by General Raoul Salan, a hero in both world wars and later the commander in chief of French forces in the wars in Indochina and Algeria. Aligning itself with another terrorist group (the National Liberation Front), the OAS set off more than one hundred bombs in Paris and other cities, climaxing with the decision to assassinate de Gaulle. Planning for the attack on de Gaulle's motorcade began immediately after the Bastille Day failure.

The arrest by French police of a young woman within hours after the attack on the road to the airport resulted in a series of captures of Salan and others involved in the OAS plot. This was followed by the collapse of the Algerian rebellion. Following a de Gaulle-arranged cease-fire with the rebel National Liberation Front, voters approved a referendum that granted Algerian independence. Ending a crisis that most historians agree could not have been resolved by any other leader, de Gaulle emerged with even more power and used it to secure a constitutional amendment to allow direct election of the president of the Republic. Given a second seven-year term, he continued an independent foreign policy that included expelling NATO (North Atlantic Treaty Organization) from France. He also condemned the U.S. war in Vietnam, urged independence for Quebec, and lent support to Arab countries in the 1967 war with Israel. At home, he proposed a "society of participation" that appeared to be part capitalism and part communism. It promised rebellious students and disaffected labor a major role in making government policies and a share in profits of industry. But in 1969, when he warned that he would resign from office if French voters did not approve a proposed referendum on a constitutional change that would make the French Senate into a strictly advisory body, and to expand the powers of regional councils, voters gave him a rare defeat. He resigned the next day.

At his home at Colombey-les-Deux-Eglises, he worked on completing what was to be a monumental set of memoirs. When a reporter summoned the courage to ask de Gaulle what would happen to France following his death, the questioner recalled that Napoleon's response to the same question had been, *"Apres moi, l'deluge."* ("After me, the flood.") Charles de Gaulle answered, *"Apres moi, vous verrez."*

("After me, you will see.") He died on November 9, 1970.

Convicted of treason, but later pardoned, General Salan died in Paris in 1984, probably wondering, along with historians, how the course of world events, and France's future, would have been different if the plots to kill de Gaulle had succeeded.

While biographers of Charles De Gaulle devoted little attention to the more than thirty plots to assassinate him between 1944 and 1962, author Frederick Forsythe used the OAS plot as the basis of a thriller that became a best-selling novel and block-buster movie. Titled *The Day of the Jackal*, the fictionalized drama reversed the actual sequence of events, presenting the ambush of de Gaulle's car first and climaxing with the failure of a hired assassin, known as the Jackal, to shoot de Gaulle during the Bastille Day ceremony. In the story, however, the gunman didn't fail because he couldn't get a clear shot, but because a French detective who had been tracking the Jackal burst into the room and killed him.

46.

DEATH OF PRINCESS DIANA

Not since the reign of England's King Henry VIII and his plottings to dispose of a series of unsatisfactory wives has the British Monarchy found itself enmeshed in so much speculation about sinister conspiracies as those surrounding the death of Princess Diana. Within minutes of the news that the beautiful, glamorous ex-wife of the heir to the British throne (Charles, Prince of Wales) and the mother of a future king of England (Prince William) had been killed in an automobile accident in Paris, France, on August 31, 1997, the idea that she had been murdered swept around the world.

Six years later, the belief that Diana died as the result of a conspiracy was given fresh impetus by her former butler, Paul Burrell. He revealed that ten months before the fatal crash, she had written to him in a letter, "This particular phase of my life is the most dangerous." She reportedly said she believed there was a plot to kill her in an "accident" in her car "in order to make the path clear" for Prince Charles to marry his long-time mistress, Camilla Parker-Bowles.

Why do so many people believe that Diana's fate was the result of a plot, and why has the so-called "fairy tale wedding" of Charles and Diana at St. Paul's Cathedral that was watched by millions of people on worldwide television turned into a story of twists, turns, and possibly murder worthy of an Alfred Hitchcock movie?

As one "royal watcher" recently observed, "Famous people meeting strange ends is a phenomenon that always seems to bring out the conspiracy theorists." A writer on the Internet site Coverups.com noted that ever since Princess Diana's tragic demise "millions of words have been written and spoken about what really happened the night she died, and why. Perhaps, not unlike the murder of [President John F. Kennedy], we will never truly know the whys and wherefores of that night."

What we do know is that Diana and her companion, Dodi (son of the multi-millionaire owner of London's Harrods department store, Mohammed Al Fayed), left the Ritz Hotel in Paris and sped away to avoid the paparazzi in a black 1994 Mercedes S–280. Diana and Dodi were in the rear seat. Behind the wheel was an expert driver, Henri Paul. Also in the front seat was Diana's bodyguard, Trevor Rees-Jones. Minutes later, the car was traveling at a high speed when it crashed in an underpass called the Alma Tunnel. Diana was alive, but died not long after she was rushed to a hospital. The only survivor was Rees-Jones.

Hours after the news flashed around the world, the first suggestion of a conspiracy was posted on the Internet in Australia. It said, "The whole thing seems too pat and too convenient." Much more believable, it stated, was that the crash had been arranged by Western governments, arms manufacturers, and the royal family.

Of all supposed plots, the most common was that Diana's death was decreed by someone at Buckingham Palace, possibly Queen Elizabeth II herself because 1) Diana's flamboyant lifestyle had become cause for embarrassment; 2) Diana was believed to be pregnant with Dodi's child and it was impermissible that the mother of a future king of England also be the mother of a Muslim child; 3) if Diana married Dodi, her sons, Princes William and Harry, would become related by marriage to a family with a dubious reputation (the Al Fayeds); and 4) Diana was such an unstable woman who knew too many secrets concerning the royal family that she presented a potential threat to the stability of the monarchy.

Credence was lent to suspicions that Buckingham Palace had been involved when Queen Elizabeth II appeared aloof from the outburst of national mourning that swept over Britain, and by the fact that the Queen's flag over the palace was not lowered to half-staff out of respect.

Similar reasons for killing Diana were attributed to MI6, Britain's secret service, either to it as an institution or to a group of "rogue agents" who took it upon themselves to protect the royal family, the throne, and the state. Conspiracists pointed to MI6's alleged record of having wire-tapped Diana's telephones and that MI6 agents had previously kept a file on former Beatle John Lennon because he was perceived in the intelligence community as a subversive and a real threat to the continuance of the monarchy.

One of the chief proponents of the "this was not an accident" theory was Dodi's father, Mohammed Al Fayed. He reportedly believed that someone in the British government had acted to prevent Diana from marrying Dodi because he was a Muslim. This theory is widely believed in the Arab world. Numerous books were published in Egypt, one of which had appeared within three days of Diana's death, asserting that the royal family and "Jewish circles" conspired to kill Diana. Anis Mansour, a former adviser to assassinated Egyptian President Anwar Al Sadat, held in an article in the Egyptian newspaper *Al Ahram* that Diana was "killed by British Intelligence to save the monarchy."

Theories as to how the "accident" was contrived range from sabotaging the brakes of the Mercedes to a radio-controlled device that would send the car spinning out of control. Central to this scenario is that the only survivor, Trevor Rees-Jones, was a former solider who had served in Northern Ireland and would have come in contact with members of MI6.

Another supposed plot makes the target of the "accident" not Princess Diana, but Dodi. In this theory the culprits are business enemies of Dodi's father who contrived to make it appear that Diana was the objective, thereby diverting suspicion from a "let's get even with the father by killing the son" scheme.

The most bizarre of the conspiracies is that Diana wasn't killed and that she had cooked up the "accident" so that she could disappear from the glare of the world's spotlight and live in peace and quiet. Never mind that Diana had welcomed press attention and that in this scheme Diana would be causing pain and turning her back on two sons, Princes William and Harry, whom she obviously adored.

47.

JACK THE RIPPER

Conspiracy buffs who speculate that the death of Princess Diana in a car crash in Paris was the work of someone in Buckingham Palace or a rogue element within Britain's intelligence service are not the first people to have attributed sinister plotting to England's royal household. For more than a century the murderous rampages of the world's most fascinating serial killer, Jack the Ripper, have been attributed by some crime historians and experts on the subject (known as "Ripperologists") to individuals who sought to cover up the fact that the murders had been committed by the deranged grandson of the most venerated monarch in British history, Queen Victoria.

Others have attributed the "Ripper" murders of several prostitutes in the Whitechapel area of London in 1888 to killers such as socialist radicals who hoped to incite a popular rebellion against Britain's aristocratic ruling class, political radicals who hoped to replace the monarchy and install a republic, a newspaperman seeking fame, and even the Masons.

Despite overwhelming evidence that Jack the Ripper acted alone, with studies and re-studies of the case by criminologists reaching the same conclusion almost every year since "Saucy Jack" terrorized the mean nighttime streets and alleys of London's East End, conspiracy buffs persistently believe that somehow the royal family and its protectors had been involved in the slashing deaths of Polly Nichols, Elizabeth "Long Liz" Stride, Catherine Eddowes, Mary Kelly, Annie Chapman, and possibly others.

One recent theory of the complicity of Queen Victoria's court was advanced in the film *From Hell*, starring Johnny Depp as Scotland Yard investigator Frederick Aberline. A previous movie, *Murder By Decree*, based on a novel by Robert Wenerka, presented a similar scenario in which the detective who cracked the Ripper case was none other than Sherlock Holmes, portrayed by Christopher Plummer. Mastermind of the plot, Queen Victoria's physician, Dr. William Gull, set out to create "Jack the Ripper" by murdering prostitutes in order to conceal the secret marriage of one of the victims and Prince Albert Victor, known as "Eddy." Because Eddy was the son of the Prince of Wales and future King Edward VII, Dr. Gull decided that the prostitute had to be eliminated because she was a Roman Catholic and had born Eddy's child. In this scenario, other prostitutes had to be murdered in order to prevent a scandal because the public knew of the nuptials and the child. The fault in this theory is that even if Eddy had wed a Roman Catholic, in violation of a law that forbade an heir to the throne from marrying a Catholic, the marriage would have been illegal because Eddy was underage and did not have Queen Victoria's consent to marry.

In another scenario, Eddy was the killer and his crimes were covered up, not only to keep the public from learning that he had been driven insane by syphilis, but that an heir to the throne was a homosexual. The problem in this is that at the time of the murders the prince was neither in London nor was he syphilitic. Yet another explanation with Eddy at the heart of the slayings has them being covered up because they were committed by James Kenneth Stephen, Eddy's tutor and homosexual partner while the prince was at Cambridge University, out of revenge because Eddy had ended their relationship. But no evidence exists that the two men ever had been lovers.

Prince Albert Victor died during an influenza epidemic in 1892.

Although Scotland Yard detectives had several non-royal suspects, the Jack the Ripper murders remain officially unsolved.

48.

THE KIM PHILBY
SPY RING

Throughout World War II and the peak years of the Cold War, Harold Adrian Russell Philby donned the mask of a dedicated, loyal, and patriotic British civil servant. But for more than twenty years as the central figure in a Soviet spy ring, centered around several bright young men who were recruited at Cambridge University in the 1930s, Philby was the most cynical, cunning, and successful traitor in Britain's history.

Born in India in 1912, he was the son of a British colonial official. Because he spoke the native language before he learned English, he was nicknamed Kim, after the boy with a conflict of identities in the Rudyard Kipling story of that name. While a student at Cambridge University's Trinity College in the early 1930s, Philby embraced Marxism and formed friendships with a group of like-minded young men (Guy Burgess, Donald Maclean, Anthony Blunt, and others). All of them were recruited by the Soviet secret service, then called the NKVD. The expectation was that such bright young members of England's elite, educated, governing class would eventually rise to significant positions that would prove advantageous to the Communist Party in general and the USSR in particular. The term in international espionage lingo for this is "mole."

In author and former intelligence officer John le Carré's best-selling novel and later TV miniseries, *Tinker, Tailor, Soldier, Spy,* concerning a hunt for a mole within the British secret service, the Soviet Union's agent is largely based on Kim Philby, who by the time of the novel had been exposed and had fled to the Soviet Union.

During the years when Philby, Burgess, Maclean, Blunt, and others were masquerading as loyal servants of crown and country, the Soviet Union's intelligence services were reaping benefits that were beyond the wildest imaginations and dreams of the recruiters of the group that became notorious in the history of international espionage as "the Cambridge spy ring."

Between 1944 and 1946 Philby worked as head of anti-Communist counterespionage for the British secret service. He was so trusted that he became secretary of the British Embassy in Washington and worked closely with the Central Intelligence Agency (1949–1951). He later worked as a journalist in Beirut. Alerted that he was suspected of espionage, he boarded a ship in Beirut, Lebanon, in 1963 and fled to the Soviet Union. His grateful employers awarded him one of its highest medals and granted him citizenship. He died there a year before the fall of the Berlin Wall signaled the ultimate demise of the Soviet Union.

Guy Burgess covered his loyalty to Soviet Communism by working first for the BBC (1936–1939 and 1941–1944), then with British Intelligence (MI5). Moving to the Foreign Office, he became a secretary under Philby in Washington until he was recalled from the U.S. in 1950 for "serious misconduct" (he was an alcoholic and made no secret of his homosexuality). He and fellow spy Donald Maclean also skipped to the USSR and emerged in the Soviet Union a few years later. Burgess eventually died in Moscow.

Donald Maclean had joined the diplomatic service and in 1950 became the head of the American Department at the Foreign Office, giving him access to top-secret information on atomic development. Warned by Philby that he was under suspicion, Maclean accompanied Guy Burgess to Moscow.

As a talent scout supplying the names of possible recruits to the Communist cause in the 1930s, Anthony Blunt worked for British Intelligence during World War II. After Philby's defection in 1964 he confessed to his involvement in exchange for immunity from prosecution, but his role was not made public until 1979. An art historian, he was employed as surveyor of the Queen's pictures and director of the Courtauld Institute of Art until his role as the "fourth man" of the Cambridge spy ring was revealed in 1979, resulting in his being stripped of his knighthood and academic honors.

The identity of the so-called "fifth man" was not known until the 1990s. Spotted by the eagle-eyed Anthony Blunt at Cambridge and introduced to Guy Burgess, John Cairncross was recruited into the Communist Party in 1937 and worked in the Foreign Office alongside Donald Maclean. While employed at the Treasury he was able to leak details about the military decoding center, Bletchley Park. Data that he supplied enabled Soviet spies to change their codes just as British Intelligence was about to crack them.

Two months before his death of a heart attack, Kim Philby told *The Sunday Times* of London that he had always felt that he belonged to the USSR. "It's my country," he said, "and I served it more than fifty years."

In 1990, in one of the Soviet government's last acts before it collapsed, Kim Philby was remembered by the USSR's postal service in a series of stamps noting "KGB heroes."

49.

THE OSS

It may be hard to believe in this age when American spy satellites seem to be keeping an eye on almost everything that happens around the globe, but there was a time not so very long ago when the United States did not have an espionage service. Immediately after World War I, the Secretary of State shut down a small intelligence operation with the comment, "Gentlemen do not read other people's mail."

That naive attitude would change as the United States prepared to enter World War II, thanks to the work of a hero of the previous war. When William J. "Wild Bill" Donovan came back from his service in the Army, he was hailed as one of the top four U.S. heroes, along with Sergeant Alvin York, "Ace of Aces" Captain Eddie Rickenbacker, and Chief of the Allied Expeditionary Forces, John J. "Black Jack" Pershing. Brushing off pleas that he run for president in 1920, Donovan went back to his pre-war law practice. After serving as the U.S. Attorney for the Buffalo District, he was chosen by President Calvin Coolidge to be acting Attorney General and held the post until 1929, then ran unsuccessfully for governor of New York in 1932. Nine years later, President Franklin D. Roosevelt acted on the suggestion of an expert in espionage, William Stephenson, that Donovan be sent to London to confer with Prime Minister Winston Churchill on American aid to Britain as England stood alone in the war with Germany. The ultimate result of this was a recommendation to FDR that the United States form an espionage agency. Roosevelt approved a plan for a "Coordinator of Information."

Donovan was put in charge with orders to report directly to Roosevelt. On June 13, 1942, the agency's name was changed to the Office of Strategic Services. For the duration of the war, OSS agents would slip behind the lines to carry out espionage and build a network of spies in Europe and North Africa. One of these spies was Allen Dulles, a future head of the CIA. He went to work in Bern, Switzerland with two unpressed suits and a letter of credit for a million dollars to set up a network of spies in Italy and Germany. At the same time, Donovan was in touch with Germany's spymaster, Admiral Wilhelm Canaris, in hopes of attaining an end to the war.

In his sixties, Donovan proved to be a genius at devising plots to thwart the Germans and Japanese. He constantly put in sixteen-hour days supervising and directing the collection of data that contributed significantly to the success of the D-Day landings in Normandy. As the Allied Forces swept into and across the continent, they were assisted by an OSS-trained "underground" of French citizens that blew up trains and bridges and provided vital information on deployment of enemy units.

With an Allied victory in sight in October 1944, Roosevelt sent a note to Donovan that asked him to provide a report on the needs of a post-war intelligence service. But Roosevelt's successor, Harry S. Truman, felt no need for such an agency. Consequently, a month after the Japanese surrender, he ordered the OSS disbanded. Of its 16,000 agents and other operatives in combat zones during the war, 2,000 were awarded medals for gallantry, 143 men and women had been killed, and about 300 captured.

Retired with the rank of major general, Donovan resumed law practice, but he was not out of the game of spy plotting for long. When the Soviet Union's activities resulted in what Winston Churchill called a Communist "Iron Curtain" descending all across Eastern Europe, and forced Truman to change his mind about the need for an intelligence service, Donovan found himself called upon to assist in the formation of the Central Intelligence Agency. Following the election of Eisenhower, he was named U.S. Ambassador to Thailand (1953–1954). Choosing to retire again, he wrote to his boss, Secretary of State John Foster Dulles (Allen's brother): "I want the President to know whatever the circumstances, my experience is at his disposal to serve the best interests of the country." Beset by failing health, he received a get well greeting from Churchill: "I well remember," it said, "the remarkable services which you rendered to our joint cause in the war years."

When Donovan was taken to CIA headquarters in late January 1959 to see his full-length portrait hanging in the agency's lobby, a witness noted that Donovan's eyes focused on the erect figure in the Army uniform, the twin stars of rank on each shoulder, the banks of bright ribbons with the blue Medal of Honor at the top. "This was the Donovan who had commanded his troops in battle at St. Mihel and the Argonne Forest," wrote the observer, "who led the OSS through the Second World War, who had served his country above and beyond the call of duty."

Dressed in his uniform, Donovan lifted his head, drew himself to attention, and, straight as a soldier, did an about-face and strode away. When he died a few days later, on Sunday, February 8, 1959, a signal went out from the CIA to its agents around the world: "The man more responsible than any other for the existence of the Central Intelligence Agency has passed away."

In devising organizations for the defense of the United States and on behalf of the cause of democracy, Wild Bill Donovan was a mastermind of conspiracies with a noble purpose.

50.

BAY OF PIGS

Running against Vice President Richard Nixon for president in 1960, John F. Kennedy accused the administration of President Dwight Eisenhower of ineffectively dealing with the Communist government "ninety miles from Florida" that had been imposed on Cuba following the Fidel Castro-led revolution. Although Eisenhower had declared that the United States would not tolerate "establishment of a regime dominated by international Communism in the Western hemisphere," what neither Ike nor Nixon could say in reply to Kennedy was that Eisenhower had directed the Central Intelligence Agency to devise a plan for overthrowing Castro.

This was to be achieved by secretly recruiting Cuban exiles, covertly providing them military training, and landing them in Cuba with the support of American naval and air power. This planning went forward on the basis of intelligence reports that once the exile army had been securely established, the Cuban people would rise up and kick out the Communists.

Presented to Eisenhower on March 17, 1960, the CIA scheme was titled "A Program of Covert Action against the Castro Regime." It included the creation of a responsible and unified Cuban opposition outside Cuba (anti-Castro exiles, based mostly in Florida), propaganda aimed at the Cuban people to encourage them to join an uprising, organizing anti-Castro forces inside Cuba, and development of a paramilitary force outside Cuba for future guerilla action. All of this was to be done "in such a manner as to avoid the appearance of U.S. intervention."

Ike approved both the plan and the spending of more than seven and a half million dollars to carry it out.

Nixon knew all of this during the campaign. Kennedy learned of the plan only after he was elected, and gave it his blessing.

During a press conference on April 12, 1961, five days before the landings were to be launched, Kennedy was asked how far the United States would go to help an uprising against Castro. Kennedy replied that "there will not be, under any conditions, an intervention in Cuba by the United States armed forces." In saying this, he was adhering to a plan that had been designed to make the impending invasion of Cuba seem entirely an effort by the exile forces with, as the CIA plan envisioned, no "appearance of U.S. intervention."

Two days after Kennedy's news conference, six ships carrying 1,500 invaders, known as Brigade 2506, sailed from Puerto Cabezas, Nicaragua, bound for Playa Giron—the Bay of Pigs—on the southeast coast of Cuba. The next day, April 17, 1961, U.S. B-26 bombers with Cuban markings bombed four airfields in Cuba. Press reports said the action had been an "uprising" by Cubans. But news accounts quickly noted that the rebels were not only encountering very strong resistance from Castro's forces, but also that there were no signs that masses of Cubans were joining the invaders. With these discouraging reports pouring into the White House, Kennedy faced the likelihood that without direct action by the United States in the form of air naval support, followed by a commitment of U.S. ground troops, the invasion was doomed.

Kennedy chose not to supply the needed support. The result was the capture of 1,189 exiles (all of whom were sentenced to 30 years in prison, then paroled upon payment by the U.S. to Cuba of $53 million in food and medicine); severe embarrassment to the Kennedy administration when it was revealed that the exiles had been trained and supplied by the United States; and a pledge from Kennedy to the Soviet Union and Castro that the U.S. would never again attempt to invade Cuba.

Historians of the Cold War agree that the failure of Kennedy to come to the rescue of the Bay of Pigs invaders, and to follow through with the plan to depose Castro, encouraged Soviet leader Nikita Khrushchev to secretly install nuclear missiles in Cuba, which led to the Cuban Missile Crisis of 1962.

An analysis by the CIA of "the Bay of Pigs fiasco" attributed the undertaking to a phenomenon shared by most conspiracies, which psychologists call "groupthink." It has been defined as a susceptibility "to radically wrong decision-making because everyone in the group is so enthusiastic about being among powerful and knowledgeable men that they neglect to check basic assumptions, to push opposing views, or to consider that they may be just plain wrong."

51

THE ASSASSINATION OF EGYPTIAN PRESIDENT ANWAR SADAT

Although Anwar Sadat was a distinguished Egyptian soldier who'd taken part in political conspiracies against the British in World War II and then against King Farouk in 1952, when he became president of Egypt in 1970 it was not the result of a plot. He assumed office after Gamal Abdul Nasser died of natural causes. Legally inheriting power in a nation that had suffered the most in wars with Israel (Egypt, for instance, lost five times as many men in the 1967 Six Day War as Syria and Jordan), Sadat put out peace-feelers to Israel that were ignored. He responded by launching troops in 1973 in an effort to drive Israel out of the Sinai Desert and with the hope that Israel would be forced to make peace at last. The result was another defeat of Egypt and its ally, Syria. Beset by domestic troubles that included several riots, Sadat decided that the time had come for a bold gamble that Israel was as weary of incessant warfare as Egypt was.

Eager to provide a "peace dividend" to both countries, Sadat told Egypt's parliament in 1977 that he was willing "to go anywhere" to negotiate peace with Israel. "There is no time to lose," he warned. "I am ready to go to the ends of the earth if that will save one of my soldiers, one of my officers, from being scratched. I am ready to go to their house, the Knesset [Israel's parliament], to discuss peace with the Israeli leaders."

Israel's Prime Minister Menachem Begin, himself a former conspirator and ex-guerilla fighter who'd fought to drive the British out of Palestine and had been imprisoned, responded with a formal invitation. Lined up to meet Sadat when his plane landed at Ben Gurion Airport were Begin; former Premiers Yitzhak Rabin and Golda Meir; Foreign Minister Moshe Dayan (who'd beaten the Arabs in 1948 and 1967); and the man known as Israel's "General Patton," Ariel Sharon, whose tanks had driven across the Suez Canal to Cairo's suburbs in 1973.

Addressing the Knesset, Sadat recalled the history of Arab–Israeli relations since the birth of the Jewish State in 1948. "We used to reject you, true. We refused to meet you anywhere, true," he said. "Yet today we agree to live with you in permanent peace and justice. Israel has become an accomplished fact recognized by the whole world and the superpowers. We welcome you to live among us in peace and security."

After meetings at the presidential retreat, Camp David, with President Jimmy Carter acting as interlocutor, Sadat and Begin signed the "Camp David Accords" on the lawn of the White House. Since 1979, a peace treaty has existed between Egypt and Israel.

For his daring stroke, Sadat was awarded the Nobel Peace Prize, along with Menachem Begin.

Sadat had hoped that peace would usher in an era of domestic harmony and economic progress in Egypt. Unfortunately, this did not happen. Despite desperate gambles to deal with domestic problems, Sadat came under increasingly bitter criticism by fundamentalist Muslim groups, not only because of the peace deal with Israel, but also because the fundamentalists wanted to transform Egypt into an Islamic state. Sadat reacted by outlawing protest demonstrations and arresting more than 1,500 opponents, many of whom belonged to militant Islamic organizations, including the Al Jihad, the Muslim Brotherhood, and Jamaa Islamiya, led by Karam Zohdi.

Eight years after Egypt had been defeated by Israel in the Yom Kippur War, Sadat chose to stage a military parade to commemorate the eighth anniversary of an event that he viewed not as a blow to Egypt, but as a victory for peace and prosperity. His opponents, though, saw the parade as an opportunity to get rid of Sadat and advance their cause of an Islamic state.

As Sadat reviewed the troops on October 6, 1981, several armed members of Al Jihad and Jamaa, dressed as soldiers, led by Lieutenant Colonel Khalid al Islambuli, jumped out of passing army trucks, opened fire into the reviewing stand with rifles, and tossed hand grenades. Sadat was killed instantly and twenty others were wounded. Surviving the attack were future UN Secretary-General Boutros Boutros-Ghali and Air Force General Hosni Mubarak.

When Mubarak succeeded Sadat as president, he launched a crackdown on the Islamic terrorists. Two members of the Sadat assassination conspiracy were shot and three were hanged. Among other Islamic militants rounded up was Sheik Omar Abdel Rahman. Years later, he would be convicted in the United States for conspiring to blow up the World Trade Center. Also taken into custody was Ayman al-Zawajiri, who became one of Osama bin Laden's top lieutenants of Al-Qaeda and helped plan and carry out the attacks on the World Trade Center and the Pentagon on September 11, 2001.

The head of Jamaa Islamiya's ruling consultative council, Karam Zohdi, who'd given the order to kill Sadat, was sentenced to twenty-five years in prison. Interviewed twenty-two years after he gave the order for the assassination, he appeared to have changed his opinion of Sadat. Expressing deep sorrow for having approved the murder, he called Sadat a "martyr." If time could be turned back, he said, he would act differently.

Those who conspired to assassinate Anwar Sadat hoped his death would immediately result in Egypt's becoming an Islamic state. This did not come to pass, but President Mubarak's government continues to this day to be attacked by fundamentalist militants.

52.

THE BENEDICT ARNOLD PLOT

In history's roster of conspirators two names stand apart as synonyms for betrayal. Both became traitors for money. Judas Iscariot sold out Jesus Christ to enemies for thirty pieces of silver. General Benedict Arnold's asking price to commit treason in the American Revolution by handing the British the fortress called West Point was 20,000 pounds (about one million dollars today). Scholars of both plots also attribute the deeds of the two turncoats to the personal disappointment with the manner in which their leaders were conducting themselves. Feeling let down when Jesus did not prove to be a leader of an armed revolt against the occupation of Israel by Rome, Judas betrayed him for thirty silver coins. Arnold appears to have had a personal reason for becoming a turncoat. As a genuine hero of the War of Independence, he believed that he was poorly treated by his superiors and that the Continental Congress had tainted the purity of the revolution by inviting an alliance with France.

Early in the war, Arnold distinguished himself by leading an assault on Quebec, Canada. Suffering a leg wound in the bold attack that failed to take the city, he emerged as a hero. During the battles at Saratoga, New York, he proved to be a brilliant strategist and again distinguished himself. But the American commander, General Horatio Gates, relieved him of his command, in part for insubordination and because Gates viewed Arnold as a "pompous little fellow."

This insult to Arnold was assuaged following British abandonment of Philadelphia when George Washington appointed Arnold to the post of commandant of the city. But by this time Arnold was an embittered figure with open disdain for his fellow officers and resentment toward Congress for not promoting him more quickly. He was also a widower who courted and married Margaret (Peggy) Shippen, described as "a talented young woman of good family." At nineteen she was half Arnold's age and pro-British. Plunging into the social life in America's largest and most sophisticated city by throwing lavish parties, he was soon deeply in debt. This extravagance drew him into dubious financial schemes that forced Congress to investigate his activities, resulting in a recommendation that he be brought before a court-martial. Arnold complained to Washington that having "become a cripple in the service of my country, I little expected to meet ungrateful returns."

Confronted with personal and financial ruin, unsure of future promotion, and disgusted with the politicians in Congress, Arnold made a fateful and ultimately disastrous decision to wipe out his difficulties by offering his services to the British. He began by writing to their commander, Sir Henry Clinton, and promising to deliver the garrison at West Point, with 3,000 defenders, in the belief that the surrender would bring about the collapse of the American cause. Standing on a promontory that commanded a narrowing of the Hudson River, the guns of the fort were in easy range of all shipping on a vital waterway that if taken over by the British would cut New England off from the rebellious colonies to the south.

To put himself in a position to deliver on his offer, Arnold persuaded Washington to place the fort under his command. In September 1780 he was ready to execute his plan. To assist him in the plot the British chose Major John André as the go-between. The two men shared more than the conspiracy to neutralize West Point. Before Arnold married Peggy Shippen, André had been her suitor. Serving with the Fifty-fourth Foot as adjutant general to General Clinton, André was also in charge of British spy operations. The plot involved coded letters and invisible ink. To make it easier for the British to take over, Arnold scattered his troops to weaken West Point's defenses. Following a meeting with Arnold on September 21, 1780, André set out for his own lines in civilian clothes and carrying identification papers in the name of "John Anderson." He was stopped by three suspicious Americans, taken to headquarters, searched, and exposed as a spy. Learning this, Arnold hastened to New York and the safety of his British allies.

Although the British commander tried to bargain for André's release, Washington would accept only one person in exchange: Benedict Arnold. Major André was hanged on October 2, 1780. He accommodated his executioner by placing the noose around his neck and tying his own handkerchief as a blindfold. His body was eventually disinterred and buried with much pomp as a hero in Westminster Abbey.

Arnold served the British in 1781 by leading devastating strikes on American supply depots: In Virginia he looted Richmond and destroyed munitions and grain intended for the American army opposing Lord Cornwallis; in Connecticut he burned ships, warehouses, and much of the town of New London, which was a major port for American privateers. Unrepentant and defending his betrayal of his native country, he died in England in June 1801.

53.

EXECUTION OF QUEEN ANNE BOLEYN

Queen Anne Boleyn, the second of King Henry VIII's six wives, was beheaded as the result of one of history's most infamous, continually fascinating, and ultimately ironic official conspiracies. On the day of her death, Boleyn calmly said to bloodthirsty spectators at the Tower of London: "Good Christian people, I am come hither to die, for according to the law, and by the law I am judged to die, and therefore I will speak nothing against it. I am come hither to accuse no man, nor to speak anything of that, whereof I am accused and condemned to die, but I pray God save the king and send him long to reign over you, for a gentler nor a more merciful prince was there never: and to me he was ever a good, a gentle and sovereign lord."

Born in 1502, Anne was the second daughter of Sir Thomas Boleyn and Lady Elizabeth Howard, making Anne the maternal niece of one of Henry's courtiers, the Duke of Norfolk. For a time, Anne's sister, Mary, was Henry's mistress. Exactly when Henry switched his attentions to Anne isn't clear, but by 1525 he was actively pursuing her while seeking a way to divorce his wife, Catherine of Aragon, because she'd failed to produce a male heir.

Anne became queen on January 25, 1553, after Henry split with the Catholic Church, put himself at the head of the Church of England, and launched what became known as the Reformation. Three years later, the formal charges that brought Anne a death sentence were witchcraft and adultery, but her fate really had been sealed for more complex reasons. Because she did not produce a son after the birth of a daughter, Elizabeth, Henry was determined to find a queen who could. The woman he had his eyes on was Jane Seymour. At the same time, members of the anti-Anne Boleyn clique at Henry's court were eager to advance their own ambitions and status by helping Henry to find a way to get rid of a woman whom they viewed as a vulgar and duplicitous social climber with no charm, no wit, and no accomplishments. She was seen as a woman with a scarlet past who had connived to become Henry's mistress during the time he was seeking to end his marriage to Catherine.

"The plot against Anne Boleyn was most carefully calculated," wrote historian E. Ives in *Faction in Tudor England* (1979). "Seymour deliberately tantalized the king, at the same time poisoning his mind against Anne. The rest of the queen's enemies joined in the chorus when and how they could."

To pave the way for Anne's downfall, a secret commission was established that included not only Henry's closest advisor and archconspirator, Thomas Cromwell, but also Anne's father and her uncle, the Duke of Norfolk. Their purpose was to investigate allegations of her sexual misconduct, including incest with her brother, Lord Rochford, and adulterous acts with Sir Francis Weston, Sir Henry Norris, and William Bererton. All were notoriously licentious. Perhaps the most unlikely of all those accused of being the queen's lovers was Mark Smeaton, a court musician who was probably a homosexual. They all paid with their lives.

Because a queen's adultery was an offense against the monarch, Anne was charged and brought to trial for treason. As Queen of England, she was tried by her peers. The death sentence was pronounced by her uncle. As a concession to her former position, she was not beheaded by axe; an expert with the sword was brought in from France. When Anne was told of this, she replied, "I have heard that the executioner is very good. And I have a little neck." She prayed that she might be sent into exile, or be allowed to end her days in a nunnery. But at eight o'clock in the morning on May 19, 1536, she became the first English queen to be executed.

She was buried on the Tower grounds in an old arrow box. Because the box was too short, her head was put in beside her. It was rumored that a few of her loyal friends smuggled her body to a graveyard in Norfolk and buried it under a plain slab. Some people say that her spirit haunts the place. If so, twenty-two years after she'd fallen victim to a royal conspiracy, her ghost had good reason to smile. Her daughter Elizabeth became Queen of England.

54

ATTEMPTED DEPOSING OF QUEEN ELIZABETH I

"Uneasy lies the head that wears the crown."

When William Shakespeare wrote those words in *Henry IV, Part II*, the English crown rested on the head of the red-haired daughter of King Henry VIII and his second wife, the ill-fated Anne Boleyn. When Elizabeth ascended to the throne in 1558 at age twenty-five, she found the royal treasury empty and a country torn between Protestants and Catholics who were eager to replace her with her Catholic cousin, Mary, Queen of the Scots, with the avowed support of Mary's mother-in-law, Catherine de Medici, Regent for Charles IX of France.

To further her claim to the English throne, Mary married her cousin, Henry Stuart, Lord Darnley, a relative of the ruling family of England (the Tudors). They had a son, James. After Darnley was implicated in the murder of Mary's Italian secretary (and possibly her lover) by a group led by Darnley and a group of Protestant nobles, Darnley was also murdered. The primary suspect was the Earl of Bothwell. Acquitted in a mock trial, he rescued Mary from Protestant captivity. For this Mary not only publicly pardoned his "seizure" of her person, but also named him Duke of Orkney, and married him.

With Scottish nobles taking up arms against her, Mary's own soldiers abandoned her. Forced to surrender, she was imprisoned at Loch Leven and coerced into signing an act of abdication that put her son on the throne as James VI.

After a daring escape, Mary raised another army, but was again defeated (1568). Seeking the protection of Queen Elizabeth, she found herself in an English prison because the presence in England of a Catholic claimant to Elizabeth's crown (through Darnley) worried Elizabeth and her advisors. They had good reasons to feel anxious. English Catholics saw in Mary a restorer of the faith that had been rejected by King Henry VIII.

For keeping tabs on those who might be planning to seat Queen Mary on the English throne, Elizabeth at first had the services of a network of spies run by William Cecil. In 1571, he learned of a plot by Roberto Ridolfi. A Florentine banker in England, Ridolfi proposed to the Pope and Spain that the Spanish land 10,000 troops at Harwich or Portsmouth at the same time there'd be an uprising of English Catholics led by the Duke of Norfolk, for the purpose of seizing Elizabeth, proclaiming Mary as Queen of England, and restoring Catholicism. When Cecil got wind of the plot, he had Ridolfi arrested and found the Italian talkative. As a result, the Spanish ambassador was sent home and the Duke of Norfolk was tried and executed.

The next foiled plot (1583) was conspired by Francis Throckmorton. An English Catholic, he was arrested with a letter to Mary in his hand. Under torture he confessed that he was engaged in a grand "enterprise" to assassinate Elizabeth. Letters found in Throckmorton's home listed names of Catholic noblemen and areas where a Catholic army could invade. Because Throckmorton had discussed his scheme with the Spanish ambassador, the diplomat was quickly sent packing.

Three years later, Cecil's successor as Elizabeth's spymaster was Francis Walsingham. Born in Kent around 1530, he'd studied at Cambridge and spent many years living in Europe. Back in England in 1559, he was elected to Parliament. A protégé of Cecil, he later served as ambassador to France and established a network of spies among French Protestants (Huguenots). His efforts earned him the post of Elizabeth's secretary of state and a knighthood. Taking over from Cecil in rooting out Catholic conspirators, he faced the most serious threat to her crown in 1586 in what is known in British history as the "Babington Plot."

Sir Anthony Babington, a young Catholic nobleman from Derbyshire, was persuaded by Jesuit priest John Ballard to enlist in the cause of putting Mary on the English throne. He was a logical choice. As a child, Babington had served as a page to Mary's jailer. Evidently a natural conspirator, Babington wrote letters to Mary that explained his plan to rescue her. Written in code, they were smuggled into her prison in a beer keg. In one of these letters he asked Mary's permission to assassinate Elizabeth. While Mary did not give her outright assent to regicide, she approved of Babington's rescue plot. Unfortunately for him and Queen Mary, Walsingham had become aware of the plot almost as soon as it was hatched. Exhibiting all the skills of espionage and what would later be known as "dirty tricks" that have enshrined him as a pioneer in the world of spies, counterspies, and double agents, Walsingham was able to intercept and decode all of the correspondence between Babington and Mary.

In August 1586, John Ballard was arrested. Questioned under torture, he gave up the details of the Babington plot. Despite a plea to Elizabeth for mercy, he was executed for treason.

Although reluctant to kill another monarch, on February 8, 1587, Elizabeth signed Mary's death warrant. Her execution by beheading at Fotheringay Castle did not go well. Unable to chop off Mary's head with one blow, the executioner was forced to use a grinding motion to complete the grisly task. She was buried at Peterborough, but in 1612 her body was moved to Henry VII's chapel at Westminster. When Elizabeth died childless, the heir to the English throne was Mary's son. He ruled as James VI of Scotland and James I of England.

55

THE GUNPOWDER PLOT

When King James I of England donned the crown in 1603, he presented to the English several problems. First, he wasn't English. He had been born in Scotland, where he'd ruled as James VI following the abdication of his mother, Mary, Queen of Scots. He believed that the "divine right of kings" placed him above laws enacted by Parliament and surrounded himself with corrupt favorites in an extravagant court. Nineteenth-century historian Thomas Macaulay described him as "made up of two men—a witty, well-read scholar who wrote, disputed, and harangued, and a nervous, driveling idiot who acted."

Although James's mother had been Catholic, he was a Protestant who'd grown up amid the turmoil of civil war, religious plots and counterplots, and was surrounded by what one historian called "as bloodthirsty a set of intriguers as could be found." Quickly at odds with a Parliament that refused to pay his debts, and lawyers who opposed him at every turn, he was also hated by the Catholics of his new realm because they felt that he had reneged on his promises to relax anti-Catholic laws and appeared determined to impose even more severe persecutions.

Consequently, at a meeting in the spring of 1604 at John Wright's house in the London suburb of Lambeth, Wright, Robert Catesby, and Thomas Wintour devised a scheme to trigger a Catholic revolt by ridding England of James; his son, the Prince of Wales; most of the government ministers; and the House of Lords by blowing them up when they gathered for the opening of Parliament on November 5, 1605. In the following months they enlisted others in the plot, including Thomas Percy, Robert Keyes, John Grant, Sir Everard Digby, Francis Tresham, Ambrose Rookwood, Thomas Bates, and Guido (Guy) Fawkes, a Catholic convert who was born in York and served as a mercenary in the Spanish Army in the Netherlands.

The original plan called for Catesby to rent a house near the Palace of Westminster and for a tunnel to be dug from there to the Houses of Parliament. When this proved an impossible task for men not accustomed to physical labor, Thomas Percy used his connections to rent a cellar under the House of Lords. The job of placing of thirty-six barrels of gunpowder, concealed beneath firewood and coal, was given to Fawkes. Posing as Percy's servant, John Johnson, he did his work efficiently and finished concealing the explosives months before he was to return to the cellar to detonate them while James and the members of the House of Commons assembled in the House of Lords for the opening ceremony on November 5.

Among those who would be seated in the chamber on that date was Lord Monteagle, but ten days before, as he sat at his dining table in his Hoxton home, he was handed an alarming letter. The person who sent it has never been identified. Some speculate it may have been from Monteagle's brother-in-law, Frances Tresham, one of the conspirators. Expressing "a care for your preservation," it said, "I would advise you, as you tender your life, to devise some excuse to shift your attendance of this Parliament, for God and man hath concurred to punish the wickedness of this time." The writer urged Monteagle to "retire yourself into your country [estate], where you may expect the event in safety, for though there be no appearance of any stir, yet I say they shall receive a terrible blow, the Parliament, and yet they shall not see who hurts them."

Although Monteagle immediately took the letter to Secretary of State Robert Cecil, Earl of Salisbury, the king's Privy Council did not order a search of the cellar beneath the House of Lords until the evening of November 4, first by the Earl of Suffolk, and somewhat later by Sir Thomas Knyvett. Fawkes greeted the searchers calmly. With the discovery of the kegs of gunpowder, he was overpowered and arrested.

Learning that the gunpowder plot had failed, Catesby, Wintour, and the other conspirators fled, but after three days were tracked to Holbeche House in Staffordshire. In the ensuing battle Catesby, Percy, Wright, and Wright's brother were killed. Other plotters were captured a few days later. While all were executed, Francis Tresham died while he was confined to the Tower of London. That he was spared public execution has resulted in speculation that steps had been taken to conceal his authorship of the letter that revealed the mass assassination plot.

It has also been proposed that the letter had been part of a plot within a plot, in which the scheme to blow up Parliament would be revealed anonymously in order to thwart the gunpowder plan, yet give the plotters enough time to escape.

Another version of the story holds that Guy Fawkes was an agent provocateur, acting on behalf of unspecified individuals who wished to alert King James to the Catholic threat.

Others contemplate that Robert Cecil, Earl of Salisbury, got wind of the plot in its early stages and waited until the last moment to expose it for dramatic effect. If so, King James I was never in danger.

Whatever the truth may be, the Gunpowder Plot is remembered throughout England on November 5 as "Guy Fawkes Day." It is marked by bonfires, burning "Guy" effigies, fireworks, and other colorful and noisy festivities. Children take part in all of this while reciting:

> *Remember, remember the fifth of November,*
> *Gunpowder, Treason, and Plot.*
> *I see no reason why Gunpowder and Treason*
> *Should ever be forgot.*

56.

PLOT TO DEPOSE MIKHAIL GORBACHEV

Since the victory of Bolshevism in Russia in the aftermath of World War I, the Union of Soviet Socialist Republics was seen by the outside world as a monolith run by ruthless dictators, from Vladimir Lenin and Josef Stalin to Nikita Khrushchev, whose boast, "We will bury you," sent chills through a world already gripped by the Cold War. Then along came Mikhail Gorbachev. In his first appearance in the West as chairman of the Presidium (parliament) of the Supreme Soviet in December 1984, Gorbachev met in London with Great Britain's Prime Minister, Margaret Thatcher. An implacable foe of Communism, she startled the world by announcing, "We can do business with this man."

Elected General Secretary of the Central Committee of the Communist Party in March 1985, Gorbachev signaled the need for a dramatic change within the USSR by declaring, "We can't go on living like this." What was required, he said, was glasnost (openness) and perestroika (reform and change to a more democratic system, starting with the top leadership of the USSR).

Appreciating that remaking his country and improving the living conditions of its people required a monumental shift from a militaristic

Cold War economy to a consumer-based system, he felt an urgent need to end a forty-year arms race with the world's other super-power—the United States. To do so, he had to deal with Ronald Reagan. A president whose entire political life had been an unrelenting assault on Communism, he had recently labeled the Soviet Union "an evil empire."

After accession to power of four traditional, hard-line Soviet leaders, and their rapidly following deaths, Gorbachev found himself elected General Secretary (1985) and in a position to test his ideas for reform. He began by issuing tough anti-alcohol laws to tackle the Soviet Union's historic problem of excessive drinking. The result was lengthy lines at liquor stores that the people named "Gorbachev's nooses." In a televised speech on May 17, 1985, he criticized industrial failures. This was followed by salary increases for scientists and engineers, along with a system of bonuses linked to efficiency and productivity.

In the following months Gorbachev faced what appeared to be an unraveling of Soviet control over Eastern Europe, unrest in the Soviet Republic of Georgia, demands by the Ukraine for independence, coal miners going on strike, a forced and humiliating defeat and withdrawal of Soviet troops after a year-long invasion of Afghanistan, and continuing obstinacy concerning arms limitations by a president who saw the USSR as an evil empire and, in a speech made on the western side of the Berlin Wall on June 12, 1987, had demanded, "Mr. Gorbachev, tear down this wall." Two and a half years later, the wall gave way to a tidal wave of freedom that was the result of Mikhail Gorbachev's glasnost and perestroika.

But in August 1991, peaceful breakaways by former satellite countries in Eastern Europe, German unification, arms agreements with the United States, and the crumbling of the Soviet Union itself, persuaded hard-liners in Moscow that Gorbachev had to go. Taking advantage of his being on vacation in the Crimea, they staged a coup.

For several hours on the night of August 20 it seemed likely that the hopes of his people for freedom were about to be snuffed out by hard-line Communist leaders of a coup d'état who called themselves the State Committee on the Emergency Situation. On their orders two days earlier, Soviet President Mikhail Gorbachev had been imprisoned in his summer house in the Crimea. With him immobilized, the junta announced that they had taken over his presidential powers. Troops and tanks converged on the main government building in Moscow, known as the White House. But as they took up their positions and prepared to storm the building, thousands of unarmed Muscovites rushed to defend it.

Alerted to these alarming developments at his residence in the Arkhangelskoye district of downtown Moscow, Boris Yeltsin, an important official in the Soviet government, hurried to the scene. As troops and tanks surrounded Moscow's White House and with the world watching breathlessly on television, thousands of Muscovites stood between the tall, floodlit building that stood for freedom and the soldiers and tanks of the Tula Division that represented the past.

When Yeltsin arrived and climbed onto the top of tank No. 110, his stance was a scary reminder to Russians who knew the history of their country in portraits of Lenin in similar poses meant to glorify the Communism that seemed, at last, to be on its way out. Unknown was just whose side Yeltsin was on.

What the crowd and the anxiously waiting world saw was an act of bravery in the form of a speech that persuaded the troops to switch sides. The next day, leaders of the coup were under arrest for treason. On Yeltsin's orders a rescue team brought Gorbachev back to Moscow, but he would no longer be the head of the Communist Party. After seventy years of ruling the Soviet Union, the Communist Party was banned by Yeltsin and its property was confiscated.

On December 1, 1991, Ukraine voted for independence. A week later, it joined with Russia and Belarus in forming the Commonwealth of Independent States. On the day before Christmas, Russia replaced the disbanded Union of Soviet Socialist Republics at the United Nations. With an empire that Ronald Reagan had been widely chastised for calling "evil" gone into what Reagan had called "the dustbin of history," its last leader resigned. Boris Yeltsin replaced Gorbachev, who had contributed greatly to the Communist Party's demise. Yeltsin inherited a nation that seven decades of Communism and forty years of Cold War had left an economic shambles.

57.

RICHARD III'S MURDER OF THE TWO PRINCES

When Richard, Duke of Gloucester, makes his entrance in the first moments of act I, scene I in William Shakespeare's *The Tragedy of King Richard III*, he announces, "Plots have I laid." Shakespeare then provided lines that described character traits meant to enshrine Richard high on the roster of history's nastiest schemers and give him the distinction of being the world's all-time most dangerous uncle.

Declaring himself in the play to be "subtle, false, and treacherous" and "determined to prove a villain," Richard lusts for the crown that rests on the head of his brother, King Henry IV, with Henry's son, twelve-year-old Prince Edward, next in line, followed by the ten-year-old Prince Richard. When Henry became ill and died unexpectedly in April 1483, at the age of forty-one, his will decreed that Richard serve as "protector" to the boy now known as King Edward V.

To further his design to claim the throne, Richard arranged to have the validity of King Edward IV's marriage questioned and ultimately nullified, making Prince Edward's claim to the throne illegitimate. As King Richard III, he had both princes confined to the Tower of London. According to an account of their fate, written by Sir Thomas More and the inspiration for Shakespeare's play, he conspired with Sir James Tyrell "that they should be murdered in their bed."

In More's story of the murders, based on Tyrell's confession several years later during his imprisonment for another crime, the murders were carried out by Tyrell, a Tower jailer by the name of Miles Forest, and Forest's horsekeeper, John Dighton. Around midnight they crept into the bedchamber and smothered the boys with pillows. In Shakespeare's play Tyrell reports the deed to Richard:

> King Richard: *Kind, Tyrell, am I happy in thy news?*
> Tyrell: *If to have done the thing you gave in charge,*
> *Beget your happiness, be happy then,*
> *For it is done.*
> King Richard: *But didst thou see them dead?*
> Tyrell: *I did, my lord.*
> King Richard: *And buried, gentle Tyrell?*
> Tyrell: *The chaplain of the Tower hath buried them;*
> *But where, to my truth, I do not know.*

The location of the princes' bodies would remain a mystery for nearly two centuries. In 1674 workmen engaged by King Charles II to dismantle a staircase in the Tower found a wooden chest containing skeletons of two children. But it wasn't until four years later, after they'd been stored at the Ashmolean Museum, that they were buried at Westminster Abbey, in an urn stating that they were the remains of the princes. In 1933, in the hope of solving the mystery of the fate of the princes, King George V gave permission for the urn to be opened and the skeletons to be examined by Dr. Lawrence Tanner, archivist at Westminster Abbey, and Professor W. Wright, a dental surgeon. Their findings were published in 1934. After the human bones were extracted from animal bones found in the urn, the doctors declared the skeletons to be of children ages twelve to thirteen and nine to eleven. Although neither the sex of the skeletons, the age of the bones, nor the cause of death could be determined, Tanner and Wright declared the bones to be the remains of the princes. Because Sir Thomas More's account of their deaths stated that they had been buried "at the stair foot," the doctors decided the find in this location was too much a coincidence for the bones to be those of any other children.

This was a blow to revisionists of Richard III's history who contend that Richard was made into a "monster" by enemies in their desire to not only depose him, but to defame him for all time as a ruthless, bloodthirsty, child killer.

Whether Richard ordered the murder of the princes in the Tower is still debatable, with a plausible case to be made by both sides of the debate.

The end to Richard's two years as king occurred during a battle with an exiled contender for the crown, Henry of Richmond. Leading an army that Henry had raised in France, he landed at Milford Haven, Wales, on August 7, 1485, and met Richard in battle on August 22 at Bosworth field, Leicestershire. In Shakespeare's drama, Richard III's words before he was killed were, "A horse! A horse! My kingdom for a horse!"

58.

FREEMASONRY

Freemasonry is the oldest secret society in the world. Its rituals and rites are said to date to the building of Solomon's Temple, and the death of the architect Hiram Abiff. Common ancient tools used in building—the trowel, plumb, level, compass, square, et cetera—are used in ceremonies because Masons find them symbolic of the building of morality and the advancement to understanding "Universal Light."

Because Freemasons impose secrecy on members regarding their rituals, they have been regarded for centuries by outsiders as sinister conspirators to take over and control the world. Masons say they are simply idealists who have banded together to study and celebrate common moral beliefs and individual improvement.

Although Freemasonry does not claim to be a religion, its beliefs are heavily influenced by eighteenth- and nineteenth-century Deism and Universalism and members must swear that they believe in a Divine Being. Consequently, Masonry is open to members of any religion.

Masons themselves debate the origins of Freemasonry. While some accounts trace it back to ancient Greece, Egypt, and Israel during the building of Solomon's Temple, these accounts are now generally discounted. What is known is that in 1717, several Masons met in London to form the first United Grand Lodge of England. As the British Empire extended to America, Masonry followed. Many of America's founding fathers were Masons. Beginning with Washington, numerous presidents have belonged to this elite group, as well as members of Congress and other officials.

That Freemasonry is shrouded in closely held rites, rituals, and an oath of secrecy that is required of members has created a mystique of mystery and a belief that the Masons are not only a group with sinister objectives, but that they are anti-Christian. This has resulted in an opposition to Freemasonry by the Roman Catholic Church, which bans Masonic membership.

The first such prohibition was enunciated in a papal bull in 1738, issued by Pope Clement XII. At one point in U.S. history, animosity toward Masonry took the form of the Anti-Masonic Party.

Masons counter the belief that it is the prototype of anti-democratic secret societies by noting that there is no overall veil of secrecy, that the degree of secrecy varies widely around the world, that Masons are public about their affiliation, that Masonic buildings are clearly marked, and that meeting times are generally a matter of public record. While this is true, central aspects of Freemasonry are kept hidden. Not only are details of rituals that take place at meetings not made public, but members are also sworn to silence on what goes on and why. Suspicions that the Masons are engaged in a mysterious conspiracy are reinforced by a Masonic system of signs of recognition, including a secret handshake.

It is of little wonder that tyrannical governments have shown hostility to Freemasonry, including the Nazis—who sent Masons to concentration camps—and Communist governments.

Masons have also been suspected of showing favoritism to other Masons. Recently, in France, the chief prosecutor accused some judges and lawyers of stalling cases involving Masons. In the 1990s in Great Britain, the Labour Party government tried unsuccessfully to enact a law requiring all public officials who were Masons to make their affiliation public.

One of the theories associated with the murderous rampage of Jack the Ripper in 1888 in London is that either Jack was a Mason, or that Masons created "Saucy Jack" in order to protect the British Royal Family. At the heart of this is *Murder by Decree*, a book and movie in which Sherlock Holmes discovered that the Ripper murders had a Masonic connection and were covered up. Many Ripperologists cling to this Masonic-connection theory.

Among the most persistent popular beliefs concerning the power of Freemasonry in the United States are that the Great Seal of the United States, the street plans and designs of U.S. government buildings in Washington, D.C., were laid out on the basis of Masonic beliefs, and that the U.S. one-dollar note contains Masonic symbols.

In the Great Seal of the United States, as pictured on the back of the dollar bill, the eagle has thirty-two feathers, the number of degrees in Scottish Rite Freemasonry. The left wing has thirty-three and is said to correspond to the Thirty-third Degree of the Scottish Rite, conferred for outstanding Masonic service. Nine feathers in the tail correspond to the nine degrees in the York Rite. The eagle is also a symbol of St. John the Evangelist, the great patron of Freemasonry. The arrows in its left talon refer to Israel's King David. The olive branch in the eagle's right talon is associated with King Solomon, who built the temple at Jerusalem. The thirteen stars above the eagle's head represent Jacob, his twelve sons, and the tribes of Israel. Thirteen stars, in double triangular form and one in the center, are symbolic of the delivery of the children of Israel from their oppressors and their attainment to a glorious freedom. The Latin *"e pluribus unum"* (out of many, one) indicates brotherhood to the Masonic fraternity.

Those who find Freemasonry on the mighty one-dollar note that the largest symbol on the bill is the portrait of George Washington. A Mason, he belonged to two Masonic lodges, was a charter "Master of Alexandria Lodge," took his oath of office as President of the United States on the Bible of St. John's Lodge of New York City, and took part in Masonic ceremonies at the laying of the corner stone of the Capitol in Washington, D.C.

Also cited as evidence of Masonry on the greenback is an unfinished pyramid. At the top of the pyramid inside a radiant triangle is the "all-seeing eye of Providence," representing that "the Grand Architect" (the Masonic phrase for God) is omniscient and watching over mankind in general and the United States of America in particular.

59

THE AARON BURR
CONSPIRACY

In an ironic coincidence in the early history of the United States, two men who became heroes in an attack on Quebec, Canada, during the American Revolution are not remembered for their gallantry in war, but for treason. General Benedict Arnold became infamous for his plot to surrender the strategically vital fort at West Point to the British. A year after President Thomas Jefferson bought the Louisiana Territory from France, his vice president, Aaron Burr, plotted to wrest it from the United States and create a new nation with himself at its head.

The son of the second president of Princeton, Burr was born in New Jersey in 1756. With the outbreak of the Revolution, he set aside becoming a lawyer to volunteer for the 1775 attack on Quebec, served in the Battle of Long Island, commanded a regiment at age twenty-one, was at Valley Forge, and led a brigade in the Monmouth Campaign (1778). He retired from the army the next year because of ill health, completed his law studies, and shared a legal practice with Alexander Hamilton. After two years as New York's Attorney General, he was elected to the U.S. Senate (1790), but served only one term. After several years in the New York legislature, he organized the Democratic Party in New York City and hoped to be elected President of the United States.

When he tied with Thomas Jefferson in the electoral college (seventy-three votes each), his former law partner, Hamilton, backed Jefferson, resulting in the House of Representatives voting to grant presidency to Jefferson and vice presidency to Burr. When he decided to run for Governor of New York in 1804, Hamilton thwarted him again by supporting Republican Morgan Lewis. Embittered, and blaming Hamilton for both losses, Burr challenged Hamilton to a duel. It took place on July 11, 1804, across the Hudson River from New York in Weehawken, New Jersey, and ended with Hamilton mortally wounded.

It was at this time that Burr launched the conspiracy to detach the Louisiana Territory from the United States. Convinced that he could do so with a small but well-trained army, and that residents of the territory would join in the effort, he sought the support of Great Britain, as he wrote in a letter to Britain's minister to the United States (Anthony Merry), to "effect a separation of the western part of the United States." On a journey to the West to recruit allies, he enlisted the support of former U.S. Senator Jonathan Dayton and a group of New Orleans businessmen. Calling themselves the Mexico Society, they favored annexation of Mexican territories in the West. But Burr's chief co-conspirator was a friend from the Revolutionary War, General James Wilkinson, who was now Commander-in-Chief of the U.S. Army. With a recommendation from Burr, Jefferson agreed to appoint Wilkinson governor of Northern Louisiana.

With a powerful ally in Wilkinson, Burr openly continued soliciting other supporters and detailed his scheme in correspondence with Wilkinson that would become known as the Cipher Letter. This proved to be a mistake. Believing that Burr's plan was doomed to failure, Wilkinson sent a letter to Jefferson outlining the conspiracy. Although he did not name Burr, the fact that Burr was actively pursuing his plan was so widely known that Burr was accused and tried for treason three times by the U.S. Court in Frankfort, Kentucky. He was acquitted each time.

On December 9, 1806, the Ohio Militia raided a boatyard in Marietta, Ohio, and captured boats and supplies that were to be used in the plot. When less than one hundred recruits showed up at the end of December to join what Burr had hoped would be a substantial army, he was undaunted and proceeded down the Mississippi River, recruiting as he went. Shortly after arriving at Bayou Pierre, about thirty miles above New Orleans, he was shown a New Orleans newspaper that announced a reward for his capture and included the decoded Cipher Letter.

After surrendering to authorities, he was arraigned and the case was referred to a grand jury. Although it did not indict him, he chose to flee into the wilderness. Captured by soldiers from Fort Stoddert on February 13, 1807, on a muddy road near the town of Wakefield, Louisiana Territory, he was taken to Richmond, Virginia, to be tried for treason.

Despite the evidence of the Cipher Letter, and testimony from individuals concerning the plot, Burr was saved by the definition of treason in the U.S. Constitution. Article III, Section 3 states, "Treason against the United States shall consist only in levying War against them, or, in adhering to their Enemies, giving them Aid and Comfort."

Because Burr had technically done neither, and with the Chief Justice, John Marshall, insisting on absolute adherence to the definition, Burr was acquitted. By now the most hated man in America, with his image being frequently burned in effigy and with several states set to charge him, he fled to Europe, where he attempted to persuade Britain and Napoleon of France to support other plots to invade the United States.

Unlike Benedict Arnold, who died in exile in England, Burr returned to his homeland in 1812 and resumed his law career. Despite having been vice president, having killed Alexander Hamilton in the most famous duel in American history, and having plotted against his country, he lived quietly and died at the age of eighty-one on September 14, 1836.

Three days later, his obituary in *Niles' Weekly Register* in Baltimore, Maryland, noted, "Few men in this country have excited more of the public attention than the deceased, in despite of the dark cloud which shrouded his once fair frame; for all admired the bravery and talents which rendered him such an important auxiliary in the early struggles of our country, and lamented that they were perverted by unhallowed ambition."

60.

ASSASSINATION OF HUEY LONG

Seven decades after U.S. Senator Huey Long of Louisiana was gunned down in a hallway in the state capital building on September 8, 1935, no one can say with certainty who fired the bullet that killed him. The official account places the blame on a lone assassin with a personal motive. In a second version, the fatal shot was fired in the confusion following the attack on Long and came from the pistol of one of Long's bodyguards. But a widely held view at the time and one that continues to fascinate historians is that Long was the victim of a conspiracy to end the life of a rambunctious, popular demagogue who posed a serious threat to the re-election in 1936 of President Franklin D. Roosevelt.

Born in 1893 in a log cabin, Huey Pierce Long studied law at Tulane University, and was plunged into politics. After serving ten years on the state's railroad commission, he was elected governor by appealing to poor farmers and factory laborers with a message of "us against them" and the slogan "Every man a king."

Known by the nickname "Kingfish," after a character on the nation's most popular radio show, "Amos and Andy," he was elected to the U.S. Senate in 1930 and kept such a tight grip on the state's political machinery that Louisiana newspaper publisher Hodding Carter wrote, "Huey Long owned Louisiana." In a political newspaper, *The American Progress,* which Long started in 1933, he wrote, "We just fight to avoid the country being opened up on a basis of a mere economic slavery for the masses, with the ruling classes greater in power and standing than ever."

He proposed a program that he called "Share the Wealth," in which he advocated "redistributing the wealth" by giving $5,000 to each "deserving family" in America, while leaving the rich "all the luxuries they can possibly use." He also proposed a thirty-hour workweek, an annual one-month vacation for every worker, old age pensions, free college for "deserving" students, and a federal program to purchase farm surpluses. By April 1935, his "Share the Wealth" clubs had close to five million members. A public opinion poll by the Democratic National Committee in 1935 showed that between three and four million Americans would consider casting votes for Long in the 1936 presidential election, posing a genuine threat to the re-election of President Roosevelt. Long was so confident that the presidency was within reach that he started dictating a book that he titled *My First Days in the White House.*

On the night of September 8, 1936, he was back in Louisiana to check up on his handpicked successor in the governor's chair, and on the state legislature that he controlled. Surrounded by bodyguards and hurrying toward the governor's office, he was approached by a slender, bespectacled man in a white suit. Drawing a small pistol, Dr. Carl Austin Weiss got off one shot before Long's protectors opened fire with their guns, killing Weiss. When Long arrived at the hospital, he was riddled with bullets. He died thirty hours later.

Because no autopsy was performed on Long, no one can say whose bullet actually killed him. Most historians attribute his death to Dr. Weiss. Others speculate that he'd been marked for death by political enemies and that Weiss had been set up, much as Lee Harvey Oswald was said to have been manipulated by conspirators to appear to have been the lone assassin of John F. Kennedy in 1963.

Those who believe that Weiss killed Long disagree about whether he attacked on his own, or whether he was part of a conspiracy. Some students of the assassination speculate that in such a conspiracy, one, or perhaps several, of Long's bodyguards were in on a plot in which Weiss would attack Long and provide an opportunity for the guards to kill both Long and Weiss. Others surmise that orders for killing the Kingfish had originated in Washington, D.C.

61.

ASSASSINATION OF EMPEROR CALIGULA

When a group of senators conspired to kill the first Roman emperor, Julius Caesar, they were motivated by politics. But while the plotters of the death of the fourth emperor, Gaius Julius Caesar Germanicus, nicknamed Caligula, claimed to have acted to end a tyrannical reign of a ruler who had gone insane, there was also a desire to even personal scores with a young man who had used his powers to humiliate and abuse everyone who was close to him.

According to a later Roman historian, Suetonius, in a gossipy book titled *The Lives of the Twelve Caesars*, Caligula was assassinated by members of his mostly German Praetorian Guard, including Arrecinus Clemens, a co-prefect of the Guard, and two tribunes, Cassius Chaerea and Cornelius Sabinus, in a conspiracy with several high-ranking members of the Senate, including Marcus Vinicius, husband of Caligula's exiled sister Julia Livilla.

Yet four years earlier (A.D. 37), Caligula had been a welcome relief from the tyrannical rule of the third emperor, Tiberius. What the Romans did not know was that Caligula had come to power by standing by as Caligula's chamberlain, a soldier named Macro, smothered Tiberius, and then arranged the killing of the next in line to succeed

Tiberius, a grandson named Gemmelus. What mattered most to the Roman people and Rome's aristocracy was that Caligula was the son of a venerated, deceased military hero Germanicus, and grandson of beloved Emperor Augustus.

For the first seven months of Caligula's reign, Roman hopes for a new Augustan era of peace, prosperity, and personal security seemed justified. Their twenty-four-year-old ruler cast aside the gloom and fear they'd experienced under Tiberius by staging lavish games, doing away with a sales tax, and abolishing Tiberius's reign of terror.

Born in A.D. 12 in one of his father's camps during a campaign against Germans, young Gaius won the hearts of Rome's legions by dressing in an army uniform and tiny soldiers' boots called *caligula*, meaning "little boots," hence Gaius's nickname. During his adolescence, he was virtually a prisoner of Tiberius on the Isle of Capri, a fact cited by most historians as a cause of the twisted character of Caligula that would emerge to the shock and horror of Romans in the seventh month of his reign, following an illness that may have been a nervous breakdown or, as some psychologists have theorized, a sudden surfacing of schizophrenia.

Instead of the enlightened emperor Romans expected, they found themselves suffering from the whims of a ruler whom they described, privately, as a monster.

"Those who helped him to the throne," Suetonius recorded, "were rewarded for their kinship and their faithful services by a bloody death. He was no whit more respectful or mild towards the senate, allowing some who had held the highest offices to run in their togas for several miles beside his chariot and to wait on him at table, standing napkin in hand either at the head of his couch, or at his feet."

Others he secretly put to death, but continued to send for them as if they were alive, only to state after a few days that they had committed suicide. When consuls forgot to proclaim his birthday a holiday, he deposed them, and left the state for three days without magistrates. He treated other officials with like insolence and cruelty. Being disturbed by the noise made by those who came in the middle of the night to secure the free seats in the Circus, he drove them all out with cudgels. In the confusion more than twenty Roman nobles were crushed to death. At a gladiatorial show he would sometimes draw back the awnings when the sun was hottest and give orders that no one be allowed to leave.

He would match worthless and decrepit gladiators against mangy wild beasts, and have sham fights between householders who were of good repute, but conspicuous for some bodily infirmity. Sometimes he would shut up the granaries and condemn the people to hunger. When cattle to feed the wild beasts that he had provided for a gladiatorial show were rather costly, he selected criminals to be devoured. Any men of honorable rank were disfigured with the marks of branding irons and then condemned to the mines, to work at building roads, or to be thrown to the wild beasts; or else he shut them up in cages on all fours, like animals, or had them hacked into pieces.

Not all these punishments were for serious offences, but for criticizing one of his shows, or for never having sworn by his genius. He forced parents to attend the executions of their sons. He once invited a man to dinner immediately after witnessing one such death, and tried to rouse him to gaiety and jesting by a great show of affability. He burned a writer of farces alive in the middle of the arena because of a humorous line of double meaning.

Having asked a man who had been recalled from an exile of long standing how in the world he spent his time there, the man replied by way of flattery: "I constantly prayed the gods for what has come to pass, that Tiberius might die and you become emperor." Thinking that his exiles were likewise praying for his death, he sent emissaries from island to island to butcher them all. Wishing to have one of the senators torn to pieces, he induced some of the members to assail him suddenly on his entrance into the Senate, with the charge of being a public enemy, to stab him with their styluses, and turn him over to the rest to be mangled. His cruelty was not sated until he saw the man's limbs, members, and bowels dragged through the streets and heaped up before him. When his grandmother, Antonia, gave him some advice, he replied: "Remember that I have the right to do anything to anybody."

He seldom had anyone put to death except by numerous slight wounds. His order was, "Strike so that he may feel that he is dying." He declared, "Let them hate me, so long as they fear me." Angered at the "rabble" in an arena for applauding a faction that he opposed, he cried, "I wish the Roman people had but a single neck."

Determined to bring an end to Caligula's reign, the plotters planned to strike when he took a luncheon break while attending the Palatine Games on January 24, A.D. 41. But when Caligula said that he was not in the mood to eat because was feeling slightly ill from an evening of excesses, they enticed him from his seat by telling him, "some boys of good birth, who had been summoned from Asia to appear on the stage, are rehearsing their parts."

Caligula agreed to go and watch them. This required him to pass through a tunnel.

"From this point," wrote Suetonius, "there are two versions of the story. Some say that as he was talking with the boys, Chaerea came up behind, and gave him a deep cut in the neck, having first cried, 'Take that.' Then the tribune Cornelius Sabinus stabbed him in the breast. Others say that Sabinus, after getting rid of the crowd through centurions who were in the plot, asked for the watchword, as soldiers do; and that when Caligula gave him 'Jupiter,' Sabinus cried 'So be it,' and as Caligula looked around, he split his jawbone with a blow of his sword."

As the emperor lay writhing upon the ground, others inflicted thirty wounds. Some even thrust their swords through his genitals. The guards then murdered Caligula's wife and infant daughter, slaughtered everyone believed to be Caligula loyalists, and named Caligula's elderly and, some Romans believed, dim-witted uncle Claudius emperor.

The new emperor's first order was that the conspirators be executed.

62.

ASSASSINATION OF
LEON TROTSKY

A news story carried by newspapers around the world on Thursday, August 22, 1940, noted, "Leon Trotsky, the exiled Bolshevik leader, died early this morning from injuries received when he was attacked in his home in a suburb of Mexico City some thirty hours earlier."

Born in 1877, Trotsky was forty years old when the Russian Revolution broke out in 1917. With Lenin he shared in organizing the movement that led to the establishment of the Soviet regime. When Lenin died, Trotsky's influence was undermined by Stalin, resulting in a more open split with Communist Party policy. Expelled from the party in 1927, he was first sent to Siberia and then deported from the USSR. As Trotsky eventually made his way to Mexico, Stalin became more and more obsessed with eliminating the "fascist hireling" and "the old man."

He ordered Lavrenti Beria, head of the secret service, "Spare no expense. Bring in whoever you want." Beria immediately passed the assignment to a veteran operative of the Foreign and Secret Political Sections of the Security Directorate, Naum Ellington, who engaged a team of Spanish-speaking agents. When their attempt at assassination with machine guns failed, he recruited a Spaniard who'd been a Soviet agent during the Spanish Civil War, Jaime Ramon Mercador. Using the name Frank Johnson, Mercador had struck up a friendship that led to a love affair with a Trotskyite named Sylvia Agelof, who'd recently replaced her sister Ruth as private secretary to Trotsky. To enlist Mercador in the plot, Ellington promised that by killing Trotsky Mercador would see his name added to the glorious honor roll of heroes of the Soviet Union.

Working in Trotsky's fortress-like house, Sylvia had no reason to suspect that her lover had become an agent of Stalin. To Trotsky and his guards, Johnson was a polite and sweet-natured young man who was sometimes helpful by offering the use of his car and serving as driver. Consequently, when he arrived at the house to ask Trotsky to review an article that he'd written, he was readily admitted. When Trotsky's wife, Natalia, asked him why he was wearing a raincoat on such a hot day, he replied that he thought there might be rain.

Concealed in the coat was a tool used by mountain climbers. Known as an alpine pick, it was about the size of a hatchet. After chatting a few minutes in a small garden at the back of the house, the two men moved into Trotsky's office. As Mercador laid his raincoat on a table in such a way as to be able to remove the ice pick, Trotsky began reading the article.

Deciding not to miss a moment that Mercador later called "the wonderful opportunity that presented itself," he said in a statement to police, "I took the ice pick from the raincoat, gripped it in my hand, and with my eyes closed, dealt him a terrible blow on the head. Trotsky gave a cry that I shall never forget. It was a long 'aaaa,' endlessly long, and I think it still echoes in my brain. Trotsky jumped up jerkily, rushed at me and bit my hand. I pushed him away and he fell to the floor. Then he rose and stumbled out of the room."

Trotsky's cry brought guards running. As they grabbed Mercador, he shouted, "They made me do it. They've got my mother. They have my mother in prison. Kill me now."

Trotsky managed to say, "No, he must not be killed. He must talk."

A letter found in Mercador's pocket, prepared by the Soviet secret service (NKVD) to make it appear that the attack was part of a Trotskyite plot, said that he'd acted because he was "disillusioned" by Trotsky.

Leon Trotsky clung to life for twenty-six hours. He died at 7:25 PM, August 20, 1940.

Two days later, the official Soviet news agency Tass reported, "The person who made the attempt belongs to the followers most closely associated with Trotsky." The Soviet newspaper *Pravda* continued the lie by stating that the assassination had been carried out "by one of his closest circle."

Tried and convicted of the murder of Trotsky, Mercador served twenty years in prison. Four years after he was released in 1960, the successor to Josef Stalin, Nikita Khrushchev, revealed in a then-secret speech to the Soviet Communist Party's hierarchy the scope of Stalin's crimes and that it had been the long arm of the NKVD that in 1940 had reached all the way to Mexico to finally rid Stalin of the "old man."

63.

CIA OVERTHROW OF
THE GOVERNMENT OF IRAN

In one of the earliest efforts during the Cold War by the United States to block expansion of Soviet influence into the oil-rich Middle East, Iran became the target of a plan carried out by the Central Intelligence Agency to oust a government that had nationalized the oil industry. The object of the scheme was Iran's Prime Minister, Mohammed Mossadegh.

With a large nose and sad-looking eyes and an aristocratic and imposing bearing, Mossadegh had been educated in France and Switzerland. A nationalist who had vehemently objected to British petroleum concessions in his country, he had been reluctantly appointed to his post by the Shah of Iran, and was named *Time Magazine's* Man of the Year in 1951. Noting that Mossadegh went to great lengths to present himself as a sickly, old, and emotional figure, and that he often wore pajamas and frequently wept in public, U.S. diplomat Averell Harriman observed, "He projected helplessness, and while he was obviously as much a captive as a leader of nationalist fanatics, he relented on nothing. Under pressure he would take to his bed, seeming at times to have only a tenuous hold on life itself as he lay in his pink pajamas, his hands folded on his chest and eyes fluttering and breath shallow. But at the appropriate moment, he could transform himself from a frail, decrepit shell of a man into a wily, vigorous adversary."

British Prime Minister Winston Churchill called Mossadegh "an elderly lunatic bent on wrecking his country and handing it over to the Communists."

Although the administration of President Harry Truman initially had been sympathetic to Iran's nationalist aspirations, his successor, President Dwight D. Eisenhower, adopted the view of his wartime friend, and ally, Churchill, whose government held that no compromise with Mossadegh was possible. Ike along with many Americans feared that Mossadegh was Communist-inspired. As a result of this, in June 1953, Eisenhower approved a British proposal for a joint operation to oust Mossadegh and replace him with a friend of the West.

To set up Operation Ajax and to coordinate plans with the Shah and the Iranian military, the CIA named its man in charge of Middle East activities. Known as "Kim" in the Agency, he was Kermit Roosevelt. A grandson of President Theodore Roosevelt, and a graduate of Groton and Harvard, he had been recruited from college for the wartime Office of Strategic Services, and went on to become a high CIA official. While serving in that capacity in the late 1940s, he met a British diplomat named Harold Philby, also nicknamed Kim. When Philby was ultimately exposed as the head of a Soviet spy ring in Britain, Roosevelt said of the other Kim what most Americans would have said about Kim Roosevelt, that he was "the last person you would expect to be up to his neck in dirty tricks."

The operation to depose Mossadegh was considered so sensitive and dangerous that Roosevelt was taken to the Shah's palace in the summer of 1953 under a rug in the back seat of a car. The plan called for the chief of the royal guards to deliver a formal notice from the Shah of Mossadegh's dismissal to his home. The scheme backfired when the messenger was arrested. When the Shah fled abroad, and Iranians poured into the streets to support Mossadegh, Roosevelt was ordered by his CIA superiors to leave the country.

Instead, Roosevelt arranged for demonstrators, most of them hired for the occasion, to swarm into the streets to protest against Mossadegh's government. When they arrived at Mossadegh's house and stormed in following a brief skirmish with guards, Mossadegh sought refuge with a neighbor. When he surrendered the next day, the Shah returned from Italy in triumph to state that he owed his throne to God, his people, his army, and to Kim Roosevelt. CIA Director Richard Helms would later write that the overthrow of Mossadegh was "the high tide of covert action."

Iran's Minister of Foreign Affairs, Hosein Fatemi, was sentenced to death and executed. Hundreds of National Front leaders, Mossadegh's Tudeh Party officers, and political activists were arrested. Several army officers were also condemned to death.

Tried for treason, Mossadegh denounced "foreign conspiracies," and after three years in prison, was kept under house arrest until his death in 1967.

Kim Roosevelt continued with the CIA until 1958, worked for Gulf Oil for six years, and served as a consultant to American firms with business in the Middle East. In 1979, he published a memoir of the 1953 plot, *Counter Coup: The Struggle for the Control of Iran.* Ironically, the book, which made no apologies for Operation Ajax, came out in the year that the Shah of Iran was deposed and replaced by an Islamic fundamentalist regime, headed by the Ayatollah Khomeini, which took Americans hostage and held them captive for 444 days. Driven into exile, the Shah died on July 27, 1980, at age sixty. Kim Roosevelt died on June 8, 2000, at the age of eighty-four.

64.

THE LINDBERGH BABY KIDNAPPING

More than seventy years after Bruno Richard Hauptmann was executed for the kidnapping and murder of the two-year-old son of aviation hero Charles A. Lindbergh, some students of what was known as "the crime of the century," which the famed muckraking journalist H. L. Mencken termed the greatest story since the Resurrection of Christ, believe that Hauptmann was in fact the victim of a conspiracy involving faked evidence to set him up to be the fall guy.

Late on the evening of March 1, 1932, Lindbergh and his attractive, pregnant wife, the former Anne Morrow, were at their home in Hopewell, New Jersey, believing that Charles, Jr. was tucked snugly in bed. But between eight and ten o'clock, an intruder had used a ladder to enter the child's bedroom and kidnap him. Left behind was a note, written in crude English and demanding $140,000 in five-, ten-, and twenty-dollar notes.

Leading the investigation by the New Jersey State Police was its superintendent, Colonel H. Norman Schwarzkopf (father of the general who would lead U.S. troops in the first Gulf War in 1991). While the police, the Lindberghs, and a shocked nation hoped for the child's safe return, Lindbergh paid the ransom money through an intermediary who handed $50,000 to a man who called himself "John" in a cemetery in the Bronx, New York. But on May 12, the baby was found dead five and half miles from the Lindbergh home. He'd been dead since the night of the kidnapping.

Although many leads were followed, and numerous suspects were questioned, the case remained a mystery for more than two-and-a-half years. The "break" came when part of the ransom money, a ten-dollar gold certificate, was used to buy five gallons of gas at a Bronx filling station. Because an attendant jotted down the car's license plate number, police were able to trace the auto to a German immigrant, Bruno Richard Hauptmann. Despite evidence in the form of floor planking in Hauptmann's home that matched the wood used to make the ladder used in the kidnapping, Hauptmann denied involvement. He stuck to his story to the moment he was electrocuted at the New Jersey State Prison in Trenton on April 2, 1936. His wife continued to maintain that her husband was not guilty for the rest of her life.

Those who also claim that Hauptmann had nothing to do with the crime assert that he was the victim of a rush to judgment by the police and prosecutor, evidence was faked, and that evidence to exonerate Hauptmann had been overlooked or suppressed. Others who doubt the official version of the case, including authors of several books, have proposed other theories concerning the real kidnappers.

The most provocative and sensational of these theories holds that the child was killed by his famous father accidentally, that Lindbergh made up the story of a kidnapping, and that he'd manufactured and planted the "evidence," possibly with the assistance of his butler, Oliver Whately.

Another contention is that the child was taken and killed by Lindbergh's sister-in-law, Elizabeth Morrow, because Lindbergh had rejected her amorous advances.

A theory that was floated at the time of the crime, and one that persists to this day, is that the plot had been carried out by the Mafia and that Hauptmann had been set up, or that the child had been taken by an infamous criminal outfit in Detroit known as the Purple Gang.

One of the first persons to suggest that the crime was the work of gangsters was mystery writer Agatha Christie. In her novel *Murder on the Orient Express*, first published in 1934, with the title *Murder in the*

Calais Coach, her private detective, Hercule Poirot, discerned that the kidnapping and murder of the daughter of a famous aviator had been the work of a mobster named Cassetti, and that he was murdered on the famous European train by a "jury" of twelve men and women who were related to or otherwise had a connection with the Armstrong family.

The basis of most of the continuing "wrong man" versions of the crime is that Bruno Richard Hauptmann was not smart enough to have committed such a complex crime involving kidnapping the most famous baby in America and arranging a complex ransom payment. Much more believable, contend the many doubters, is that the hapless Hauptmann became the victim of two conspiracies. The first was a sophisticated plot by the actual criminals in which he was set up. The second was a scheme by the police and the prosecutors to save face in their failure to solve the crime quickly by framing Hauptmann.

Although several attempts have been made by defenders of Hauptmann to reopen the case, the official explanation, that Bruno Richard Hauptmann acted alone, still stands.

65

THE BARKER GANG

A staple of the sort of novels written by Agatha Christie was the mysterious and deadly woman. The femme fatale! Countless mystery and detective novels have been rooted in the rule *cherchez la femme.* Look for the woman! For Sherlock Holmes, Miss Irene Adler would always be "the woman." To Dr. Watson she was forever "of dubious and questionable memory." Even Dashiell Hammett's hardboiled private eye, Sam Spade, was duped for a time by the devious Brigit O'Shaughnessy in his novel *The Maltese Falcon.* In Hammett's *Red Harvest* the sleuth known only as "the Op" noted of a certain dame, "She looked as if she were telling the truth, though with women, especially blue-eyed women, that doesn't always mean anything."

Although "Ma" Barker had brown eyes, she stands alone in the annals of American crime as the mastermind of numerous conspiracies to stick up banks, rob payroll deliveries and post offices, and two of the most sensational kidnappings of the 1930s. Born in 1872 near Springfield, Missouri, Arizona Donnie Clark married a sharecropper named George Barker and bore four sons: Herman, Lloyd, Arthur (nicknamed "Doc"), and Fred. When they were old enough to hold guns, they began lives of crime. Herman's career was brief. After killing a policeman during a robbery of a store in Newton, Kansas, on

November 19, 1927, he committed suicide. Lloyd was caught attempting to rob a post office in Oklahoma in 1922 and was confined in Leavenworth prison in 1922. Released in 1947, he was killed by his wife two years later.

Ma's other sons, Arthur and Fred, formed the basis of what became known as the Barker Gang. Whether Ma was really the brains behind the gang is a matter of dispute. Certainly there was no doubt in the mind of FBI Director J. Edgar Hoover. He wrote that Ma and her sons, and Alvin Karpis and his cronies, "constituted the toughest gang of hoodlums the FBI ever has been called upon to eliminate." Looking over the record of these criminals, Hoover was "repeatedly impressed by the cruelty of their depredations," including murders of policemen, the machine gun killing of an innocent citizen who got in the way during a bank robbery, kidnapping and extortion, train robbery, mail robbery, and the protection of high police officials bought with tainted money.

Barker Gang member Alvin "Creepy" Carpis expressed a different view of Ma Barker. In his autobiography, *The Alvin Karpis Story*, he wrote, "The most ridiculous story in the annals of crime is that Ma Barker was the mastermind behind the Karpis-Barker gang." Karpis claimed that the legend grew after her death. "She wasn't a leader of criminals," he wrote, "or even a criminal herself. There is not one police photograph of her or set of fingerprints taken while she was alive. She knew we were criminals but her participation in our careers was limited to one function. When we traveled together, we moved as a mother and her sons. What could look more innocent?"

What is clear is that wherever the two Barker boys went, Ma was with them and knew what they were up to. In the definition of "conspiracy," her presence and foreknowledge of her sons' activities made her an accomplice in some of the boldest crimes of the 1920s and 1930s. Among their heists were stickups of numerous banks.

Accompanied in their crimes by Alvin Karpis and similar desperadoes, they committed not only the crimes cited by Hoover, but two of the most sensational kidnappings in an era when individuals were grabbed and held for ransom with shocking regularity.

The first to be snatched by the Barkers was William Hamm, Jr. A millionaire Minnesota brewer, he was taken on June 15, 1933, and held for a ransom of $100,000. Thirteen months later, the gang grabbed Minneapolis banker Edward G. Bremer. Bremer was ransomed for $200,000.

Fate and the FBI caught up with Arthur "Doc" Barker on a street in Chicago on the night of January 8, 1935. After G-man Melvin Purvis searched him and found that Doc was not carrying a gun, Doc explained that he'd left it at home, then asked, "Ain't that a hell of a place for it?"

Refusing to give up the whereabouts of his brothers and mother, Doc was sentenced to Alcatraz prison in San Francisco Bay, but on June 12, 1939, during an attempt to escape, he was riddled with bullets fired from a guard tower and instantly killed.

Although Doc had refused to put the FBI on his family's trail, when agents searched his apartment, they found a map of Florida that sent the G-men scurrying to a resort in Oklawaha on Lake Weir. As agents surrounded a cottage, they heard Ma Barker say to her son Freddie, "All right! Go ahead!" With her permission given, he opened fire with a Thompson machine gun.

When the shooting ended about an hour later, Melvin Purvis entered the cottage to find Freddie dead with eleven bullet holes in him. Ma had three wounds, the last of which, through her heart, had been self-inflicted.

Opening Ma's handbag, Purvis found crisp new currency in the amount of $10,200.

66.

BURKE AND HARE

In the mid-1690s in Scotland, the dissection of bodies of executed criminals in the name of science was a routine practice. This was a convenience for medical schools as well as the authorities, who wouldn't have to pay for burials. The arrangement was later expanded to include the cadavers of unidentified people who died on the streets. A century later, when Edinburgh's College of Surgeons had so many students that there weren't enough bodies to meet the demand, opportunists saw an easy way to line their pockets by robbing graves at St. Cuthbert's, one of Edinburgh's oldest churches with an attached graveyard. Those who plundered the burial sites became known as "Resurrectionists."

In the early 1790s two such characters entered British folklore by providing dead bodies without having to go through the trouble of digging them up.

Born in the county of Cork in 1792, William Burke eventually abandoned a wife and family and moved to Edinburgh to work on the construction of the Union Canal. He soon met another Irishman, William Hare. Little is known about Hare's past, except that he was a brutal man with no education and may have been a soldier. After the canal was complete in 1822, Hare became a hawker and while working he became friendly with a lady named Margaret Log, or Logue, whose husband owned a lodging house. Shortly after Mr. Log died, Hare married Margaret and inherited the lodging house. Burke met his female partner, a woman by the name of Helen MacDougal, while he was working on the canal. When the canal was finished, he tried farm work, hedging, ditch digging, and shoemaking.

When an old soldier named Donald who had been staying at the Hares' lodging house for some time was found dead, Hare felt cheated because the old man had owed him rent. When a coffin was delivered for the old man's body, Hare filled it with bark from a tannery and placed the body in a sack. He and Burke then took it to the College of Surgeons where a student directed them to Dr. Robert Knox. The surgeon paid them seven pounds, ten shillings, and did not ask where the body came from.

Born in Edinburgh in 1791, Knox had attended high school until 1810, when he enrolled in medical classes at Edinburgh University and specialized in anatomy. He graduated four years later at the age of twenty-three and became an assistant surgeon in a military hospital in Brussels, treating casualties of the Battle of Waterloo. After several years of military service and travels in South Africa, he returned to Scotland in 1821 as a skilled surgeon. At the peak of his career in Edinburgh he had over five hundred students.

With Knox asking no questions about the origin of the bodies provided by Burke and Hare, they soon delivered another guest of the lodging house. Possibly an Englishman from Cheshire, he had become ill with jaundice. Burke and Hare suffocated him. The third victim, an old woman, was lured into the lodging house by the Hares with an offer of drink. When she was drunk, Hare placed his hands on her mouth and Burke lay across her body. Dr. Knox "approved" of the corpse because it was "so fresh," and still asked no questions.

The next victim, Mary Patterson, was a beautiful teenage prostitute. She was strangled while she was drunk. When Burke and Hare arrived with the body, one of Knox's students remarked that he had seen a girl similar to her. Burke dealt with this by saying that Mary had drunk herself to death and he had bought the body from an old woman.

Over the next three months Burke and Hare became even bolder, even taking the bodies to Dr. Knox during the day. Their tally soon reached ten victims, including Jamie Wilson. Known as "Daft Jamie," he was a simple-minded nineteen-year-old young man who was described as big and strong, but with the mind of a child. When he fled his home after a disagreement with his mother and went to live on the street, surviving by doing odd jobs and receiving charity from people who took pity on him, he had the misfortune of meeting Burke and Hare. Burke's official confession states that Hare's wife brought Jamie off the street for a drink while Burke was at a local tavern. After being lured to the lodging house, he was strangled. When the body was taken to the medical school, several students said they recognized Jamie. But Dr. Knox denied that it was him and quickly ordered the dissection.

The last Burke and Hare murder took place on Hallowe'en. While Burke was in a local tavern, an old woman came in begging for money. Burke talked to her and learned that her name was Mary Docherty and that she had come from Ireland in search of her lost son. Burke deceived her into thinking he was a distant relative and invited her to his house.

They had a fine party that night, with lots of dancing and drinking. At the time Burke had an ex-soldier by the name of James Gray and his family staying with him. Burke asked if they could stay with Hare that night so the old woman could use their room. They agreed. When Mrs. Gray returned in the morning she found Burke acting suspiciously by a bed with a pile of straw atop it. Later that day Burke went out to replenish his supply of whiskey. Still suspicious, Mrs. Gray went over to the bed, lifted the pile of straw, and uncovered the naked corpse of Mrs. Docherty, with bloodstains around the nose and mouth.

Although Burke, Helen MacDougal, and the Hares were interviewed, the police decided there was insufficient evidence to bring a charge of murder. In the hope that Hare and his wife would provide it, they offered them immunity if they would turn King's evidence. The Hares eagerly agreed. Burke was charged with Docherty's murder and those of Jamie Wilson and Mary Patterson. The trial began on Christmas Eve with both of the Hares, along with other witnesses testifying against Burke. Evidence was provided in the form of clothing from the victims and Jamie's snuffbox. The jury took fifty minutes to find Burke guilty. The charge against Helen MacDougal was declared "not proven" and she was set free.

William Burke was sentenced to hang and his body publicly dissected. On January 28, 1829, a crowd of 25,000 people watched the execution. Even more lined up to see his body on display, followed by a public dissection, and his skeleton exhibited as a reminder of his "terrible crimes." Spared imprisonment because of his deal with the prosecution, Hare was released from custody. Choosing not to risk being put to death by irate citizens taking the law into their own hands, he fled to London. There, according to unconfirmed reports, he was either attacked by a mob and thrown into a lime pit, or became a destitute blind beggar wandering the city and was never seen again.

Mrs. Hare and Helen MacDougal also disappeared into obscurity. Knox was never charged with a crime, but after angry Edinburgh citizens rioted outside his house shortly after the trial, and with dwindling registration for his classes, he moved to Glasgow and later to London, where he died in 1862.

Although Burke and Hare are in the annals of crime as "Resurrectionists," and a popular horror film starring Boris Karloff and Peter Lorre was based on them, Hare firmly denied that they had been gravediggers. They were merely a pair of murderous conspirators who had killed at least sixteen people—more victims than Jack the Ripper.

They and the doctor who bought their macabre wares are remembered in a grim bit of English folk poetry:

> Up the close and down the stair,
> In the house with Burke and Hare.
> Burke's the butcher, Hare's the thief,
> Knox, the man who buys the beef.

67.

MURDER, INC.

When Burton B. Turkus died on November 22, 1982, at the age of eighty, few outside the world of police, prosecutors, and historians of organized crime would have been able to identify him or explain his contribution in exposing and breaking up a branch of organized crime known as "Murder, Inc." Set up in the 1930s with the blessing of the bosses of organized crime, known to the public and among law enforcement as the Mafia, and to its members as "the syndicate," it was run out of Brooklyn, New York, by Louis "Lepke" Buchalter with the purpose of eliminating anyone the gang leaders designated.

"There was no method of murder their fiendish ingenuity overlooked," wrote Turkus in an account of how Murder, Inc. had operated for two decades. "They used the gun, the strangling rope, the ice-pick—commonplace tools for homicide. There was the unimaginative mob-style ride, the shotgun blast on the lonely street. And there were the bizarre touches, too. Dozens [of victims] were dropped into quicklime pits. Others were buried alive, cremated, roped up in such a way that they strangled themselves by their own struggles for life. The killers thought they had come up with an especially appropriate effect the night they tied a slot machine to the body of a pinball operator who was 'cheating' and dropped him into a resort lake. The Syndicate's tentacles reached everywhere and anywhere."

The existence of the "death department" of the national crime cartel became known to Turkus, an assistant district attorney in the homicide bureau in Brooklyn, when a killer by the name of Abe "Kid Twist" Reles decided to bargain his way out of a date with the electric chair by spilling the beans on not only murders he'd committed, but on those that had been ordered by gang leaders from coast to coast.

With a calm demeanor that Turkus described as the nonchalance of a "skilled artisan, proud of his craft," Reles said, "I can tell you about fifty guys that got hit; I was on the inside."

Born in 1907, Reles grew up in the gangs of Brownsville, Brooklyn, and was eventually brought into Murder, Inc. by Lepke. The information he provided gave Turkus evidence against not only Lepke and Anastasia, but also gangland assassin Charlie "Bug" Workman, believed to have handled the mob-ordered killing of Dutch Schultz.

"Reles's song was a full-length opera," Turkus noted. "In two days, he had taken a trail of triggers and rackets to cities a thousand miles away. In five days, he was wearing out stenographers, and they had to be put on in relays. By the eleventh day, he was going at such a rate that investigation of extortions he exposed had to be set aside in order to keep up with his listing of homicides. At the end of the twelfth day, he had confessed the incredible total of twenty-five notebooks, chockfull of shorthand record."

Reles rattled off names, places, facts, and data of killing after killing, recalling not only the people involved, but "decent people who had an unwitting part in some angle of a crime." He was, Turkus reported, "an extrovert with an outsize ego," who "derived much pleasure from the horror he stirred up with tales of the terrible deeds of himself and his buddies."

Turkus wrote, "Kid Twist's aria reached its crescendo in the incredible disclosure that there actually existed in America an organized underworld, and that it controlled lawlessness across the United States. For the first time in any investigation anywhere, the lid was lifted to lay bare a government-within-a-government, in which the killings and the rackets worked hand in hand in a national combine of crime."

In an effort to keep Kid Twist out of the clutches of the deadly men he was singing about, Turkus arranged to stash him in the Half Moon Hotel on Coney Island with several New York police detectives providing protection. Early on November 12, 1941, as the trial of Anastasia was about to open, Reles was found dead five stories beneath a window of his sixth-floor room. Knotted sheets dangling from the window, although not nearly enough to reach the ground, made it seem that he'd fallen while trying to escape.

Although the truth will never be known, crime historians agree that he was either thrown from the room by one of the policemen assigned to protect him, or by a third party as the cops looked the other way. One theory is that Reles was given the heave-ho from room 623 by the deputy police commissioner, Frank C. Bales, and that Lucky Luciano had paid $50,000 for one of the most dramatic rubouts in gangland history.

Kid Twist's demise has provided the most famous wisecrack in the colorful chronicles of American gangsterism: "The canary could sing, but he couldn't fly."

68.

THE NIGHT OF THE LONG KNIVES

Just before dawn on June 30, 1934, a long line of automobiles carrying Adolf Hitler and a large contingent of the black-shirted Nazi police known as the SS (Schutzstaffel), arrived at the Hanslbauer Hotel on the shore of Tegernsee in the town of Wiessee. The purpose of their secret journey was to eliminate the leadership of a force of thugs and street brawlers, the Sturm Abtelung (storm troops). Led by one of Hitler's earliest backers, Ernst Roehm, the SA men wore brown uniforms and swastika armbands and had provided the muscle to carry Hitler to power. Having built a force that was larger in number than the German military, Roehm boasted in January 1934, "Hitler can't walk over me as he might have done a year ago. I've seen to that. I have three million men." He also had significant enemies, not only within the top ranks of the Nazi Party, but also among field marshals and generals who feared that Roehm intended to use his position as leader of the SA to demand that Hitler merge the army (Wehrmacht) and the SA and put him in command. "If Hitler is reasonable I shall settle the matter quietly," said Roehm. "If he isn't, I must be prepared to use force, not for my sake, but for the sake of our [Nazi] revolution."

Although there is disagreement among historians as to whether Roehm was planning to use the SA to stage a coup, or simply using it to force Hitler to meet his demand that the SA take over the army, there is no doubt that when Hitler arrived at the lakeside hotel in Wiessee, he was convinced that Roehm and the SA leadership, many of whom were known homosexuals, were not simply enjoying what Roehm had called "a period of complete relaxation," but were planning to make their move. Hitler would later explain that he personally had led the raid on the Handlbauer Hotel because he had received reports that the SA intended to launch a "surprise attack" on that very morning. "In these circumstances I could make but one decision," he said. "Only a ruthless and bloody intervention might perhaps stifle the spread of the revolt."

What Hitler and his raiding party found, noted William L. Shirer in a monumental history, *The Rise and Fall of the Third Reich*, was Roehm and his lieutenants peacefully slumbering in their beds. "So far did the SA chiefs seem from staging a revolt," Shirer recorded, "that Roehm had left his staff guards in Munich. Their appeared to be plenty of carousing among the SA leaders but not plotting."

One of the SA leaders and a young SA officer were discovered naked in bed, ordered out of the hotel, and shot. Hitler then barged alone into Roehm's room with a whip in his hand and arrested him. When the man who had stood at Hitler's side as a trusted and loyal friend, and, according to Shirer, had done more for "the launching of the Third Reich" than anyone but Hitler himself, refused to commit suicide, he too was executed.

Describing a meeting with Hitler the next day, Hitler's architect and the future Minister of Armaments, Albert Speer, wrote in his 1970 book, *Inside the Third Reich*, that Hitler had been extremely excited and inwardly convinced that he had come through a great danger. Again and again, Speer wrote, Hitler scribed how he had forced his way into the hotel, "not forgetting, in the telling, to make a show of his courage."

Speer quoted Hitler: "We were unarmed, imagine, and didn't know whether or not those swine might have armed guards to use against us. I alone was able to solve this problem."

Shirer notes that although Hitler expressed "disgust" at discovering SA men engaging in homosexual acts, and used this as further justification of executions, Hitler had known "from the earliest days of the party that a large number of his closest and most important followers" were homosexual, that he had "not only tolerated, but defended" them, and more than once "warned his party comrades against being too squeamish about a man's personal morals [as long as] he were a fanatical fighter for the movement."

Quoting a line from a popular song of the day, Hitler called his attack on the SA "The Night of the Long Knives."

It resulted in more than 150 SA leaders being rounded up and shot against a wall of the Cadet School at Lichterfelde. Others who were not in the SA, but were seen as enemies by other Nazi leaders, were also executed. Persons deemed to be enemies of the state, and many who had been marked for death as personal enemies, were murdered all over Germany and as far away as Paris, France.

Shirer noted, "Many were killed out of pure vengeance, others were murdered apparently because they knew too much, and at least one because of mistaken identity." How many were liquidated in the purge was never established.

With most of the killing accomplished by July 1, 1934, Hitler had removed what he had decided was an obstacle to the solidification of his power. In doing so, he had cleared the way for the complete backing of an army that would be the keystone of his plan to expand the Third Reich by conquest. To be certain that the army knew its place in the new Nazi order, Hitler required every officer and soldier to swear an oath, not to Germany, but to Hitler himself.

In a speech to the Reichstag (parliament) on July 31, in which he revealed the scope of the Night of the Long Knives, Hitler justified himself by declaring, "If anyone reproaches me and asks why I did not resort to the regular courts of justice, then all I can say is this: In this hour I was responsible for the fate of the German people, and thereby I became the supreme judge of the German people. Everyone must know for all future time that if he raises his hand to strike the State, then certain death is his lot."

By the time of the destruction of Hitler and the Nazi regime in 1945, the death toll would be scores of millions.

69.

ASSASSINATION OF LORD LOUIS MOUNTBATTEN

On a sunny, almost windless August 29, 1979, at the fishing village of Mullaghmore overlooking Donegal Bay on Ireland's northwest coast, Lord Louis Mountbatten was enjoying an annual Irish vacation. Dressed in faded corduroys and a rough pullover, he pulled up to a boat dock around 11:30 AM with his daughter, Lady Patricia Brabourne, her husband, his mother, and their twin sons Timothy and Nicholas. Fifteen-year-old boat boy Paul Maxwell cast off the moorings, and the diesel-powered boat, *Shadow V*, glided past the harbor's walls to proceed along the coast. After going a few hundred yards, the boat was stopped to allow him to inspect lobster pots. A moment later, an enormous explosion blew the boat to pieces, killing Lord Mountbatten, Nicholas, and Maxwell.

Within hours of the assassination, a three-vehicle convoy of British soldiers moving along a highway just inside the Ulster border was blown up by an IRA bomb that killed eighteen soldiers, the largest number of British troops lost in a single incident in Northern Ireland. The next day, another bomb went off at a bandstand in Brussels, where a British military band was to give a concert as part of the

Belgian capital's millennium celebrations. In the previous decade IRA attacks had killed nearly 2,000 people and injured 21,000.

Louis Mountbatten was the great-grandson of Queen Victoria, a hero of the Royal Navy in both world wars, the protégé of Winston Churchill, one of the planners of the naval portion of the D-Day invasion of France on June 6, 1944, and last viceroy of India. But perhaps his most significant role in the history of the United Kingdom was in slyly arranging for the older daughter of his cousin, King George VI, to meet the man Elizabeth would marry—the dashing, handsome Prince Philip of Greece, who happened to be his nephew.

Born at Windsor, England, on June 25, 1900, Louis Francis Albert Victor Nicholas Battenberg was the son of Prince Louis of Battenberg and Queen Victoria's great-granddaughter, Princess Victoria of Hesse. But as anti-German fervor gripped Britain during the First World War, the Germanic family name was changed to the more English-sounding Mountbatten. Joining the Royal Navy in 1916 as "officer cadet," Louis trained at Dartmouth and saw action on HMS *Lion* and HMS *Queen Elizabeth*. As aide-de-camp to the Prince of Wales after the war, he traveled to the Far East, Australia, and India. He married in 1922 to the vivacious, beautiful Edwina Ashley, and continued his naval career. Retaining a close relationship with the Royal Family, Louis and Edwina were a popular couple in a whirl of titled English society and entertainment celebrities on both sides of the Atlantic that crowned them the "fabulous Mountbattens." Promoted to captain in 1932, Mountbatten held that rank at the start of World War II as commander of the destroyer *Kelly*. Despite being torpedoed several times in the Mediterranean, he was such a heroic figure that Winston Churchill rewarded him with the new post of Chief of Combined Operations, with responsibility for assisting in the planning of the invasion of Europe. Later appointed Commander of Allied Forces in Southeast Asia, he was on a par in authority with General Douglas MacArthur. After receiving the formal surrender of 750,000 Japanese troops at Singapore, he was second only to General Sir Bernard Montgomery in the esteem of the British people. His reward was appointment by King George VI as Viceroy of India (the last). Returning to England in 1948, he rejoined the Navy. Named Fourth Sea Lord and commander of the Mediterranean Fleet (1952–55), he eventually was the first Chief of Defense Staff (1959). But it was as a Royal match-maker that he would have a significant and lasting effect on the history of Great Britain. With the marriage of Elizabeth to Lieutenant Philip Mountbatten of the Royal Navy on November 20, 1947, he not only saw Philip wedded to the crown with the title Duke of Edinburgh, but himself revered by the queen and her four children, especially Prince Charles, as a favorite uncle and cherished advisor. After serving as chairman of the Defense Staff, he was governor and lord lieutenant of the Isle of Wight. After his retirement from active service, he became a tempting target of the Irish Republican Army (IRA).

When Thomas McMahon and Francis McGirl observed the boat, they were surprised to discover that it was not guarded. Moored with about a dozen other small craft at the public dock, it was easily boarded. They planted a bomb, and quickly departed. But then their luck ran out. Two hours before the boat exploded, they were stopped at a routine roadside checkpoint seventy miles away on suspicion of driving a stolen car. McMahon was convicted of the murder of Mountbatten and two others on the boat, but was released in 1998 as part of a truce known as the "Good Friday Agreement."

70.

THE ALGER HISS CASE

On August 25, 1948, during the first hearing of the House Un-American Activities Committee (HUAC), Chairman J. Parnell Thomas looked at two men seated at the witness table. Alger Hiss was a handsome, svelte intellectual brimming with self-confidence. A former high-ranking official in the State Department, he had been one of President Roosevelt's advisors at the 1945 Yalta Conference with Josef Stalin and Prime Minister Winston Churchill. Hiss had been held in such high esteem in diplomatic circles that he had been under consideration to be the first Secretary General of the United Nations. The second witness on that day, Whittaker Chambers, was a nervous, glum-looking, and chubby figure whose middle-class family had a thread of insanity running through it.

As a troubled youth of questionable sexual identity, Chambers had become enthralled with Communism in the 1920s. A devoted member of the Communist Party of the U.S.A. in the 1930s, he'd been editor of its periodical, *The New Masses*. Eventually repelled by the brutalities and excesses of Stalinism, he broke with the Party and settled on a farm in Maryland and lived in fear that the Party considered him a traitor and had marked him for death. From 1940 to 1948 he was Senior Editor at *Time Magazine*. Claiming that he had known Alger

Hiss by a Communist Party name, "Mr. Crosley," and that Hiss was not only a Communist, but also a traitor who had spied for the Soviet Union, Chambers told the committee that Hiss had been "the closest friend" he'd had in the Party.

Asked by committee member Richard Nixon to explain his reasons for testifying against Hiss, Chambers answered, "The story has spread that in testifying against [him] I am working out some old grudge, or motives of revenge or hatred. I do not hate Mr. Hiss. We were close friends, but we are caught in a tragedy of history. Mr. Hiss represents the concealed enemy against which we are all fighting, and I am fighting, but in a moment of history in which this nation now stands, so help me God, I could not do otherwise."

Since Hiss vehemently denied having ever been a Communist and having never known Chambers, one of them was lying. "As a result of this hearing," declared Chairman Thomas, "certainly one of these witnesses will be tried for perjury."

Evidence assembled by the committee soon showed that Hiss had lied about not knowing Chambers. Among the proof was a roll of microfilm of State Department documents that was meant to be passed to the Soviet Union. Hidden in a hollowed-out pumpkin on Chambers's farm, they were turned over to Nixon and became known as the "Pumpkin Papers."

Although Hiss was charged with perjury, tried, and convicted, his supporters continued to insist he was the innocent victim of a conspiracy of anti-Communist "witch hunters" in an era of Cold War hysteria motivated by a baseless fear of the Soviet Union and an unfounded belief that the U.S. government had been infiltrated by disloyal Americans.

Denounced and excoriated, accused of mental illness, dismissed from *Time*, and unable to get other work, Chambers retreated to his farm and contemplated suicide.

Two years after Hiss's conviction, however, Chambers published an autobiography. Titled *Witness*, it not only became a best seller then, but also remained in print as one of the foundation stones of the conservative movement in the Republican Party. At the same time, Hiss and his supporters continued to proclaim that Hiss had been an innocent victim of Red-baiting by HUAC, Nixon, and Senator Joseph McCarthy.

Detested by the political left, with the money from his book gone, and unable to sell other writings, Chambers died of a heart attack on July 9, 1961. He remained a tainted figure until 1984, when President Reagan recognized his role in the long struggle against Communism with a posthumous award of the Presidential Medal of Freedom. Three years later, the Maryland farm where Chambers revealed the existence of the Pumpkin Papers that sealed Alger Hiss's fate and branded him a traitor, was placed on the National Register of Historical Places.

The final chapter in the saga of Chambers and Hiss was written in the aftermath of the demise of the Soviet Union. As files of the USSR's secret service and other classified archives were thrown open in the early 1990s, documents and memoranda dating back to the 1930s and 1940s showed that Alger Hiss had, indeed, been at the center of a Communist conspiracy that had flourished in the top echelons of the U.S. government. In 1995, the U.S. National Security Agency released a trove of Soviet messages that had been intercepted during World War II. They contained references to Hiss's valuable services to the Soviet Union as its "leading" spy in the American government for ten years.

71.

THE HOLLYWOOD TEN

Although the House Un-American Activities Committee that unmasked Alger Hiss as a traitor had been created in 1938 primarily to look into the influence of Nazi and fascist organizations in the United States, HUAC was not made a permanent committee until 1945. When the Republican Party won control of Congress in the 1946 elections, the committee's chief purpose was to investigate not only Communist infiltration of the government, but in all aspects of American life.

One of the first items of concern to HUAC was whether the American movie industry was rife with writers, producers, directors, and others who were Communists or sympathetic to the Soviet Union, and to what extent they had conspired to inject "subversive" propaganda into Hollywood's films.

Although an investigation by the earlier committee in 1940 found no credible evidence of Communist activity in the movie industry, the new chairman, J. Parnell Thomas, chose to take another look into the issue by opening hearings in the autumn of 1947. He began by summoning forty-one witnesses. Of these, nineteen were considered "unfriendly" because they announced that they would not cooperate with the investigation. When hearings began on October 27, 1947, ten witnesses appeared before the committee. They were writer John

Howard Lawson, who had previously testified in 1940; fellow writers Alvah Bessie, Lester Cole, Ring Lardner, Jr., Albert Maltz, Samuel Ornitz, and Dalton Trumbo; writer/producer Adrian Scott; writer/ director Herbert Biberman; and director Edward Dmytryk. All agreed that they would not only refuse to answer questions, based on the U.S. Constitution's guarantees of freedom of speech and right of association, but would also use their appearances to thwart the committee.

Again and again during the nationally televised hearings, when the men who had been named by headline writers as the "Hollywood Ten" were asked if they were or had ever been a member of the Communist Party, replies took the form of challenges of the committee's right to even pose the question, along with assertions to the effect that the only "un-Americans" in the room were the committee members.

All were found to be in contempt of Congress. When the Supreme Court refused to reverse their convictions, they went to prison. The reaction of movie studio executives was adoption of a resolution against employing Communists that sympathizers of the Ten termed "the blacklist." With the exception of Dmytryk, who later cooperated with the committee, none of the Ten had his name in the credits of American movies until the 1960s, after producer Otto Preminger hired Dalton Trumbo to write the screenplay for *Exodus.*

Had the Ten answered the question truthfully, they would have replied "Yes." Each had been at one time, or still were, Communists.

Since the exposure of the Hollywood Ten, their defenders have attempted to depict them, in articles, books, and several movies, as heroic champions of the Constitution, while playing down their Communist loyalties. Allan Ryskind succinctly stated the counter-argument to claims that they were victims of anti-Communist zealots. A son of playwright Morrie Ryskind, who willingly testified in 1947 against the Communist infiltration of the Screen Writers Guild, Allan wrote in an article in the weekly newspaper *Human Events* that far from being "just good-hearted innocents" each of the Ten "had been an active Communist," and that each had been issued a Communist Party (CP) card, had paid dues to the Party, met in secret gatherings, embraced CP projects, gave money and/or time to Party causes, and invariably followed the Party line dictated by Moscow.

"When the 1947 hearings rolled around, the Soviet Union, Communism, and the American Communist Party were fundamentally known quantities," Ryskind wrote. "Any student of the USSR knew—or certainly should have known—about the Soviet-manufactured famine, the slave labor camps, the trumped-up purge trials, the mass executions, and the cloak of terror that Stalin had imposed on his own countrymen," yet, the Ten "excused or endorsed" these atrocities, and then sought to avoid responsibility for where they chose to place their loyalties by wrapping themselves in the very Constitution of the nation that the Soviet Union and the Communist Party of the United States had conspired to subvert and eventually destroy.

72.

THE BELTWAY SNIPERS

When James Martin left a grocery store on October 2, 2002, and was shot to death with a rifle fired from a long distance opposite a shopping mall in Montgomery County, Maryland, not far from Washington, D.C., his murder was barely noticed outside the immediate area. But when similar fatal sniper attacks occurred in Maryland malls and on a street in the nation's capital over a period of fifteen hours, followed on October 4 by the wounding of a woman as she left a craft store in a mall in Spotslyvania, Virginia, millions of Americans from coast to coast who learned of the shootings on TV and radio newscasts immediately recalled terrorist attacks on the World Trade Center in New York and the Pentagon on September 11, 2001.

Fears that the wave of killings within easy access to the circumferential highway around the District of Columbia known as the Beltway might also be the work of foreign terrorists were made more plausible as sniper attacks were reported almost daily at gas stations, restaurants, supermarkets, and at a school. Because the shootings took place within the Beltway region, news organizations labeled the attacker the "Beltway Sniper." An investigation task force of local, state, and federal law enforcement agencies, headed by Montgomery County's

Chief of Police Charles Moose, initially believed that they were look-ing for a lone gunman.

Witnesses provided a few slim leads, including descriptions of a white van leaving the scene of several shootings in which victims appeared to have been chosen at random. But when the sniper left messages at some of the murder locations, they appeared to suggest that the killer may have had an accomplice. At several scenes, Tarot cards were found. One of these was the "Death" card on which the shooter had written, "Dear Policeman, I am God. Do not tell the media about this." Long handwritten notes were left at other locations in sealed plastic bags. One of these that demanded payment of ten million dollars warned, "Your children are not safe, anywhere, at any time."

In an attempt to open a dialogue with the sniper, Chief Moose used the news media to reply to the sniper's messages and to appeal to the shooter to respond by calling a phone number that the police had provided for that purpose. Meanwhile, tips from the public flooded into other hotline numbers. Some of these provided information that led federal authorities to conduct searches in places far from the Belt-way area. By October 24, the task force was concentrating on a sus-pect, John Allen Muhammad, an Army veteran, along with a seventeen-year-old friend, John Lee Malvo.

When investigators learned that Muhammad had bought a blue 1990 Chevrolet Caprice, attention shifted from the white van. After a description of the Caprice was broadcast, along with the names and descriptions of the two suspects, a truck driver who pulled into a rest stop on a Maryland highway spotted the Caprice and alerted police. When they arrived, they discovered Muhammad and Malvo asleep in the Caprice. Found in the car was a .223-caliber Bushmas-ter rifle with a sighting scope, a rifle tripod, ammunition, maps marked with shooting locations, and other evidence indicating that Muhammad and Malvo were the killers. Examination of the trunk of the car revealed that a hole had been cut to allow the rifle to be fired while the shooter was in a prone position. Found in a laptop computer was a map that indicated the two men had planned more than two-dozen other murders. On sites stretching south to Raleigh, North Carolina, were notes such as "good spot" and "many ways out."

During their three-week rampage, they'd killed ten men and women and wounded three others, including thirteen-year-old Iran Brown as he arrived at the Tasker Middle School in Bowie, Maryland. Ballistics tests confirmed that eleven of the fourteen bullets recovered from victims and at the scenes of shootings were related to the Bushmaster rifle.

On an audiotape played at the trial of Lee Malvo in Virginia on November 18, 2003, for the murder of an FBI analyst, Linda Franklin, outside a Home Depot store, Malvo told police that he had pulled the trigger in all the attacks and that he had "intended to kill them all." His defense lawyers contended that he should not be found guilty by reason of insanity because he had been brainwashed by Muhammad. As Malvo's trial was starting, Muhammad was in another Virginia court and awaiting a decision on whether he would receive a death sentence from the jury that had convicted him of murdering Dean Harold Meyers at a gas station. But these were only the first of many trials facing the Beltway Snipers.

While Muhammad and Malvo were not the terrorists that millions of Americans feared in the first few days of their murderous escapades, the effect of their conspiracy had been the same as those who had used airplanes as weapons to commit thousands of murders a year earlier. For twenty-three days, Muhammad and Malvo had virtually paralyzed the U.S. capital city and had frightened an entire country not because they were part of a conspiracy of foreign terrorists, but because they were a pair of serial killers who plotted their crimes from twisted personal motives.

73.

THE MENENDEZ BROTHERS

When Lyle and Erik Menendez were charged with killing their parents, Jose and Kitty, in the living room of their $3.5 million home in Beverly Hills, California, on August 20, 1989, their nationally televised trial in 1994 was the most sensational prosecution of such a murder since the trial of Lizzie Borden a century earlier. In both cases, prosecutors alleged that the motive was a desire to inherit the father's wealth. But there were significant differences in the cases. Lizzie stood accused of using a hatchet on her father and stepmother, doing it alone, and blaming the murders on a mysterious intruder who may have acted out of hatred for Lizzie's father. Lyle and Erik were charged with having plotted to use shotguns and suggest that their father had been the target of either his enemies in the entertainment business or the Mafia. Lizzie Borden became an immediate suspect because she'd been in the house at the time. Lyle and Erik said that they had been out for the evening and returned to discover their parents' bodies.

Their story was given credence by a frantic phone call from Lyle to the police. Sobbing, he blurted, "They shot and killed my parents."

As news organizations swarmed to cover the murders, reporters and cameras found two attractive young men. Lyle was a twenty-one-year-old college student. Erik was eighteen and a talented tennis player with potential to become a pro. The idea that such a handsome and personable pair might have committed the crimes seemed ludicrous, but as the police investigated various theories as to who might have done it, to no avail, the involvement of the brothers became more and more a possibility. They noted that rather than exhibiting a period of mourning, Lyle and Eric had gone on a spending spree. From an inheritance of an estate estimated at $14 million, they had bought expensive watches, clothing, and a luxury condominium, and Lyle had purchased a restaurant in New Jersey, where he was a student at Princeton. Yet what seemed to be suspicious activity of a pair of murderers profiting from their crimes could be explained as the understandable reaction of callow youths exhibiting shockingly poor judgment.

Evidence that the police were right in their suspicions came in the form of several tapes that had been secretly made by Erik's psychologist, on which Erik had confessed to the murders. When Lyle learned of this, he made what Dr. Jerome Oziel interpreted as a threat that if the doctor disclosed Erik's confession, he might wind up as dead as Jose and Kitty. Ultimately, it wasn't Oziel who disclosed the existence of the tapes to the police, but Oziel's mistress. In a turn of events that the brothers' plan to murder their parents could not have anticipated, she and Oziel had a falling-out, resulting in her disclosure of Erik's confession.

With Lyle and Erik arrested, what would ordinarily have been the end of the case became a national fixation. When their trial was carried live on television, the brothers' attorneys chose to present them as terrified victims of years of sexual abuse by their father, with Kitty allowing it to continue. The brothers claimed that because they'd feared Jose was planning to silence them by killing them when they returned to their home on the night of August 20, 1989, they bought shotguns and used them in self-defense.

The prosecution contended that Lyle and Erik were not motivated by fear, but a desire to claim their inheritance. To do this, they'd used fake identification to buy the guns in San Diego and had attempted to concoct an alibi that at the time of the murders they'd been to a movie. To the district attorneys, the evidence of their guilt was overwhelming. The key to their case was that after attacking their parents, the brothers returned to their car, reloaded the guns, and went back to finish them off. But when Lyle and Erik took the witness stand to tearfully relate their stories of years of Jose's sexual abuse, and their belief that Jose had planned to kill them, the two juries that heard the cases simultaneously (and millions of TV viewers) proved sympathetic. The result was two hung juries.

Lyle and Erik were brought to trial again in 1996, but with all of Jose's estate having been consumed by legal expenses and their spending spree, their defense was paid for by the State of California. Because the judge in both cases banned the defense attorneys from using the sexual abuse/self-defense strategy, and with one jury in the second trial, Lyle and Erik were convicted of first-degree murder. They were sentenced to life in prison without parole.

While confined in different prisons, they both got married. On January 31, 1997, Erik wed a young woman who had become a pen pal. The ceremony was conducted by phone. Lyle also married a former pen pal on November 21, 2003, in a ceremony held within his prison. Neither is allowed conjugal visits.

As to Lizzie Borden, after her jury found her not guilty she lived on her inheritance to an old age without having married.

74.

MURDER OF MALCOLM X

When Malcolm X rose to speak in Harlem's Audubon Ballroom on February 21, 1965, he had been described in numerous news stories and magazine articles on his life and activities as an advocate of "black power" who'd become the most controversial black figure in America by advocating the use of violence. He was depicted as a serious rival to Martin Luther King, Jr. for the leadership of the civil rights movement, a person of intense interest to the FBI and CIA as a possible threat to domestic peace and national security, and foe of organized crime because of his fight against Mafia drug trafficking in black neighborhoods. He was also viewed by Elijah Muhammad, the head of the Nation of Islam (Black Muslims), as a dangerous traitor.

A school dropout who had drifted into petty crime, gambling, drug dealing, and hustling business for brothels, and who had done time in prison, he was born Malcolm Little in Omaha, Nebraska, on May 19, 1925. Converted to Islam while incarcerated he abandoned the "slave name" Little for the Muslim surname X, and joined the Nation of Islam. Throughout the 1950s he was credited with expanding its membership from about four hundred to more than ten thousand.

By the early 1960s he was not only the most famous Black Muslim in the country, but a dynamic voice whose militant tone caused blacks in the civil rights movement to fear that his advocacy of black power and black separatism would frighten and alienate the movement's white allies.

Much of this concern appeared to be justified when Malcolm said that the assassination of President John F. Kennedy was "chickens coming home to roost" in a society that tolerated white violence against blacks. Negative reaction to the statement was so vociferous among both whites and blacks that Elijah Muhammad suspended Malcolm and forbid him from speaking on behalf of the Nation of Islam for ninety days.

Three months later, Malcolm announced that he was quitting the Nation to form the Harlem-based Muslim Mosque, Inc., and a multinational Organization of Afro-American Unity. Following a pilgrimage to the Muslim holy city of Mecca, Malcolm returned to the U.S., changed his name to El-Hajj Malik El-Shabazz, and became increasingly critical in public of his former mentor, Elijah Muhammad, by raising questions about the Nation of Islam's finances and accusing Elijah of philandering and fathering at least eight children with secretaries.

This open split drew a warning in the Black Muslim newspaper, *Muhammad Speaks*. Written by Nation of Islam minister and spokesman Louis Farrakhan, it said that only those who "wish to be led to hell, or to their doom," would follow Malcolm. It continued, "The die is cast, and Malcolm shall not escape, especially after such evil, foolish talk about his benefactor."

As a result of the break with the Black Muslims, Malcolm received several death threats, and, on the night of February 14, 1965, his house was firebombed.

A week later, as he addressed a few hundred of his followers at the Audubon Ballroom, three black men rushed up the center aisle and opened fire with a shotgun and two pistols, inflicting ten bullet wounds in Malcolm's chest, thigh, and ankle, including two shotgun blasts that shattered his heart and aorta. He died while undergoing surgery.

Although three Black Muslims, Talmadge Hayer, Norman 3X Butler, and Thomas 15X Johnson, were convicted of the assassination and sentenced to life in prison, and despite Hayer having admitted being hired on behalf of the Nation of Islam, conspiracy seekers proposed that the murder was ordered by others. Some said it was a Mafia hit. Others asserted that it was an operation of American counterintelligence (COINTELPRO) to prevent him from meddling in U.S. relations with African governments, or to keep him from charging the United States in the International Court of Justice at The Hague of human rights violations.

As in the murders of the Kennedys and Dr. King, these conspiracy theories remain alive as alternative explanations for Malcolm X's death, and, like the victims of those assassinations, he has been memorialized in monuments, street names, books, and movies as a martyr.

75.

ALIENS AMONG US

According to a public opinion survey conducted for *Time Magazine* and the Cable News Network in 1994, 80 percent of Americans believe that for more than a half a century the U.S. government has been concealing not only that it possesses space craft from somewhere beyond Earth, but also that it has the dead bodies of extraterrestrial creatures.

If true, the largest and most significant conspiracy of all time would have involved every American president since Harry S. Truman, hundreds of officials of the Defense Department, and many thousands of federal employees.

This belief in a government cover-up of its knowledge of the existence of alien beings from outer space has its roots in what has become known as the "Roswell Incident." On July 3, 1947, following the observance of strange flashes in the night sky and the sound of an explosion by residents of the small town in New Mexico, a local rancher discovered what he believed were remnants of a UFO (unidentified flying object) that had crashed in the desert. Convinced that he'd found a "flying saucer," the farmer carried a large piece of the debris home and stored it in a garage. The discovery was reported by the local press and repeated from coast to coast.

A few days later, Air Force officials arrived from Roswell Air Force Base to investigate the find and the supposed "crash site." The area was immediately secured.

Although the air base issued a press release announcing that a "flying disc" had been discovered, the headquarters of the Air Force in Washington quickly explained that the debris was part of a weather balloon. Reports by residents of four small coffins being carted away by the government fueled a belief that they contained the corpses of alien creatures, that autopsies had been conducted, and that the bodies were preserved in a hangar at a super-secret Air Force base.

As the number of believers in a conspiracy to conceal proof that "aliens" had been killed near Roswell grew, the U.S. government issued denials in the form of reports on "investigations" that were dismissed by UFO believers the moment they were published as a continuation of the cover-up. In a lengthy re-examination of the Roswell Incident, released in 1994 and titled "Case Closed," the Air Force stuck to its story that an experimental weather balloon had crashed, that the "bodies" were actually anthropomorphic (human-like) test dummies, and that the "unusual" military activities in the New Mexico desert were U.S. government tests of new and secret types of aircraft, conducted primarily from the Groom Lake Air Force Base.

About ninety miles north of Las Vegas, Nevada, this super-secret installation was officially named the "United States Air Force Flight Test Center," but because it was on maps as "Grid 51," it became widely known as "Area 51." Among the aircraft tested there were the U-2 spy plane and so-called "stealth" fighters and bombers that can't be detected by radar. But to the conspiracy believers, Area 51 is at the very heart of the half-century government plot to keep secret not only that aliens had crashed at Roswell, but that space travelers continue to visit Earth, that contact has been made between them and us, and that the Air Force has been studying and experimenting with their space craft.

Other believers that aliens are among us have contended that the only explanation for the construction of the pyramids in Egypt and other architectural and scientific accomplishments of early civilizations is that they had the help of "ancient astronauts." Some even find evidence of extraterrestrials in events in the Bible, such as Ezekiel seeing "a wheel" in the sky and "angels" going up and down a ladder between Heaven and Earth.

Those who scoff at assertions that we are regularly observed by aliens note that the UFO phenomenon began as a result of Cold War anxieties that started in the mid- to late 1940s and continued until the demise of the Soviet Union. They point out that most UFO sightings have coincided with releases of science-fiction movies dealing with hostile space invaders, including *The Thing*, about a crashed flying saucer in the Arctic, and *The Day the Earth Stood Still*, with a spacecraft and its occupant landing in Washington, D.C., both in 1951; *It Came From Outer Space* (1953); and numerous others through the decades, from *Close Encounters of the Third Kind* to *2001: A Space Odyssey*, in which early earthlings were presumably endowed with inquiring minds by a force from outer space.

Other believers in the existence of unearthly visitors go far beyond observing UFOs to claim that they have been abducted by aliens at night, carried off in spacecraft, subjected to medical and sexual experiments, and returned to their beds. Another supposed example of the proof of otherworldly visitations are "crop circles," in which intricate geometrical patterns appear overnight in fields of corn and wheat as the result of alien activity.

In the *Time*/CNN poll of 1,024 adults, 54 percent said they believe that intelligent life exists beyond Earth, 64 percent said they believe that aliens have contacted humans, and 37 percent said they believe aliens have contacted the U.S. government. Yet 91 percent of those in the survey told the pollsters that they'd never had contact with aliens and knew no one who had.

76.

THE DEATH OF MARILYN MONROE

When a news bulletin flashed around the world on August 5, 1962, that Marilyn Monroe had been found dead in the bedroom of her home in the Brentwood section of Los Angeles, the official cause of death was declared to have been an accidental overdose of barbiturates. To the millions of her fans, this seemed to be a plausible explanation for the death of a movie star they had come to know not only as a glamorous, beautiful, and talented screen actress, but a woman whose entire life had been personally and professionally troubled.

Born Norma Jean Mortenson on June 1, 1926, in Los Angeles, she'd spent most of her childhood and adolescence in an orphanage and foster homes. Because her father had abandoned her, she used her mother's last name, Baker, until she married an aircraft factory worker, James Dougherty, in 1942 at the age of sixteen. When he went to sea in the merchant marine, she also took a job in the airplane industry. In 1946, she quit that job, divorced Dougherty, became a full-time model, and in 1949 was paid fifty dollars to pose nude for a calendar that became the most pinned-up picture since a photo of fully clothed movie star Betty Grable had set the hearts of American soldiers, sailors, and airmen fluttering during World War II. Signed to a movie contract by 20th Century Fox, she changed her name to Marilyn Monroe. After several minor roles, primarily as a "dizzy blonde," she found herself catapulted to star status in two 1953 films, *Gentlemen Prefer Blondes* and *How to Marry a Millionaire*. The next year, she became the bride of one of the most famous men in America, former New York Yankees star Joe DiMaggio, but the marriage lasted less than a year. Determined to overcome her image as a sex symbol, she began studying at the Actor's Studio, resulting in a critically acclaimed role in *Bus Stop* in 1956. That year, she married America's most renowned playwright, Arthur Miller. In 1959 she starred in *Some Like It Hot* as a banjo-playing singer in a women's band.

By now the biggest female star in the world, Marilyn split with Miller in 1961 and began earning a reputation in Hollywood as an unreliable and troublesome performer who dealt with her personal problems by taking various drugs.

It was also no secret in the film capital that she had become fascinated with the nation's new president, John F. Kennedy, and that she and JFK had moved beyond a public friendship to a secret sexual relationship. According to people who claimed to know about it, when JFK broke off the relationship, Marilyn shifted her affections to Robert Kennedy.

With revelations after Marilyn's death that she had been involved not only with JFK, but also with Attorney General Robert Kennedy, doubts quickly arose surrounding the circumstances of the drug overdose that killed her. Questions were asked as to whether her death was accidental, a suicide because JFK had broken off the affair, or a murder. Those who suspected the latter to be the truth attributed it to various conspiracies.

Some believed that Marilyn was killed by Robert Kennedy's enemies in organized crime. To other conspiracy seekers, Marilyn had to be killed because her romances with the Kennedys presented a potential scandal.

Her biographer, Donald Wolfe, explained, "Marilyn Monroe was in a position to bring down the presidency. She was cognizant of Jack Kennedy's marital infidelities and other private matters. She had his notes and letters and was privy to Kennedy's involvement with [Mafia boss] Sam Giancana. That the Kennedy brothers had discussed national security matters with the film star added to an astonishing array of indiscretions."

While the actual events surrounding Marilyn Monroe's death will probably never be known, crime historian Rachael Bell noted that what is known for certain is "a living legend mysteriously died before her time, in a mist of confusion, scandal and uncertainty."

77.

SYMBIONESE LIBERATION ARMY

Begun in 1973 by prison-escapee Donald "Cinque" DeFreeze, the Symbionese Liberation Army (SLA) was an interracial leftist revolutionary group. With a coiled, seven-headed cobra as its symbol, it adopted a motto that vowed, "Death to the fascist insect that preys upon the life of the people." Responsible for the November 6, 1973, murder of the superintendent of schools in Oakland, California, Dr. Marcus Foster, in violent protest of a plan to issue school identity cards, the SLA gained national notoriety on February 4, 1974, by kidnapping publishing heiress Patricia (Patty) Hearst. Two days later, a local radio station received an SLA communiqué saying the group had "served an arrest warrant" that called her the daughter of a "corporate enemy of the people."

A second letter a few days later was accompanied by an audiotape on which Hearst said, "Mom, Dad, I'm okay." She reported that she was kept blindfolded, had been treated well, and cautioned police not to attempt a rescue operation, which could endanger her or them. The communiqué demanded that Hearst give every poor person in California $70 in free food. Randolph Hearst, the chairman of the Hearst Corporation, estimated the cost of such a distribution would be $400 million. Instead, he set up a $2 million "People in Need" program.

To the shock of the Hearst family and the amazement of the entire country, when Patty was heard again on tape (April 3, 1974), she called the food distribution "a sham" and her father a "corporate liar." Declaring that she had been given a choice between returning to her family or "joining the forces of the Symbionese Liberation Army and fighting for my freedom and the freedom of all oppressed people," she stunned everyone by announcing she had "chosen to stay and fight" and had adopted the "revolutionary" name "Tania."

Twelve days later, as the SLA robbed a bank in San Francisco of $10,692, and shot two bystanders, surveillance cameras photographed Hearst carrying a carbine and shouting orders at terrified customers. While the Hearst family and Patty's fiancé said that she had obviously been brainwashed, the U.S. attorney general denounced her as a "common criminal" and the FBI sent out posters seeking her apprehension as a "material witness."

While federal and local law enforcement searched in the San Francisco area, the SLA moved to Compton, a poor black neighborhood of Los Angeles, and began stockpiling weapons. When two members of the gang, William and Emily Harris, were spotted attempting to steal an ammunition case in a sporting goods store on May 16, 1974, Patty was the lookout in a van and armed with a machine gun. As the Harrises fled, she opened fire. After ditching the van and stealing several cars, they hid out in a motel. When the van was located, police found a parking ticket that led them to the house in Compton.

As more than four hundred police officers and FBI agents surrounded the small stucco house and called on the SLA members inside to surrender, a standoff began that was broadcast on television from coast to coast. In an attempt to force the occupants to come out, tear-gas canisters were fired into the house. Moments later, the house was ablaze. When two SLA members emerged, they were shot by police who feared they were about to get fired on. With the fire out, searchers found the bodies of DeFreeze and three others. But Hearst and another SLA member had escaped.

The next time Patty was heard from, in a taped message sent to an LA radio station, she praised those who had been killed. On the same tape, William Harris boasted, "The SLA is not dead and will not die as long as there is one living, fighting member of any oppressed class, race, sex, or group left on the face of the earth."

Tracing the remnants of the SLA to a pair of apartments in San Francisco, the FBI made its move on September 18, 1975. After arresting the Harisses as they were jogging, the agents closed in on Hearst's apartment. Taken into custody, she raised a clenched fist in her mug shot and gave her occupation as "urban guerilla." Put on trial for bank robbery, she was no longer a defiant "Tania," but the Patty Hearst who had been "brainwashed" by DeFreeze into believing the FBI would kill her if she returned to her parents. Convicted, she served two years in prison before President Jimmy Carter commuted her sentence.

The Harrises served six years for kidnapping Hearst and additional crimes. In 2002, they and other members were convicted of killing a man during an SLA bank robbery in 1975. Other members of the SLA were imprisoned for lesser offenses. A few remained fugitives for years under different names but were eventually tracked down and brought to justice.

78

MURDER AT THE MALL

When a Brink's armored truck pulled up in front of a bank in a shopping mall in the village of Nanuet in Rockland County, New York, on October 20, 1981, a red van was parked nearby. Inside was Mutulu Shakur. Formerly named Jeral Wayne Williams, he was a veteran of several armored car and bank robberies in New York and New Jersey. Calling himself a "black nationalist" and running an acupuncture clinic at Lincoln Hospital in New York City, he had devised a scheme to help the cause of "black self-determination" by sticking up banks and armored cars and "redistributing" the money to various black causes. With him in the van were Cecilio "Chui" Ferguson; Samuel Brown, also known as Solomon Bouines; Samuel Smith, aka Mtayari Sundiata; and Donald Weems, using the name Kuwasi Balagoon.

Calling themselves "The Family," they had ties to the Black Panthers and the Black Liberation Army. For the Nanuet operation, code-named "The Big Dance," they were armed with shotguns, automatic rifles, and 9mm handguns. Firing as they bounded from the van, they killed one of the guards, Peter Paige, and seriously wounded his companions, Joseph Trombino and James Kelly. After loading bags of money containing millions of dollars into the van, they sped off in the direction of a Korvettes shopping mall about half a mile away on

Route 59. In its parking lot, other gang members waited in a medium-size U-Haul truck that had been rented by David J. Gilbert in the Bronx. A white long-time member of the Weatherman Underground, he was a fugitive from Colorado on charges of assault and possession of explosives. With him was Kathy Boudin, his wife, who had been on the run since a Weatherman Underground bomb factory had blown up in Greenwich Village, New York, in 1970. The plan called for the Brink's loot to be switched from the van to the U-Haul truck. The black participants in the robbery would either hide in the back of the truck or switch to other cars for a getaway. Assumed was that police would be looking for a red van and pay no attention to a white couple in a U-Haul truck.

The escape plot went awry when a young college student who was working on a school assignment in a house overlooking the Korvettes parking lot saw the van pull in and watched men with rifles jump out, remove several bags of money, and toss them in the U-Haul and a yellow Honda sedan. Her report to the police resulted in a broadcast alert and responses from all law enforcement agencies throughout Rockland County. Roadblocks were set up on likely escape routes, including entry ramps of the New York State Thruway. Stationed at one of these checkpoints, Nyack police officers Waverly Brown and Brian Lennon, Sergeant Edward O'Grady, and Detective Artie Keenan signaled the U-Haul to pull over. As Lennon aimed a shotgun toward the truck, O'Grady asked the white couple to step out.

Leaving the truck, Boudin raised her hands and pleaded with the cops to lower their guns because they were making her "nervous." O'Grady said to Lennon, "Put the shotgun back. I don't think it's them." As Lennon walked back to his police car and Detective Keenan attempted to open the rear door of the U-Haul, it flew open and six men bounded out. In a fierce gun battle, Brown was killed instantly. O'Grady would die in a hospital an hour and a half later.

As Lennon continued to fire despite being outgunned and outnumbered, and with the entry ramp blocked, Kathy Boudin attempted to escape by dashing across the Thruway, only to be spotted and grabbed by an off-duty New York Corrections Department officer, Michael Koch. As she was taken into custody, other gang members in cars were pursued by police in the kind of chases that residents of tranquil Rockland County had seen only in movies. Ironically, one of these high-speed races ended when a getaway car crashed into a wall in front of the Nyack home of actress Helen Hayes.

With most of the gang captured, investigators learned that they were not only remnants of the Weathermen, but also former members of the Black Liberation Army (BLA). Violent extremists in the 1970s, they had specialized in shootings of uniformed police officers, including ambush murders on May 20, 1971, of New York City police officers Joseph Piagentini and Waverly Jones, and the January 28, 1972, killing of officers Gregory Foster and Rocco Laurie outside a restaurant in Manhattan. During searches of "safe houses" that the suspects had visited after the robbery, investigators found leads to other members of the BLA and the Weathermen.

Raids in other parts of the country netted another fugitive, Cynthia Boston, in Gallman, Mississippi. Located in a ranch house owned by another radical organization called the Republic of New Africa, she had not been an active participant in the robbery, but she was charged with conspiracy. Two other suspects, former Weathermen Jeffrey Jones and Eleanor Raskin, were arrested in the Bronx and charged with unlawful flight to avoid prosecution after cops found bomb-making material in their Hoboken apartment in 1979. Over the next several months, the FBI located and arrested Donald Weems, "Chui" Ferguson, and Edward Joseph, also called Jamal Baltimore, in a raid on a Bronx apartment. The planner of "The Big Dance," Jeral "Mutulu Shakur" Williams escaped and later fled to California. Arrested in Los Angeles on February 13, 1986, he was convicted in a federal court in New York in May 1988 and sentenced to sixty years.

When the most famous of the gang, Kathy Boudin, was convicted and sentenced to twenty years to life, she showed no remorse for her life as a terrorist and fugitive for twelve years. She told the court, "The meaning of my life has come from being part of a worldwide tradition of fighting for a more just and humane world."

Rockland County District Attorney Kenneth Gribetz gave the court a different account. Calling her methods "violent and despicable," he compared her life with the men who had died as a result of her participation in a string of terrorist conspiracies. "Peter Paige, Edward O'Grady, and Waverly Brown were also concerned and compassionate human beings," he said. "Unlike Miss Boudin, however, they had sought to brighten, rather than destroy. In the final analysis that is the distinguishing factor—how one transforms ideals into action—that sets the civilized apart from the uncivilized world."

Twenty years later, to the shock and disgust of those who had suffered at the hands of the conspirators in "The Big Dance," the New York State parole board let her out of prison in 2003. As she walked out of the prison, a police officer said, "Kathy Boudin needs to know that when she's sleeping safely tonight, she's being protected by police officers just like the ones that she was involved in murdering."

79.

WALKER SPY RING

The most damaging acts of treason involving members of one family since the Julius and Ethel Rosenberg case began in 1968 when John Anthony Walker, Jr. lost all of the money he had put into a café in South Carolina and decided that the easiest way to replenish his funds was by selling American military secrets to the Soviet Union.

Born in 1938, Walker enlisted in the Navy in 1955 and became a communications specialist with assignments in two nuclear-powered missile submarines (1962–1966) and as a U.S. Navy Chief Warrant Officer stationed in Norfolk, Virginia, home of the world's largest naval base. As the "watch officer" in the message center on the staff of Submarine Force, Atlantic Fleet, he had top-secret cryptographic clearance that provided him access to some of America's most closely guarded naval secrets. His material proved so valuable that the Soviets paid him $4,000 a month. Delivery of documents, microfilm photographs, and other data was made by means of weekly drops in secluded areas in Maryland and Virginia. Payments, instructions, and "wish lists" were picked up in other locations.

After several years of solitary spying, as Walker neared retirement after twenty years in the Navy, he recruited his son. Yeoman Third-Class Michael Lance Walker was serving on the nuclear aircraft carrier *Nimitz*. Also recruited were Walker's brother, Arthur, a retired navy lieutenant commander employed by a military contractor; and a friend Walker had made while in San Diego, Senior Chief Radioman Jerry Alfred Whitworth. The motive for all of them was money. Walker also attempted, with no avail, to recruit his daughter, Laura, while she was in the army and stationed at Fort Gordon in Georgia.

Walker was so pleased with himself and the work of his spy network that he boasted in a message to one of his handlers, "No member of the organization or prospective members has any of the classic problems that plague so many in this business. We have no drug problems, alcoholic problems, homosexuality. All are psychologically well-adjusted and mature."

While John Walker could brag about his abilities and longevity at espionage and setting up a spy ring, he was unable to succeed in keeping his ex-wife, Barbara, and his daughter from reporting his treason. Alarmed that he had recruited Michael and had attempted to bring Laura into the ring, Barbara contacted the FBI. Unfortunately, her report that her husband was "a dangerous spy" was dismissed as the act of a spiteful woman. But when a routine account of the accusation was read by Joseph Wolfinger of the FBI's counterintelligence division in Norfolk, Virginia, an investigation was ordered.

Through surveillance of Walker and the use of wiretaps, and based on interviews with Barbara and Laura, FBI agents accumulated enough evidence to make their move. On May 20, 1985, John Walker was arrested and charged with espionage, as were his son, brother, and Whitworth. To avoid the death penalty, Walker agreed to testify against Whitworth and received life in prison. Whitworth got 365 years and a fine of $410,000. Arthur was given three life terms and fined $250,000. As part of Walker's plea agreement, Michael Walker was sentenced to twenty-five years. He was released in 2000 after serving fifteen years.

It is estimated that during a period of seventeen years, Walker handed more than one million documents to his Soviet handlers that contained information on weapons, detection systems and naval tactics, submarine training and operations, and other data. According to the secretary of defense, Caspar W. Weinberger, the information provided Soviet "gains in all areas of naval warfare." The FBI stated that billions of taxpayer dollars were expended to repair the damage he and his accomplices had done, and that no one could ever "assess the extent to which Walker's treasonous acts jeopardized the lives of tens of thousands of our military men and women."

80.

ENRON

When Enron announced in December 2002 that it was filing for bankruptcy, the failure of the goliath energy-supply corporation sent shock waves throughout the global economy that evoked comparisons to the 1929 Stock Market Crash and the collapse of Communism in 1989. The news also added the firm's name to an ignominious roster of conspiracies from Teapot Dome in the 1920s to Watergate in the 1970s that are synonyms for corruption and scandal. But the difference between Enron and the effects of illegal granting of government oil reserves and the political skullduggery of Watergate was that the demise of Enron resulted in financial ruin for thousands of the firm's employees and countless investors in the U.S. and around the world.

Formed in 1985 as a company that provided natural gas through pipelines, Enron quickly became one of America's dominant energy traders and a choice stock for investors. As the firm accrued prestige and power, along with significant relationships with government officials, its executives began engaging in what was described by the Enron Fraud InfoCenter as "ever more complicated contracts and [business] undertakings," combined with "alleged illegal, off-the-balance-sheet transactions, and partnerships" to "conceal Enron's growing debt problem." Set up as a resource and an opportunity for victims of the scandal to research the scandal and learn their "legal rights associated with Enron fraud," the Fraud InfoCenter's Internet website noted, "By the time investors, employees, and the public learned of the company's crisis, the downward spiral was virtually unstoppable."

Among Enron's dubious activities was the formation in 1987 of a firm called Chewco. Formed by Enron executives, including Chief Financial Officer Andrew Fastow, it was bought out by Enron at an inflated price, plus $1.5 million in management fees and other payments to the company's ostensible owners that were shared with Fastow. The acquisition resulted in a rise in Enron's value, at least on paper. Ten years later, Fastow and Enron's chief executive officer, Jeffrey Shilling, arranged the acquisition of an Internet start-up firm (RhythymNetConnections) through a complex scheme to manipulate the books to mask what was actually an Enron liability as an asset.

While Enron's top executives and other insiders appeared to have known what was going on, it was a former vice president for corporate development, Sherron Watkins, who warned in August 2001 that the firm faced problems because of "a wave of accounting scandals" involving auditing firms that either had overlooked the financial irregularities of clients, or had colluded in covering them up. Among the accounting companies under scrutiny was Enron's auditing firm, Arthur Anderson, LLP. The result was an announcement by Enron in October 2001 that it was worth $1.2 billion less than the value it had claimed.

Two months later, the company filed for bankruptcy. The consequence was not only the unemployment of Enron employees in the United States and around the world, but the loss of investments in the firm by mutual funds and thousands of individual investors, many of whom found themselves financially wiped out. Because the failure had been precipitated by fraud, the participants soon found themselves facing prosecution under federal conspiracy laws and others related to money laundering and securities, wire, and mail fraud.

Among those accused were Enron's founder and former chairman and CEO, Kenneth Lay; CEO Jeffrey Skilling (CEO from February to August 2001); Andrew Fastow; two former treasurers, Jeffrey Mc-Mahon and Ben Glisan, Jr.; and executives of Greenwich NatWest bank.

Convicted of obstruction of justice, the Arthur Anderson company went out of business.

Providing one of the most brazen examples of Enron's greed, a former energy trader, Timothy Belden, who pleaded guilty to conspiracy, told how Enron had profited from an energy crisis in California by taking energy from the state to avoid price controls, transmitted it elsewhere to garner a profit, and then sold it back to California at inflated rates.

Although Enron ranks as one of the most egregious business conspiracies in American history, with thousands of its investors losing millions of dollars and a shadow of doubt cast on the honesty of all corporations, the scandal provided comedians plenty of fodder for jokes.

Late night host David Letterman asked, "Are you getting a kick out of the Enron scandal? I find this interesting that whenever a big crisis starts, people start showing up in church. So, Ken Lay shows up at church this weekend. Church officials are still looking for the collection plates." On the *Tonight Show*, Jay Leno quipped, "This past Sunday, former Enron CEO Ken Lay went to church in Houston. On the way out, a reporter asked him how he thought it was going to work out. Lay said, 'With God's help we'll get through it.' To which, the Devil said, 'Hey, I thought we had a deal.' "

81

RUBOUT OF BUGSY SIEGEL

When a teenage, Jewish, good-looking, tough, and dangerously hot-headed thug from the streets of the Williamsburg section of Brooklyn, New York, named Benjamin Siegel (shortened from Siegelbaum) met a sixteen-year-old, skinny, brainy, Russian-born Jew named Meyer Lansky (shortened from Suchowljansky) on October 24, 1918, the pair began a thirty-one-year partnership in crime that would expand to include Sicilian-born Charles "Lucky" Luciano. Through treachery and murder, the trio would take control of a criminal organization known to the public and law enforcement agencies as the Mafia. Called "the syndicate" by its organizers (and later "La Cosa Nostra," meaning "this thing of ours," by its mostly Italian/Sicilian members), it became the most successful and longest running crime conspiracy in the history of the United States.

Along with a handsome face, muscular build, and a desire to get rich quick illegally, Ben brought to his criminal exploits such an explosive and violent temper that it soon earned him the underworld nickname "Bugs." Although in gangland parlance to "go bugs" was a term of respect for courage and daring, he regarded it as a slur. Beginning his life of crime as an extortionist on the streets of Brooklyn, and serving as a killer for the syndicate, he made it clear that anyone who'd dared to call him "Bugs" or "Bugsy" in his presence would quickly suffer very unpleasant consequences. To his companions in crime, he would be either "Ben" or "Mr. Siegel."

Regarding his role as a murderer for the mob, he explained to a friend who feared that innocent people might become victims, "We only kill each other."

Four decades before a fascinated press gave the nattily dressed mob boss John Gotti the nickname "Dapper Don," Ben Siegel made himself a fashion plate by wearing expensive suits as he toured the nightspots of New York, Miami, and Hollywood. As much a celebrity as stars of stage and screen, he dined and drank with socialites and wagered huge sums at the horse races with the nation's rich and famous. His goal in his life of crime, he explained, was to attain class.

"That's the only thing that counts," he told his plain, quiet, and spotlight-avoiding pal and partner in crime, Meyer Lansky. "Without class and style, a man's a bum. He might as well be dead."

Having been organized to take advantage of the continuing thirst of Americans for booze during the "great dry spell" known as Prohibition, when the ban on selling liquor was repealed in 1933, the mob bosses concentrated on other activities, including gambling and extortion. Realizing that an area where they did not control shakedown rackets was the West Coast, the syndicate's "commission" decided to dispatch Siegel to remedy the situation by taking over an operation that blackmailed mischievous and otherwise errant movie stars. Soon after arriving in the film capital, Siegel discerned greener pastures in shaking down the motion picture studios by taking control of the union that represented extras and threatening to shut down productions unless the studios paid up. "The odd thing," noted one crime historian, "is that instead of being loathed in the film community, Siegel became a sought-after dinner guest, a so-called mystery man with exciting, sinister connections."

Pleased with Siegel's success, the commission turned its attention to the West Coast's formerly independent bookmakers and placed their plot for "organizing" them under syndicate control in Siegel's hands. While he did not disappoint them, he proposed that even more profits could be made for the mob in the form of a gambling casino in a remote spot in the desert named Las Vegas in the state of Nevada.

Holding out the prospect of patronage by the rich and famous from Hollywood, and no interference from the Nevada government, he persuaded the bosses to finance construction of a hotel and casino that he intended to call the Flamingo, after his nickname for his girl-friend, Virginia Hill. The bosses provided $3 million, but on the date that the Flamingo was to open in 1946, not only was construction incomplete, but a rainstorm also kept a host of moviedom celebrities from showing up.

When business at the Flamingo eventually picked up, Lucky Luciano personally informed Siegel at a meeting in Havana, Cuba, that he expected immediate return of the $3 million. Siegel told Lucky to go to hell and went back to Los Angeles.

At 10:30 PM on June 20, 1947, as Siegel was chatting with an associate, Allen Smiley, in the parlor of Virginia Hill's palatial house on Linden Drive in Beverly Hills, several .30-30 bullets fired from a rifle drilled through a plateglass window. One slammed into Bugsy's head with such a force that one of the slugs blasted out an eye and propelled it across the room.

Although no one was charged with the rubout, there is no doubt among mob historians that the flashy gangster whose entire life had consisted of a string of conspiracies met his end as the result of one.

82.

LEOPOLD AND LOEB

Trumpeted in newspaper headlines in 1924 as the crime and the trial "of the century," the kidnapping and murder of fourteen-year-old Bobby Franks in Chicago began as a conspiracy by the pampered nineteen-year-old sons of two of the city's richest families to commit "the perfect crime."

Bonded in a homosexual, sadomasochistic relationship, the dominant Richard Loeb and subservient Nathan Leopold believed they were so intellectually superior that not only could they experience getting away with the "thrill" of abducting and killing the child of another wealthy family, but also profit from it by collecting a $10,000 ransom payment.

The handsome son of a retired Sears Roebuck vice president, and the youngest man to graduate from the University of Michigan, Loeb had become obsessed not only with the reading of detective stories, but also planning crimes. Leopold's interests were in ornithology and the study of philosophy. The son of a millionaire box manufacturer, he was a University of Chicago law student and planning to enroll at Harvard Law School. His interests in birds had garnered him recognition as the nation's leading authority on the endangered Kirtland's warbler. His passion for philosophy had led him to a fascination with

Friedrich Nietzsche's criticism of moral codes and his belief that moral legal obligations did not apply to "the superman." In Leopold's mind, Dick Loeb was not only just a superior individual, but also the love of his life.

What is clearest about the motives of the youths, noted legal historian Douglas O. Linder in an account of the case written in 1997, "is that Leopold's attraction to Loeb was his primary reason for participating in the crime." Leopold later wrote, "Loeb's friendship was necessary to me—terribly necessary." He said that his motive "was to please Dick."

"Murder was a necessary element in their plan to commit the perfect crime," wrote Linder. "They spent hours discussing and refining a plan that included kidnapping the child of wealthy parents, demanding a ransom, and collecting the ransom after it was thrown off a moving train as it passed a designated point."

Around five in the afternoon on May 21, 1924, as Bobby Franks was walking home from school, a rented gray Winton automobile pulled up near him. Loeb invited him to get into the car to discuss a tennis racquet. As the car drove away, he was killed with a chisel. Whether he was sexually assaulted was never made clear. Leopold and Loeb then drove to a marshland near the Indiana line, stripped Franks naked, poured hydrochloric acid on his body to make identification more difficult, and stuffed the body in a drainage culvert.

When Leopold and Loeb returned to the Loeb home, they burned Franks's clothing in the basement. That evening, Mrs. Franks received a telephone call from a "George Johnson." It was Leopold, telling her that her son had been kidnapped, was unharmed, and that she should expect a ransom note soon. The following morning, a special delivery letter demanded $10,000 in old unmarked bills and advised the Franks to expect more instructions that afternoon. A call from George Johnson at three o'clock directed Mr. Franks to expect a taxicab to arrive at his home and that he should take it to a drugstore in South Chicago. But as Franks prepared to comply, a call from the police informed him that Bobby's body had been discovered.

Near the corpse lay a pair of horn-rimmed glasses with an unusual hinge that was traced to a Chicago optometrist who had written three such prescriptions, including one for Nathan Leopold. When questioned, he said that he must have lost the glasses during one of his frequent birding expeditions. Asked to demonstrate how they might have fallen out of his pockets, he was unable to dislodge them from his coat after several tries.

With Leopold and Loeb asserting that on the day of Bobby's disappearance they had been "picking up girls in [Leopold's] car and driving out to Lincoln Park," the police were about to let them go when two additional pieces of evidence were discovered. The most damaging was typewritten notes obtained from a member of Leopold's law school study group. The type proved to be a match to the type on the ransom note. Police also obtained a statement from the Leopold family chauffeur that destroyed their alibi. He was certain, he said, that the Leopold car had not left the garage on the day of the murder.

When the youths confessed, their admissions differed only on who had killed Bobby. They accused each other. With their sons arrested, the Loeb and Leopold families engaged the country's most famous defense attorney, Clarence Darrow. Immediately changing their guilty pleas to not guilty, guaranteeing them a jury trial, he proceeded to justify the press's designation of the case as the "trial of the century" by launching an attack on the death penalty that stands in the estimation of legal experts and trial historians as the most brilliant and moving plea for life in the annals of American justice.

With Leopold and Loeb found guilty by the jury, sentencing was up to the judge, John R. Caverly. "Where responsibility is divided by twelve, it is easy to say 'away with him,' " Darrow said to the court. "But, your honor, if these boys are to hang, you must do it. It must be by your cool, premeditated act, without a chance to shift responsibility."

After two weeks of deliberation, Caverly sentenced them to life in prison for the murder, plus ninety-nine years for the kidnapping. Loeb's term ended in 1937 with his death at age thirty-two after his cellmate attacked him with a straight razor, probably because Loeb had made a sexual advance. Leopold was paroled in 1958. To escape hounding by the press about the release of a movie adapted from a best-selling novel based on the case (*Compulsion*, by Ira Levin), he moved to Puerto Rico and published his autobiography, *Life Plus 99 Years*, and a volume on the birds of Puerto Rico. He died on August 30, 1971, at age sixty-six of a heart attack.

83.

MURDER OF RASPUTIN

One of the most documented assassination schemes of the twentieth century, the conspiracy to murder a strange monk and mystic named Grigory Rasputin in Russia in 1916 was launched by aristocrats in an effort to end his powerful influence on Czar Nicholas II and his wife Alexandra. One of the most bizarre palace plots of all time, it was unique not only for the fascinating personality who became the target, and the boldness and cunning of the plotters, but also how the execution of the plan took on aspects of a gruesome farce.

Born on January 10, 1869, in Prokovskoe, a small Siberian village on the banks of the Tura River, Grigory Efimovich Rasputin gained a reputation for drunkenness, womanizing, and debauchery that continued after he discovered religion and became a monk. When he arrived in the Russian capital, St. Petersburg, he gained the friendship of relatives of the Czar. Summoned to appear before Alexandra, he appeared to have the power to stop to the bleeding of their son, Alexis, who suffered from hemophilia.

As Rasputin's influence upon the royal family grew, many Orthodox clergymen who had initially supported him became skeptical about the relationship. They were not alone. Others who distrusted him circulated a rumor that he and Alexandra had a sexual relationship. When the Czar's secret police reported these stories, Rasputin was exiled to the provinces, but soon after he had departed, Alexis had another bleeding crisis that almost killed him. Brought back to the capital, Rasputin found that his influence was greater than ever.

When Russia entered the First World War, and Nicholas joined his armies at the front and day-to-day handling of governmental affairs fell to Alexandra, it was believed that Rasputin had become "the true lord of All the Russias." It's at this juncture that the plot to remove him took shape. At the heart of the conspiracy were the Czar's cousin, Grand Duke Dimitri Pavlovich, and Prince Felix Youssoupov, husband of Nicholas II's niece, Princess Irina Alexandrovna of Russia. To lure Rasputin to his doom, Youssoupov invited him to his vast palace with the promise that Rasputin would be introduced to Felix's beautiful wife Irina. No doubt with lustful hopes in his mind, Rasputin arrived at the Youssoupov palace on the evening of December 16, 1916.

The plan called for Rasputin to be lured into a cellar and offered poisoned cookies and wine. Although Rasputin was not interested in the cookies at first, claiming they were too sweet, he drank some wine, but then had a change of mind about the cookies. When nothing happened, the amazed and shocked Felix pulled out a pistol and shot him.

Believing Rasputin was dead, he raced from the cellar to inform the other plotters that the deed was done. When they sent him back to make sure Rasputin was dead, Rasputin lunged up from the floor and attempted to strangle Youssoupov. As the prince fled in terror, Rasputin struggled from the cellar and outside. While he crawled toward a gate, he was shot again, then bludgeoned and kicked in the head.

Confident of success, the plotters bound the body in a carpet and dumped it in the Moika Canal of the Neva River. When the body was discovered and pulled out of the water, his death was determined to not have been from the poison, the shootings, and the beating, but the result of drowning.

While punishment for the conspirators was exile, the aristocracy saw Youssoupov and Pavolvich as heroes who had saved Russia. But to the vast majority of Russia's people, Rasputin had been regarded as a "man of the people." As a result, his death became another example of the abuses of aristocrats and members of an imperial family who were out of touch with the needs of the population that erupted into a revolution that deposed the Czar, but in the end led to the takeover of Russia in a conspiracy by Bolsheviks, the murders of the Czar and his family, and more than seventy years of Communist rule.

84.

MURDER OF THOMAS À BECKET

The assassination of Thomas à Becket, the archbishop of Canterbury, on December 29, 1170, as he prayed at the altar of his cathedral, was not only one of the most dramatic events in the long history of the relationship between the British monarchy and religion, but also painful proof to King Henry II of the wisdom of the warning "Be careful what you wish for, you might get it."

Born in London between 1110 and 1120, but of French ancestry and having completed his education at the University of Paris, Becket came to the attention of Henry because of his zeal and efficiency as archdeacon of Canterbury. When the office of chancellor became vacant, the then-archbishop, Theobold, recommended Becket. The king found him to be such an excellent government administrator, genial companion at game-hunting and feasting, and a lively partner in bouts of regal carousing, that when Theobold died in 1162, Becket found himself elevated, reluctantly, to the most important religious post in Henry's realm.

In making Becket archbishop of Canterbury, the king expected that Becket would be as genial a cleric as he'd been as chancellor. In naming his good friend and faithful courtier, Henry assumed that

Becket would be a forceful ally in Henry's desire to impose the supremacy of the crown on the Church of England, particularly on the question of which had the power (church or crown) to punish "criminous" church officials. To Henry's shock and consternation, Becket took his job seriously and sided with the Church.

While Henry demanded the Church's subservience, Becket insisted upon exemption of the Church from all civil jurisdiction. When Henry convened the clergy on October 1, 1163, at Westminster and demanded compliance, Becket stood firm on "saving the rights of the Church." Furious at being rebuffed, the king called another assembly at Clarendon on January 30, 1164, at which he repeated his demands in the form of sixteen "constitutions" requiring abandonment of the clergy's independence. Becket refused to sign.

Summoned to appear before a "grand council" at Northampton on October 8, 1164, to answer charges of contempt of royal authority and "malfeasance" as chancellor, Becket denied the right of the assembly to judge him, appealed to the Pope, and fled to France and the protection of King Louis VII. Eventually threatened with excommunication, Henry hoped for a reconciliation that would remove the prospect of excommunication and permit Becket to return to England.

Still unwilling to yield his position, Becket went back anyway. Prepared to promulgate the order of excommunication against Henry and bishops who had sided with Henry, he landed at Sandwich on December 3, 1170, and arrived two days later at Canterbury. Learning of this, Henry exclaimed (reportedly), "Will no one rid me of this troublesome priest?"

Interpreting Henry's anguished cry as an invitation, if not an outright order, to act against Becket, four knights (Reginald Fitzurse, Hugh de Morville, William de Tracey, and Richard le Breton) set out for Canterbury. When they arrived on December 29, 1170, they barged into the cathedral, found Becket kneeling in prayer at the altar, drew swords, and hacked him to death.

Expressing shock at the murder, and denying complicity, Henry was so overcome with remorse that he did public penance as imposed by the Pope by walking to Canterbury in sackcloth and ashes to be flogged by monks. But his greatest punishment is that his thirty-five-year reign is chiefly remembered in history books for his quarrel with

Becket and the words he'd uttered in frustration that resulted not only in Becket's death, but Becket's canonization in 1173 as a saint.

Thomas à Becket also garnered literary immortality. In Geoffrey Chaucer's *Canterbury Tales*, written between 1387 and 1400, the pilgrims are on their way to pray at the shrine of Saint Thomas Becket. (The word "canter" to describe the fast gait of horses on the road to Canterbury also entered the English language as a shortened version of the term "Canterbury gallop.") Nine centuries after Becket's death, the assassination was depicted in poet T. S. Eliot's play *Murder in the Cathedral* and later by Jean Anouilh in the drama *Becket*, followed by the 1964 movie based on it that starred Richard Burton as Becket and Peter O'Toole as Henry. Four years later, Peter O'Toole again played Henry in the film version of William Goldman's Broadway play *A Man For All Seasons*, dealing with the contest between Henry and his queen, Eleanor of Aquitaine (played by Katharine Hepburn), over which of their sons—Richard, John, and Geoffrey—would succeed him.

Although Henry II remains in Becket's shadow, he proved to be a significant monarch. By the end of his reign, the jury system of twelve citizens had been established, the English for the first time became accustomed to paying taxes and expecting fair treatment from the government, and Ireland had been added to the realm.

AMERICAN HOSTAGES
IN IRAN

When President Dwight D. Eisenhower approved a plan called Operation Ajax in 1953, he authorized the Central Intelligence Agency to overthrow an Islamic revolutionary government in Iran for the purpose of thwarting a potential takeover of the oil-rich country by the Soviet Union and imposing a pro-American government in Tehran. Placed on the so-called "Peacock Throne," the shah, Mohammed Reza Pahlavi, proved to be exactly the friend that the United States desired in the Cold War. But he was also a monarch who kept a grip on the people he ruled by using all the time-tested devices of tyrants. Iranians who were deemed a threat to his power were either killed, thrown into prison, or driven into exile.

Among those who were expelled from the country was a Shiite cleric, the Ayatollah Ruhollah Khomeini. Finding refuge in Paris for fourteen years, he maintained communication with his followers and became the spiritual and political leader of a revolutionary movement to oust the shah and establish a fundamentalist Islamic government. When a combination of these religious zealots, victims of the shah's repressions, Iranian nationalists, and revolutionaries who called themselves "students" took to the streets in larger and increasingly violent protests in 1978, the shah fled the country. Khomeini returned to Iran and it became an Islamic state.

With relations between Iran and the United States already severely strained, they reached a breaking point in the autumn of 1979 when the Iranians learned that the hated, exiled, and ill shah had been admitted to the United States for medical treatment. When demands that he be returned to Iran to stand trial for the atrocities of his twenty-five-year reign proved fruitless, students, in what appeared to be a spontaneous reaction, attacked the U.S. embassy on November 4, 1979, and seized more than seventy Americans.

In a takeover that was actually a well-planned and executed plot to use the captives to demand the shah's return, Americans watched television news reports with increasing outrage as U.S. citizens were bound and blindfolded and paraded in the streets of Tehran.

After a few weeks of stalemate, in which nineteen of the captives were released, leaving fifty-three in the hands of the students, President Jimmy Carter responded to what was now being called the "Iran hostage crisis" by freezing Iranian government assets in the United States and elsewhere, and cutting off imports of Iranian oil. Although diplomatic efforts were pursued, it became clear by March 1980 that none of the rival groups in Iran could dare to defy Khomeini.

As frustrated and angry Americans in a presidential election year demanded forceful action by the Carter administration to "free the hostages," the president authorized an attempt to rescue them. It ended when three of eight helicopters failed to reach Tehran during a sandstorm. Eight rescuers were killed in an attempt to evacuate them.

With Americans obsessed with the hostages, and as the news media underscored what appeared to be U.S. government impotency by keeping count of the number of days since the hostages were taken, the crisis became an issue, along with soaring inflation and other economic problems, in the presidential campaign of the Republican candidate, former California Governor Ronald Reagan. While the hostages loomed large in U.S. politics, two events beyond the control of the U.S. government contributed to a change in the attitude of Iranians. Their demands for the return of the shah became moot when he died in Egypt. More importantly, Iran found itself in a war with its neighbor, Iraq. With the United States supporting Iraq, and feeling the pinch of the U.S. economic retaliation, the Iranians began looking for a way out of the hostage dilemma.

As a consequence of the financial pressures and the war with Iraq, and after Reagan's defeat of Carter, the Iranians welcomed the assistance of Algerian intermediaries in an effort to break the deadlock. These talks led to a U.S. agreement to release almost $8 billion in Iranian government assets and a promise by Iran to free the hostages.

After 444 days in captivity, in an obvious gesture of Iranian contempt for Carter, the fifty-two hostages departed Iran just as Reagan's inauguration as president was getting underway on the steps of the Capitol in Washington, D.C., at noon on January 20, 1981.

86.

ASSASSINATION OF RAFAEL TRUJILLO

As armed forces of the United States were fighting to destroy dictatorships in Germany and Japan during World War II, Secretary of State Cordell Hull was asked to explain why the United States supported Rafael Trujillo's brutal rule of the Dominican Republic. "He may be a son of a bitch," said Hull, "but he's our son of a bitch."

Born in San Cristobal on October 24, 1891, Trujillo joined the Dominican army in 1919 and proved to be an effective soldier. Promoted to captain in 1922, he became inspector of the First District the following year, major commander in 1924, then lieutenant colonel and chief of staff of the national police and colonel and commander of police in 1925. When the police were transformed into a national army in 1927, with the aid of the United States, he was named brigadier general. Three years later, he masterminded a revolution against President Horacio Vasquez. When an election was held to choose a new president, he guaranteed that he would win by using strong-arm tactics to garner 99 percent of the ballots cast by 55 percent of registered voters. Following a devastating hurricane later that year, he used the calamity as an excuse to suspend the constitution and get rid of political opponents. He also decreed that when the ruined capital city, Santo Domingo, was rebuilt, its name would henceforth be Ciudad Trujillo.

With political power came mastery of the country's economy, providing wealth and lives of luxury for himself and members of his family in the form of monopolies in sugar, salt, milk, beef, and tobacco, along with control of the insurance industry, national lottery, and the press. Known and feared by the Dominican people as *El Jefe* (the chief) and the *Generalismo*, he proved to be as ruthless a dictator as Nazi Germany's Hitler, Fascist Italy's Mussolini, and their ally in Spain, Francisco Franco, but with the significant exception of El Jefe being regarded by the United States government not only as "our son of a bitch," but by American corporations as a friend they could do business with. Consequently, when Trujillo's military defeated an attempt by exiled Dominicans to overthrow his regime in 1949, the crushing of the "Luperon Invasion" was welcomed. Although a second try at ousting him on June 14, 1959, by leftists, encouraged by the victory of Fidel Castro in ousting Cuban dictator Fulgencio Batista, also ended in a failure, the resistance continued in the form of the *Catorce de Junio* (Fourteenth of June) movement.

With aid provided by Venezuelan President Manuel Betancourt, the group planned to assassinate Trujillo while he attended a cattle fair on January 21, 1960. Learning of the plot, Trujillo's secret police rounded up the leaders, including five Roman Catholic priests. When Trujillo was informed of the role played in the plot by Betancourt, he approved a plan to kill Betancourt and sent a team of assassins to assassinate him with a bomb. The plot was a failure.

Increasingly alarmed that disaffection in the Dominican Republic with Trujillo might result in a successful revolution by leftists following the pattern of Castro in Cuba, and that it might install a second Communist government in the Caribbean, President Eisenhower and his successor, John F. Kennedy, authorized the Central Intelligence Agency to contract non-leftist dissidents and others with personal grudges against the dictator and offer them assistance in any scheme to remove him, including assassination.

Using carbine rifles supplied by the CIA, a group of gunmen fired on Trujillo's car on a stretch of deserted highway on May 30, 1961, and killed him. The following day, Trujillo's son, Ramfis, assumed control of the government and ordered the assassins and their accomplices in the plot tracked down. Within a month, the conspirators and anyone suspected of involvement were in custody, with six of them taken to Ramfis Trujillo's hacienda, tied to trees, shot, cut up, and fed to sharks at a nearby beach.

The thirty-year Trujillo reign ended in mid-November 1961 when Ramfis fled the country under U.S. military guard as ships of the U.S. Navy's Atlantic Fleet arrived in Santo Domingo Harbor. During the next three years, American hopes for stability in the Dominican Republic were dashed in a series of military takeovers and the outbreak of civil war. On April 28, 1965, the third U.S. president to deal with the problem of stabilizing the country, Lyndon B. Johnson, sent in the U.S. Marines to take control. They were joined a year later by troops of the Organization of American States.

Struggling to emerge from the shadow of Trujillo, with the establishment of a democratic process in 1978, the Dominican people have found that the survival of democracy on the island they share with Haiti is closely linked to the country's economic fortunes and their ties to the United States. While the knowledge of the Dominican Republic among most Americans is limited to an appreciation of numerous Dominican baseball players who have become stars in the major leagues, and the Dominican Republic as a source of excellent cigars, the Dominicans continue to cope with the nature of the nation's domestic politics and with finding its economic and political role in a world in which dictators such as Trujillo are a dwindling number.

87.

THE BLACK HAND

When twenty-two-year-old Ignazio Saietta left his hometown of Corleone, Sicily, for New York City in 1898, he took with him a reputation as a sadistic killer for the local Mafia that had earned him the nickname *Lupo* (wolf). He also left with a scheme to get rich at the expense of Italians who had preceded him to America and succeeded in realizing their dreams of building a better life. His plan wasn't new. The Sicilian Mafia had been squeezing money from countrymen by demanding payoffs and promising them violence if they didn't comply. These threats were made in letters that bore the black imprint of a hand *(la mano nera)*.

Within days of stepping off the boat in New York, Saietta was sending out Black Hand notes to prosperous Italian immigrants in Greenwich Village and East Harlem. To form a bond with two other Black Hand practitioners, Ciro Terranova and his brother, Vincenzo, who ran a Black Hand racket in Brooklyn, Saietta married their sister in 1910. The nuptials also resulted in the wedding of the Saietta-Terranova families to another gang, headed by Giuseppe Morello.

Although other Black Hand gangs plagued Italian communities in Chicago, New Orleans, and other cities, Saietta's criminal and familial alliances became the foundation of what would become the American

Mafia and the root of the present-day Genovese family, one of the five original New York Mafia gangs. While plundering Italian communities through its extortion scheme, Saietta's Black Hand organization expanded its criminal activities by taking over the Unione Siciliana. Set up to assist immigrants who didn't speak English, it functioned as a bank and an insurance company. These financial services were used by Saietta to facilitate another of its activities, counterfeiting U.S. currency. The Unione Siciliana headquarters also became an ideal place for eliminating Black Hand rivals and uncooperative extortion targets. When it was searched by the police in 1901, the corpses and body parts of sixty murder victims were found. The building entered the annals of New York City crime as the "Murder Stable."

The policeman who led the raid was Lieutenant Joseph Petrosino. Born in Italy in 1860, he had known of the Black Hand's activities there and hadn't been surprised to learn that it had been transplanted to New York. But when he discovered that one of Saietta's extortion victims was opera star Enrico Caruso, and that threats sent to the world's most famous Italian (except the Pope) had resulted in Saietta collecting 10 percent of Caruso's earnings for several years, he confronted Saietta. Shoving a pistol against the gangster's head, he warned, "If you bother Mr. Caruso anywhere on earth, I will find you and blow your brains out."

When the New York police were feeling pressure from Italians to crack down on the Black Hand, and criticized for "English-speaking, English-thinking" methods, the NYPD set up a special Italian branch in 1906 and put its only Italian-speaking officer (Petrosino) in charge. A year later, the unit was renamed the "Italian Legion." Promoted to lieutenant, making him the highest-ranking Italian-American police officer in the United States, Petrosino made breaking up the Black Hand a personal crusade. In pursuit of that goal, he traveled to Palermo with photos of known Black Hand members suspected of having fled there from New York.

Alerted to Petrosino's presence, the Sicilian Mafia unleashed a team of assassins to find him. Gunned down on March 12, 1909, he again made history as the only New York City cop to be killed in the line of duty in another country. His killers were never found.

The criminal reign of Lupo Saietta ended the following year. Convicted of counterfeiting, along with Joe Morello, he was sentenced to thirty years in federal prison. Paroled after serving ten, he found that his gang had been taken over by Joe Morello's brothers, Nicholas and Vincenzo, and Ciro Terranova. A year later (1921), after a struggle for the control of the crime family that included several rubouts and attempted assassinations, Saietta's gang passed into the hands of Joseph Masseria. Allied with Salvatore Lucania, also known as Charles "Lucky" Luciano, Masseria ruled organized crime until he was eliminated by Benjamin "Bugsy" Siegel on Luciano's orders. When Luciano was sent to prison, the family was controlled by Vito Genovese and is still identified as such.

Arrested for racketeering in 1936, Saietta was ordered to the federal prison in Atlanta to serve the remainder of his thirty-year counterfeiting sentence. Released two years later because of poor health, he lived in obscurity for eleven years. With the distinction of having been one of the twentieth century's most vicious mass murderers, and having been the first head of a crime "family," he died of natural causes in Brooklyn, New York, on January 13, 1947.

88

RUBOUT OF
PAUL CASTELLANO

In every decade of the twentieth century, law-abiding Americans in the nation's largest cities could count on learning of outbursts of warfare between rival factions of the world's oldest and longest criminal conspiracy. Whether it was called the "Black Hand," "Syndicate," "Mafia," "La Cosa Nostra," the "Mob," the "Underworld," and what law enforcement agencies termed "Organized Crime," the evolving and eventually nationally coordinated web of gangsters regularly engaged in outbursts of violence, mayhem, and assassinations of competing mob bosses. During one of these eruptions in the 1940s, one of the most vicious of the Mafia's killers, Benjamin "Bugsy" Siegel, assured a general public that was at once scared, fascinated, and outraged not to be concerned. Shortly before mob gunmen rubbed him out in Los Angeles, he had offered the assurance, "We only kill each other."

While Siegel relished being in the limelight as he blasted his way to the top of the mob in Manhattan as Lucky Luciano's handsome, debonair, and gun-happy ally, homely-looking and publicity-shy Carlo Gambino was constructing a gang in Brooklyn that became the largest of the five New York Mafia gangs and still bears his name.

When "Don Carlo" died in 1976 at the age of seventy-four (natural causes), most "Gambino family" members who expected control of the gang to go to Gambino's second-in-command (underboss), Anielo "Neil" Dellacroce, were shocked to learn that their new boss would be Gambino's son-in-law.

Born in Brooklyn in 1915, Constantino Paul "Big Paulie" Castellano shared Gambino's desire to avoid the kind of notoriety that had surrounded mobsters in the years of Luciano and Siegel. A rarity among underworld figures in that he'd never been arrested and avoided public attention as scrupulously as his father-in-law, he saw himself not as a traditional gang boss, but as a businessman running a company with legitimate worldwide interests. Although many of the family's members were unhappy with their new boss—including an ambitious ally of Dellacroce named John Gotti, who thought Dellacroce should have inherited control of the family—as long as Castellano had Dellacroce's loyalty, there was nothing they could do. That situation changed on December 2, 1985, with Dellacroce's death from lung cancer.

Seizing the moment, Gotti began plotting Castellano's assassination. As explained by Gotti's chief lieutenant, Sammy "the Bull" Gravano, in *Underboss*, a book co-authored by crime-writer Peter Maas, "We concluded that nine days before Christmas, around five to six o'clock at night, in the middle of Manhattan, in the middle of the rush hour, in the middle of the crush of all them shoppers buying presents, there would be literally thousands of people on the street, hurrying this way and that. The hit would only take a few seconds, and the confusion would be in our favor. Nobody would be expecting anything like this, last of all Paul."

Gravano was right. Shortly after he and Gotti arrived at the corner of Third Avenue and Forty-sixth Street, about a quarter of a block from Sparks Steak House, between Third and Second, they watched Castellano's car, driven by trusted aide and bodyguard Thomas Bilotti (unarmed), and signaled the quartet of killers by walkie-talkie. Castellano arrived expecting to have dinner with Dellacroce's nephew. Barely out of the car, he was greeted by four men. Dressed in identical trench coats and Russian style fur hats, they pulled guns and opened fire at point-blank range. An instant later, Bilotti was gunned down. Confident that witnesses would have been looking at their matching outfits and not at their faces, the killers ran to Second Avenue and got away.

Having masterminded and carried out one of the most spectacular rubouts in the history of the Mafia, Gotti and Gravano drove slowly past the murder scene. With Castellano's blood pouring onto the sidewalk and into the gutter from six bullet wounds, and Bilotti lying in the street, Gravano said, "He's gone."

Having made himself the undisputed boss of the Gambino family, John Gotti ruled with a flair for publicity and basked in the nickname "Teflon Don" for years because of the inability of federal prosecutors to put him in prison. When the FBI ultimately obtained a tape-recording of Gotti plotting to have Gravano killed to keep him from testifying in a federal trial, Sammy the Bull cut a deal to reduce his sentence for more than a dozen murders in exchange for providing testimony against Gotti. Convicted on charges that included five murders, Gotti was sentenced to life without parole, but continued to rule the Gambino family, first through his son, John Jr., and then through his brother Peter. With them facing federal prosecution, and serving his sentence in solitary confinement in the federal government's toughest prison at Marion, Indiana, the man who had carried out one of the most sensational rubouts in the more than one-hundred-year history of Mafia conspiracies in the United States died of cancer on June 11, 2002.

89

THE JAMES BROTHERS

When a telegraph message reached the offices of the *New York Evening Post* on April 3, 1882, that the notorious leader of a gang of murderous train and bank robbers, Jesse James, had been shot in the back and killed while hanging a picture in the parlor of his Missouri home by a traitorous friend, the newspaper's renowned editor, Carl Schurz, followed a time-tested maxim of journalism that held, "When the choice is between the truth and legend, print the legend."

Contributing to an idealized portrait provided by eastern writers of the country's most famous bandit and central figure of outlaw gangs in the West as an American version of Robin Hood whom writers of popular dime novels and articles had romanticized as the leader of outlaw gangs in the West, Schurz wrote, "All the great robbers of old times, and of other countries, lived in caves, or in mountain fastness, to which it was difficult for troops to pursue them, or they kept to the sea in long, low, rakish black schooners. James, however, lived in a comfortable house, surrounded by a loving family, and went off on his expeditions apparently as a business man goes off to collect debts or to solicit orders."

A bandit for fifteen years, Jesse Woodson James was born on September 8, 1847, in Kearney, Missouri. In 1863, at age seventeen, he followed his older brother Frank in enlisting in the Confederate cause by joining Quantrill's Raiders. Operating as guerillas, they attacked and pillaged Union towns. Tagged with the nickname "Dingus," and participating in raids and outright massacres whose primary purpose was to enrich their rapacious leader, William Clarke Quantrill, he got through the war unscathed until after the defeat of Robert E. Lee's army in April 1865. As he was trying to surrender, he was mistakenly shot in the lung by a Union soldier. Recuperating in the care of a cousin and his future wife, Zerelda Mimms, he was unable to accompany Frank James and a friend, Cole Younger, in sticking up a bank in Liberty, Missouri in February 1866 that netted them $57,000. Joining the gang a year later, Jesse participated in several robberies of what was now widely known and feared in Missouri and Kentucky as the James-Younger gang.

After six years of knocking off banks, often at great risk to their lives from armed guards and lawmen, Jesse proposed an easier and decidedly safer method of enrichment in the form of railroads. The result was the first stickup of a train. Stopping a Chicago and Rock Island Line train near Adair, Iowa, on July 21, 1873, by removing a portion of the track, they looted the safe in the express car of $2,000, helped themselves to the money and valuables of passengers, and killed the train's engineer. On January 31, 1874, they robbed an Iron Mountain Railway train in Wayne County, Missouri.

Because of these heists, and the murder of the engineer, the railroad companies brought in the Pinkerton National Detective Agency. Hundreds of agents fanned out to search for the gang. When agents located their hideout at Roscoe, Missouri, on January 31, 1874, Jim Younger was captured and his brother John was killed. In a shootout during a raid on another hideout on January 25, 1875, Jesse and Frank barely escaped. Undaunted by the close call, and despite being hunted by the Pinkertons, they formed another gang that included Cole, Jim, and Bob Younger, Bill Chadwell, Charlie Pitt, and Clell Miller. Riding into Northfield, Minnesota, on September 6, 1876, to hold up the bank, they were ambushed by townspeople. Only Jesse and Frank avoided death, serious wounds, or capture.

After lying low for three years and passing part of that time working at a gold strike in California, and befriending brothers Bob and

Charlie Ford, the bandit siblings many Americans romanticized as "the James boys" renewed their escapades with a new gang. After the holdup of a Chicago and Alton Line train in October 1879, they pulled four railway heists in 1881. By now Jesse was using the alias Tom Howard. Living in St. Joseph, Missouri, he appeared to be an upright and respectable citizen, fine husband, and good father of a boy, Jesse, and a girl, Mary.

Why Bob and Charles Ford took advantage of Jesse's turned back to kill him as he was hanging a picture in the parlor of his house on April 3, 1882, remains debatable. Some believe the Ford brothers conspired to collect a reward of $10,000. Others say Jesse was romantically involved with Bob Ford's wife. Even more fascinating was a widely held belief that the man Ford killed wasn't really Jesse James, but that Jesse lived to old age in Guthrie, Oklahoma. A theory that the body lying under Jesse's tombstone isn't Jesse was dispelled in 1995 through a DNA test that indicated a 99.7 percent probability that it's him.

Sentenced to hang for Jesse's murder, the Fords were pardoned by Missouri's governor. Two years later, Charles committed suicide. Robert Ford was killed during a barroom brawl in Creede, Colorado, in 1892.

Frank James turned himself in to the law on October 5, 1882. Tried for the murder of a passenger during the robbery of a Chicago and Rock Island Line train in Missouri in 1881, he was acquitted. He never went back to banditry and died peacefully at age seventy-two on March 21, 1916.

90

THE FALCON
AND THE SNOWMAN

When boyhood friends Christopher John Boyce and Andrew Daulton Lee conspired to provide top-secret information on new American spy-in-the-sky technology to the Soviet Union in April 1975, they were motivated by a combination of a desire for money, lack of ambition, superficial and naive knowledge about international affairs, and contempt for what they believed was a decline in the country's social and political standards. They had also forged a bond through an interest in falconry and smoking marijuana.

Although intellectually gifted, with an IQ of 142, Boyce had been a lackluster student at Harbor Junior College and had dropped out of Loyola University in 1973. With the assistance of his father (a former FBI agent employed as director of security for a large California firm), he was hired as a $140-a-week clerk by TRW. An aerospace corporation located at Redondo Beach, California, it developed intelligence-gathering satellites and their code systems for the Central Intelligence Agency, including a system called Rhyolite. Designed to orbit at 18,000 miles and detect sounds of missile engines in China and the Soviet Union, eavesdrop on coded electronic communications, and relay the data to CIA ground stations in Australia and Great Britain, it was regarded by the U.S. intelligence community as the most significant technical development in espionage since the cracking of a Nazi military code machine in World War II.

Within five months of being hired by TRW, Boyce was given top-secret clearance and assigned to work in the "Black Vault," with the responsibility of making daily changes of the Rhyolite-controlling cipher keys. Boasting of his new position while smoking marijuana with Lee, who was now a cocaine addict and drug dealer, he noted the irony of a twenty-one-year-old, marijuana-smoking, college dropout having been entrusted with one of America's most-guarded secrets. Pondering this, he mused, "That stuff would be worth a lot of money to a foreign power."

Excited about the possibility of making easy money, they agreed that Lee would fly to Mexico City and offer their services to the Soviet Union. A week later, Lee approached a guard at the Soviet Embassy, and announced that he could provide information "of interest" to the USSR. Admitted to the embassy, he handed a wary attaché (Boris Alexei Grishin of the KGB) a twelve-inch paper tape used in the TRW code machines that contained Rhyolite data. After an examination of the tape, Grishin handed Lee $250 to cover his travel expenses and promised to pay $10,000 for each delivery of material.

After about a year of such transactions, Boyce suspected that Lee was cheating him of his full share of the money (Lee was in fact keeping $7,000 of each payment) and went to Mexico City for his first meeting with Grishin. The meeting ended with an agreement that for $75,000 Boyce would provide data on development of a U.S. satellite spy system code-named Pyramider.

Before Boyce could deliver the material, Lee showed up at the embassy with the intent of satisfying his need for a cocaine fix by selling filmstrips of TRW secret documents.

Stopped by Mexican police on suspicion that he was a terrorist, he was searched. When the film was found, he was turned over to agents of the FBI. Confessing his role as courier in the espionage conspiracy, he revealed the source of the data. Picked up in Los Angeles, Boyce admitted to copying thousands of documents that Lee had delivered to the Soviets. Convicted in 1977, Boyce was sentenced to forty years in federal prison. Lee was given life.

Three years into his term, Boyce and two other prisoners escaped from the federal prison in Lompoc, California, and went on a bank robbery spree throughout Idaho, Washington, and Montana. Captured a few weeks later, he was returned to prison to complete his sentence.

While Andrew Daulton Lee was released on parole after eleven years (in 1998), Boyce served more than a quarter of a century. Freed in March 2003, to be on parole until 2046, he offered an explanation of why he had betrayed his country. "When you're young," he said to reporters, "you crave danger or are willing to put yourselves in dangerous situations."

During Boyce and Lee's incarceration, a book about their exploits, *The Falcon and the Snowman: A True Story of Friendship and Espionage*, by Robert Lindsey, became a best-seller and was made into a successful movie starring Timothy Hutton as Boyce and Sean Penn as Lee.

Asked about the code names derived from Boyce's interest in falconry and Lee's cocaine use, Boyce said, "It's a snazzy title for a book and a movie, but I don't have any recollection of someone calling me that."

91.

SACCO AND VANZETTI

Eight decades after Nicola Sacco and Bartolomeo Vanzetti were hanged for the murder of a shoe-factory paymaster and a guard in the town of Braintree, Massachusetts, on April 15, 1920, historians and legal experts continue to debate whether the Italian immigrants had been criminal conspirators who got what they deserved, or victims of a national hysteria based on fears of foreigners, socialists, communists, and anarchists.

Known as the "Red Scare," it resulted from a widely held conviction that a conspiracy of radical elements existed for the purpose of attacking and destroying American institutions. It was during a period following World War I, wrote social historian Frederick Allen Lewis, when millions of Americans thought that a "Red revolution might begin in the United States the next month or week, and they were less concerned with making the world safe for democracy than with making America safe for themselves."

Although the arrests of Sacco and Vanzetti for the robbery and murders had attracted little attention from the press beyond Massachusetts in the weeks following the holdup, when the two admitted anarchists were convicted and sentenced to death on July 14, 1921, their plight became a rallying point not only for radical sympathizers in the U.S. and around the world, but also for thousands of observers of their trials who believed they had been the victims of misconduct by the police and prosecution and prejudice by the judge.

As demonstrations took place across Europe, including a protest at the U.S. embassy in Paris that required the mobilization of 10,000 police and 18,000 French soldiers, intellectuals in the United States and elsewhere voiced outrage and formed committees in an effort to overturn the judgment. Joining in the movement were writers John Dos Passos, Upton Sinclair, Thomas Mann, and Dorothy Parker; poet Edna Saint Vincent Millay; playwright George Bernard Shaw; historian H. G. Wells, philosopher Bertrand Russell, scientist Albert Einstein, and thousands of other Americans.

With the financial aid of scores of celebrities, lawyers for Sacco and Vanzetti filed an appeal on grounds that evidence had been manipulated, that non-English-speaking witnesses had been intimidated or tricked, and that Judge Webster Thayer had been openly biased. This belief was reinforced when Thayer rejected the first appeal for a new trial in October 1924, followed by denials of five similar motions. When a statement by a convicted murderer that he had been the one who committed the murders was offered, Thayer found the confession "untruthful."

Asked to review the trial proceedings, the highest court in Massachusetts found nothing in the record of Thayer's handling of the case to support allegations of legal error or judicial discretion. Following formal sentencing of Sacco and Vanzetti on April 9, 1927, an attempt to save their lives by an appeal to Governor Alvan T. Fuller to commute the sentences resulted in the governor's appointment of a committee to review the case. Headed by Harvard University President Abbott Lawrence Lowell, it interviewed 102 witnesses, in addition to those who had testified in the trial. After two months of investigating, the committee concluded that the pair had received a fair trial.

Following a final appeal to the U.S. Supreme Court that was turned aside on the basis on the Court's lack of jurisdiction, Sacco and Vanzetti were executed in the Massachusetts electric chair on August 23, 1927.

Writer Edmund Wilson saw in the outcome of the case "the whole anatomy of American life with all its classes, professions, and points of view and all their relations" that "raised almost every fundamental question of our political and social system."

"The importance of the Sacco-Vanzetti case remains not only because it called into question some of the fundamental assumptions of American society," wrote historian Robert D'Attilio, "but because it calls into question some of the assumptions of American history."

On the fiftieth anniversary of the execution, Massachusetts Governor Michael Dukakis issued a proclamation absolving them.

92

RUTH SNYDER
AND JUDD GRAY

When "Roaring Twenties" New York newspaperman Damon Runyon learned that a Queens housewife, Ruth Snyder, and her corset-salesman lover from New Jersey, Henry Judd Gray, had conspired to murder her husband Albert, the art editor for *Motor Boating Magazine*, so she could collect on Albert's $96,000 life insurance policy, he joined an army of reporters in rushing across the East River to provide their sensation-hungry readers with every juicy detail of the killing. None rose as brilliantly to the job as the country's famous chronicler of the colorful "guys and dolls" of the steamy side of Broadway and the city's shady underworld of gamblers, bootleggers, and speakeasies.

When the pair went on trial on April 19, 1927, in what Runyon called, "for the want of a better name, The Dumb-Bell Murder," he began his account by describing Snyder as a "chilly looking blonde with frosty eyes and one of those marble, you-bet-you-will chins." Gray was "an inert scare-drunk fellow that you couldn't miss among any hundred men as a dead set-up for a blonde, or the shell game."

Lovers since Ruth met Judd in a Manhattan speakeasy in 1925, they'd begun planning to eliminate Albert in late 1926. Soon after, Albert found himself nearly killed when his car fell off a jack while he was repairing it and was almost asphyxiated when a gas jet was "inadvertently" left open. Describing how they finally succeeded on the night of Sunday, March 20, 1927, Runyon wrote, "They killed Snyder as he slumbered, first whacking him on the head with a sash weight, then giving him a few whiffs of chloroform, and finally tightening a strand of picture wire around his throat so he wouldn't revive. This matter disposed of, they went into an adjoining room and had a few drinks of whiskey, and talked things over. They thought they had committed 'the perfect crime,' [but] it was the most imperfect crime on record."

When Judd's first blow failed to kill Snyder, Ruth grabbed the sash weight and finished the task. To make the murder appear to have been committed by a burglar, they upset furniture and made drawers look as if they had been ransacked. Judd then headed for a hotel in Syracuse to resume selling girdles to stores specializing in women's garments. When Ruth called police, she reported the theft of some jewelry. Unfortunately the items were discovered hidden under a mattress. They also found the bloodstained sash weight, a check made out to H. Judd Gray, and Gray's tie clip. After a life insurance policy on Judd with a double-indemnity clause in case of accident or murder, with Ruth named as the beneficiary, was found in her safe deposit box, she admitted to the murder. Quickly picked up, Judd also immediately confessed. Blaming the plot on Ruth, he depicted himself as a victim who had been seduced and coerced because Ruth had "hypnotized" him with "drink, veiled threats, and intensive love."

"It was stupid beyond imagination," Runyon wrote of the murder plot. Of its author, he noted, "Her eyes are blue-green, and as chilly looking as an ice cream cone. If all that Henry Judd Gray says of her action the night of the murder is true, her veins are ice water."

Newspaper headline writers called her "The Iron Widow" and "The Bloody Blonde."

On May 9, 1927, the jurors needed only an hour and a half to convict her and Judd. The date set for their execution in the electric chair at Sing Sing prison was January 1928. Judd went first (January 22). As the juice surged through him, his shoes caught fire.

At the moment that the switch was thrown to execute Ruth on January 29, a reporter for the *New York Daily News*, Thomas Howard, crossed his legs in the front row of observers, pulled up a trouser leg to unveil a small camera he'd strapped to his ankle, and snapped one picture. It appeared on the newspaper's front page in the next edition under the headline DEAD!

While the sensational photo and Damon Runyon's vivid accounts of the murder and trial enshrined Ruth Snyder and Judd Gray in the ranks of inept conspirators, another reporter of the case, James M. Cain, found the plot and its central figures so fascinating that he used them as an inspiration for two best-selling crime novels, *Double Indemnity* and *The Postman Always Rings Twice*, that have become classic crime films.

93.

THE PURPLE GANG

Often overshadowed in histories of crime during America's Prohibition era by exploits of the Al Capone gang in Chicago and Lucky Luciano's mobsters in New York, the Purple Gang of Detroit was no less high profile in their methods of operation and savagery in dealing with its rivals and enemies. It evolved in the years immediately following World War I from packs of juvenile delinquents, most of them the children of recently immigrated Russian Jews.

Although the origin of the gang's name is uncertain, author and historian Paul R. Kavieff attributed it to a conversation between two shopkeepers whose stores had been frequent targets of the gang's shoplifting and vandalism. In disgust, one of the shopkeepers exclaimed, "These boys are not like other children of their age, they're tainted, off color." "Yes," said the other. "They're rotten, purple like the color of bad meat, they're a Purple Gang."

Led by four brothers, Abe, Joe, Raymond, and Isadore (Izzy) Bernstein, the Purples, as they were known, were never a tightly organized criminal syndicate, but a loose confederation of predominantly Jewish members. With the start of Prohibition, they began hijacking liquor loads from older and more established gangs of bootleggers who'd smuggled the hooch from Canada. Kavieff notes that it was "common practice for the Purples to take a load of liquor and shoot whoever was with it."

With their numbers swelled by the influx of mobsters from other cities who flocked to Detroit to cash in on the golden harvest of bootlegging, the Purple Gang prospered enough to move into other rackets. During a period of strife in the Detroit laundry and cleaning industry, known as the Cleaners and Dyers War, the Purple Gang used bombings, beatings, and murder on behalf of whatever competing labor union leaders hired them. When the turmoil resulted in "the Purple Gang Trial" of 1928, all Purple Gang defendants were acquitted. Emerging from the trial unscathed, the gang became the dominant force in the Detroit underworld and ruled it from 1927 to 1932. During this period, it controlled Detroit's vice, gambling, liquor, and narcotics trade, along with running the wire service that provided racing information to all of the Detroit horse betting parlors and bookies. Noting that the gang even became suppliers of Canadian whiskey to the Capone organization in Chicago, Kavieff explained that after Capone was told by the Detroit underworld to keep his operation out of the city, Al decided it was more prudent to make the Purples his liquor agents rather than go to war with them. After Capone's massacre of enemies in Chicago in the St. Valentine's Day Massacre, several Purple Gang members became suspects. Because the gang also specialized in kidnapping for ransom, it was initially suspected of carrying out the Lindbergh baby abduction. It's believed that in its years of operations, the gang was responsible for at least five hundred murders.

Like other gangs of the 1920s and 1930s, the Purples provided colorful characters who contributed to the lore of the "tough guy." When twenty-three-year-old Sam Drapkin became one of a very small handful of gangsters to survive a bullet during a "one-way ride" in February 1932, he was asked by a Detroit detective to name the gunman. Lifting his head from a hospital bed pillow, Drapkin answered, "Santa Claus shot me." It was not his first experience with the business end of a gun. In July 1927, at age eighteen, he was hit nine times in a machine gun attack. Said to have "a charmed life," he outlived most of his Purple Gang pals. He died in 1965 at the age of fifty-six.

The end of the Purple Gang's power began in 1931 with the murder of three Purples by members of their own gang because they'd violated an underworld code by operating outside the territory allotted to them by the Purple Gang leadership. Called the "Little Jewish Navy," Hymie Paul, Isadore Sutker, and Joe Lebowitz owned several boats used for liquor smuggling, but when they decided to strike out on their own, they were lured to an apartment on Collingwood Avenue on September 16, 1931. Believing they were going to a peace conference with the Purple Gang leaders, they went unarmed and were shot to death by the men they had gone to meet. When a bookie named Sol Levine, who'd transported them to the fatal rendezvous, was arrested soon afterwards, he turned State's witness. Arrested for what was known as the Collingwood Manor Massacre, three of the Purples involved in the murders, Irving Milberg, Harry Keywell, and Raymond Bernstein, were convicted of first degree murder and sent to prison for life.

Although the Purple Gang remained a power in the Detroit underworld until 1935, the prison sentences of its top leadership and intergang rivalries that followed eventually depleted the gang's ranks and operating strength. This vacuum opened the door for the forerunner of the present Detroit Mafia to step in and fill the void.

94.

THE TONGS

When the work of thousands of Chinese who had been encouraged to immigrate to the United States in the middle of the nineteenth century to fill a need for cheap laborers in the building of railroads in the West was completed, they remained in the country and settled in sections of large cities that got the name "Chinatown." While sustaining themselves economically with the introduction of the "Chinese laundry" and adding Chinese food to the American dinner menu, they sought to retain and nurture their national identity through three types of associations. The first was familial. Organized by surname, they assisted new immigrants by providing work and social support upon arrival. The second type, the merchant association, was a combination of labor union and civic benevolent society designed to help fight discriminatory legislation, create mutual aid networks, and ensure that workers were properly treated. The third form, the Tong (meeting hall), proved to be a means by which hard-working Chinese became the victims of a reign of terror.

A Chinese variation of the Sicilian Black Hand, the Tongs demanded payoffs to provide "protection" to individuals, merchants, and operators of gambling and opium dens. Any businessman who refused to comply was subjected to beatings, kidnapping of relatives, arson, and bombings. This extortion business became so lucrative that Tongs began competing for control of territories. So-called "Tong Wars" erupted in Chinatowns throughout the U.S. from the 1850s to the 1930s. One of the most famous of the conflicts was in New York City and lasted for thirty years. The On Leon Tong leader was Tom Lee. The Hip Sing Tong was led by Mock Duck, described by journalist and New York historian Herbert Asbury in his 1927 book, *The Gangs of New York*, as "a bland, fat, moon-faced little man who was ambitious to rule the district as Emperor, and became the terror of Chinatown."

These Tong leaders and their men protected themselves with chain-mail shirts, carried pistols, and tucked hatchets in the spacious sleeves of their garments (hence the term "hatchet man"). Mock Duck, noted Asbury, was "a curious mixture of bravery and cowardice" who at times fought bravely, "squatting on his haunches in the street with both eyes shut, and blazing away at a surrounding circle of On Leons with an utter disregard of his own safety." At other times he fled New York for the safety of Chicago or San Francisco. When a truce was arranged in 1906 by a New York State judge, a huge celebration unfolded at which Tom Lee drank 107 mugs of rice wine. Within a week, the war was on again, requiring the judge (with the help of the government of China) to step in again. The truce he obtained stuck until the outbreak of an even larger Tong War in 1909 that raged off and on throughout the 1920s. Tom Lee died in 1917 at the age of seventy-six. Mock Duck retired from the battlefield in the 1930s and died at age sixty-two of natural causes on July 24, 1941.

While Tongs still exist in the United States, they are not like those of their colorful street-fighting ancestors. Today's groups have close ties to international organizations called "Triads" that run illegal immigration networks in which Chinese are smuggled into the United States and forced to work in sweatshops or in prostitution to pay the fee. Tongs also engage in illegal gambling and heroin dealing, almost exactly what they were doing when the associations first originated in the United States more than 150 years ago.

According to author Martin Booth in *The Dragon Syndicates: The Global Phenomenon of the Triads* (2000), what began more than two thousand years earlier in China has culminated in the greatest potential criminal threat the world has ever known. Chinese Triads, with links to U.S. Tongs, engage in extortion, gambling, international prostitution, immigrant smuggling, money laundering, fraud, corruption, arms-dealing, and narcotics. Originally little more than societies founded on mutual self-interest, Booth asserts, the Triads have evolved into a criminal fraternity bound by archaic oaths and quasi-religious rituals that can visit on transgressors and opponents "death by a thousand cuts."

95.

GERMAN-AMERICAN BUND

An American pro-Nazi organization founded in 1936, the German-American Bund, also known as "Friends of the New Germany," traced its roots to the Teutonia Society of the 1920s. Based in the predominately German-American Yorkville section of New York, with a branch in Los Angeles, it was led by German-born Fritz Julius Kuhn. Claiming to be 100 percent American and for the "constitution and flag," while promoting anti-Semitism and "white gentile-ruled, truly free America," it had as its purpose the turning of American public opinion in favor of the "New Germany" of the Nazis. While it claimed to have a national membership of 50,000 at the peak of its influence, the FBI put the figure at 6,600.

Emulating Germany's Nazis, Bund members wore three kinds of uniforms. The rank and file donned black trousers, black caps, and white shirts with red-white-and-black swastika armbands. A troop of strong-arm thugs who protected Bund marches and demonstrations wore olive drab military-style outfits. The top leaders sported actual German uniforms. Among its activities were publishing a newspaper and magazine, operating youth camps patterned on the "Hitler Youth" of Germany, organizing street demonstrations, and holding rallies.

At the largest of these public meetings, held in Madison Square Garden, an audience of 22,000 heard Kuhn heap scorn on President Franklin D. Roosevelt, New York's Mayor Fiorello LaGuardia, and New York District Attorney Thomas E. Dewey for being pro-Jewish. FDR was "President Rosenfeld." LaGuardia, whose mother was Jewish, was called "the Jew lumpen LaGuardia." Dewey was "Jewey." Because this rally and others resulted in violent clashes between Bundists and their opponents, an official report of the New York State Legislature noted that the Friends of New Germany, "chiefly through the stupidity of its leaders, brought a great deal of unfavorable publicity upon the organization."

When nationally syndicated columnist Heywood Broun warned in 1937 that there was "a considerable body of Nazi-like storm troopers here in America, drilling and holding rifle practice," and that "their loyalty is palpably directed toward Hitler," FDR directed the justice department to investigate. While the FBI reported in 1938 that Bund activities had a "tendency to be subversive," it noted that they did not violate federal laws and were protected by the Bill of Rights of the U.S. Constitution.

Partly as a result of publicity surrounding the Bund, the U.S. House of Representatives authorized a committee to investigate the influence of Fascist and Communist groups within the United States. Headed by Congressman Martin Dies, it eventually became known as the House Un-American Activities Committee (HUAC). It probed Communist infiltration in the federal government, conducted an investigation into whether former State Department official Alger Hiss was a Soviet spy, and investigated Communist influence in the movie industry.

Frustrated and angry that the Bund could not be shut down by the federal government on the basis of its program of hate and Nazi sympathies, Mayor Fiorello LaGuardia and District Attorney Thomas E. Dewey decided to start an investigation into the group's financial structure for "sales tax irregularities." After Dewey's men descended on the Bund headquarters on May 2, 1939, the group's newspaper screamed in a headline, JEW YORK DEMOCRACY IN ACTION. Called before a grand jury on May 18, Kuhn refused to testify and was indicted for tax fraud. He then fled the state, only to be captured in

Pennsylvania on his way to Mexico. After a six-week trial, he was convicted of embezzlement of Bund funds and given two to five years in prison. While he was serving his term, the United States was fighting a war with Germany, other Bundists were in prison, and the Bund was outlawed by the U.S. government. Returned to Germany after the war, Fritz Kuhn, a man who'd believed he could become the Nazi ruler of the United States, died in 1951 in obscurity.

96.

PLOT TO ASSASSINATE PRESIDENT TRUMAN

When two members of the Puerto Rican Nationalist Party, Oscar Collazo and Griselio Torresola, traveled from the Bronx, New York, to Washington, D.C., on November 1, 1950, they believed that if they could kill President Harry S. Truman, the assassination would advance the cause of Puerto Rican independence. A skilled gunman, Torresola had taught Collazo how to load and handle a pistol.

Because the Truman family had moved into a government residence (Blair House, across Pennsylvania Avenue from the White House) while the executive mansion was being renovated, the pair of would-be assassins planned to approach Blair House from opposite directions and shoot their way inside. Observed by Secret Service agents and White House policemen, they drew their weapons and began a gun battle in which one of the guards, Private Leslie Coffelt, ignored a bullet wound and got off a shot that hit Torresola in the side of the head, killing him instantly. Coffelt died later in a hospital.

Two other policemen, Donald Birdzell and Joseph Downs, were each hit more than once but recovered from their wounds. While Collazo had been able to reach the steps of Blair House before collapsing with a gunshot wound to the chest, it was later found that only one shot fired by Collazo had hit anyone (Birdzell). Torresola had wounded the three White House policemen.

During a battle that lasted less than three minutes, about thirty shots had been fired.

As the shootout began, Truman was napping in an upstairs bedroom. When he rushed to a window to see what was happening, an agent yelled to him to get back from the window and get down. An account of the assassination attempt in the Truman presidential library noted, "The President obeyed."

Ten minutes later, Truman left Blair House by a backdoor to deliver a scheduled speech at the dedication of a statue at Arlington National Cemetery in Virginia. "A president has to expect such things," he calmly informed an aide as he arrived. He later said to Admiral William Leahy, "The only thing you have to worry about [when you're President] is bad luck. I never have bad luck." In an interview with Merle Miller, author of *Plain Speaking: An Oral Biography of Harry S. Truman*, he explained, "Getting shot at was nothing I worried about when I was President. It wouldn't have done the slightest good if I had. My opinion has always been that if you're in an office like that and someone wants to shoot you, they'll probably do it, and nothing can help you out. It just goes with the job, and I don't think there's any way to prevent it."

At a trial in 1951, Collazo ignored his attorney's advice that he plead insanity and gave an impassioned oration from the witness stand on the "brutal exploitation of Puerto Rico" by the United States. The jury found him guilty of murder, attempted assassination, and assault with intent to kill. Because his conspiracy with Torresola had made him a principal in the murder of Coffelt, Judge T. Alan Goldsborough sentenced him to death. A higher court upheld the verdict, and the Supreme Court refused to hear the case. The execution was set for August 1, 1952. On July 24, Truman commuted the sentence to life-imprisonment.

Two years later on Capitol Hill, three Puerto Rican Nationalists, Lolita Lebron, Rafael Cancel Miranda, and Andres Figueroa, opened fire from seats in the visitors' gallery of the U.S. House of Representatives. Shooting German automatic pistols and waving the Puerto Rican flag, they shouted, "Puerto Rico is not free." By the time they were overpowered and disarmed, they had wounded five members of Congress. They were sentenced to life terms.

A quarter of a century later, President Jimmy Carter commuted all the sentences.

Collazo returned to Puerto Rico and died there on February 20, 1994, at the age of eighty.

97.

THE BILLIONAIRE BOYS CLUB

Symbolic of the greed and the "me generation" of the 1980s, the Billionaire Boys Club was a conspiracy involving a group of privileged, bright young men that began with financial fraud and extended to kidnapping and two murders. Envisioned by its founder, Joe Hunt, as an investment company that would also be a social club for him and his friends, the BBC initially included two of his classmates, Dean Karny and Ben Dosti, at the prestigious Harvard prep school in Los Angeles.

"In an era and place where image was everything," noted one account of the rise and fall of the BBC, "it was not difficult for three attractive and well-dressed young men from an elite background to charm gullible investors into giving up their money. In reality, Hunt was not investing this money at all. Instead, he was using whatever he brought in to pay the rent, throw lavish parties, and build up his fleet of cars."

In an article for the Court TV "Crime Library" website, Katharine Ramsland noted that Hunt "liked to persuade people that life was best lived and business best done according to what he called 'paradox' philosophy." A combination of situational and utilitarian ethics, it held that the end justified the means. In Hunt's view, whatever had to be done to attain one's objective was not only permissible, but also required. Through a combination of personal charm, the force of his personality, 1980s hedonism, and raw opportunism, he recruited additional BBC members who were always young men with "good breeding" and from wealthy families who were eager to embrace Hunt's ideas for living luxuriously on the money of wealthy people who were quick to believe that Hunt and the BBC would make them even richer.

When this idyllic life became threatened by Hunt spending the backers' money, rather than investing it, and increasing pressures on the group to settle debts, Hunt began a business relationship with another wheeler-dealer, Ron Levin, who proved to be as much a con-man as Hunt. When promises of fast profits made to Hunt by Levin weren't fulfilled, Hunt decided to capture him, force him to sign a check for $1.5 million, and then kill him. After a plan that he wrote down in a detailed, step-by-step, "things to do" list was carried out on June 6, 1984, in Levin's home, his body was stuffed into the trunk of a BMW, taken to Soledad Canyon (about an hour's drive from Los Angeles), and dumped. To Hunt's surprise and dismay, expectations that Levin's check would resolve the BBC's financial dilemma were dashed when Levin's New York City bank refused to honor it.

A few weeks later, a newly recruited BBC member, Reza Eslaminia, suggested to Hunt that a quick way out of the money crunch would be to kidnap Reza's father, Hedayat Eslaminia, and force him to sign over his assets to Reza. The son reasoned that because Eslaminia was a rich Iranian political exile living in California, the police would attribute the abduction and murder to agents of Eslaminia's enemies in the Iranian government of Ayatollah Khomeini.

Dressed in brown UPS uniforms on the night of July 30, 1984, Hunt, Karny, Dosti, and a former security guard, Jim Pittman (enlisted in the plot because of his strength), drove to the Eslaminia home, knocked out Eslaminia with a dose of chloroform, and put him in a trunk in the back of a rented U-Haul truck. The scheme went wrong when they arrived at a "safe house" where they planned to force Eslaminia to sign over his assets. They found that he had died of suffocation. With their extortion plot thwarted, they removed the body from the trunk, wrapped it in a tarpaulin, and left it in Soledad Canyon.

Deeply troubled by what had occurred, Dean Karny contacted the police. Based on his testimony, Hunt, Dosti, and Reza Eslaminia were sentenced to life without parole. Because of a technical error at trial, Reza Eslaminia was ordered released in 1998 by the U. S. Ninth Circuit Court of Appeals in San Francisco. Dean Karny was given a new identity and prosecutors helped him to pursue a legal career. Despite numerous appeals, and a cost to the state of California of more than $2 million, Joe Hunt remained behind bars.

In 1987, the NBC television network dramatized the BBC in a miniseries starring Judd Nelson as Joe Hunt. Two years later, during the trial of Lyle and Eric Menendez for the shotgun murders of their parents for an inheritance, the brothers claimed they had been inspired by the story of the Billionaire Boys Club.

98.

FIXING THE 1919 WORLD SERIES

A conspiracy that resulted in the worst scandal in the history of professional baseball began on the eve of the 1919 World Series between the Chicago White Sox and the Cincinnati Reds. On September 18, Sox first baseman, Chick Gandil, invited a big-time gambler, Joseph "Sport" Sullivan, to his room in Boston's Hotel Buckminster and offered him a very tempting proposition. For $80,000 for himself and additional sums to other players whom Gandil would bring into the scheme, Sullivan would be assured of a windfall in winnings by wagering that the White Sox would lose the best-of-nine-games world championship contest.

While the revelation that some of the heavily favored to win Sox were prepared to throw the Series came as a welcome surprise to Sullivan, there was no need for Gandil to explain their willingness. Among the best players in the American League, they were paid no better than the game's worst. It was also widely-known that the club's owner, Charles Comiskey, had promised the team a bonus for winning the 1917 pennant, but instead of money, he had delivered a case of cheap champagne. The Sox were also rankled because Comiskey had promised pitcher Eddie Cicotte that if he won thirty games, he'd collect an extra $10,000. But when Cicotte racked up win number twenty-nine, Comiskey benched him.

Having made the deal with Sport Sullivan, Gandil approached Cicotte, who said he was in if he received $10,000 up front. Cicotte then enlisted pitcher Lefty Williams, shortstop Swede Risberg, and utility player Fred McMullin. Although Buck Weaver listened to Gandil's pitch, he chose not to participate. According to Gandil, the team's star, "Shoeless" Joe Jackson, agreed to take $10,000, but this was denied by Jackson. He said that he refused, but that Gandil told him it didn't matter, because the fix was in.

While Gandil was lining up teammates, Sport Sullivan was unable to personally cover the front money that was demanded. As a result, he brought in others, including the country's most notorious gambler. Known in the criminal underworld as "Mr. Big," and a man who provided financing to America's top gangsters, Arnold Rothstein had a reputation for betting on anything "that I can fix." Journalist Gene Fowler wrote that Rothstein's veins held "a solution of arsenic in ice water." Rothstein's lawyer, William J. Fallon, said Rothstein was "a man who dwells in doorways; a mouse waiting for his cheese."

Hungry for a big payoff guaranteed by the fix, Rothstein provided most of the cash for Sport Sullivan to deliver to the amenable Chicago players. On the evening before Game 1, pitcher Cicotte found $10,000 under his pillow in his hotel room. The next day, he hit the Reds' leadoff batter, Morrie Rath, to signal the gamblers that the fix was on. As the Series went on, with the White Sox disappointing their fans by losing five games, and surprising the sportswriters by not taking the Reds to a quick defeat, rumors spread about something being fishy.

Although speculation concerning a fix continued throughout the winter and into the 1920 season, it was an investigation by a grand jury into reports that the Chicago Cubs had thrown three games to the Philadelphia Phillies in 1920 that opened the door to a probe of the White Sox. Summoned to testify, Cicotte and Jackson confirmed there had been a fix. Gandil admitted nothing. When the investigation ended, eight White Sox (now being scorned by public and press as "the Black Sox"), and several gamblers (except Rothstein) were indicted for conspiracy to defraud the public. After transcripts of the grand jury confessions by Cicotte and Jackson were mysteriously lost, all eight players were acquitted because of a lack of evidence.

Meanwhile, the baseball club owners had disbanded its three-man governing commission and replaced it with Kenesaw Mountain Landis. As the game's first commissioner, he was given almost unlimited power to regulate the sport. Flexing his muscles, he brushed aside the jury's acquittal of the eight players and suspended them from the game for life. "Regardless of the verdict of juries," he declared, "no player who throws a ball game, no player who undertakes or promises to throw a ball game, no player that sits in conference with a bunch of crooked players and gamblers where the way and means of throwing a game are discussed and does not promptly tell his club about it, will ever play professional baseball."

One of the enduring stories to come of the "Black Sox Scandal" is that a teary-eyed boy looked up at Shoeless Joe Jackson and pleaded, "Say it ain't so, Joe."

Years later, Jackson said, "Charlie Owens [a sportswriter] of the *Chicago Daily News* is responsible for that [story], but there wasn't a bit of truth in it. It was supposed to have happened the day I was arrested in September of 1920, when I came out of the courtroom. There weren't any words passed between anybody except me and the deputy sheriff. Nobody else said anything to me. It just didn't happen, that's all."

99.

PROTOCOLS OF
THE ELDERS OF ZION

The most notorious forgery of a document for political purposes in the twentieth century, the "Protocols of the Learned Elders of Zion" has been used to foment hatred of Jews in every part of the world. Consisting of twenty-four sections containing the "secret plans" of a "conclave of Jewish leaders" in the last years of the nineteenth century to take control of the world, the document was the invention of the secret police (*Okhrana*) of the government of Czar Nicholas II. According to an "editor" of one version of the Protocols, the document had been stolen from a Zionist office in France. Another edition stated that it had been read at the First Zionist Congress in Switzerland in 1897. But Professor Norman Cohn in his book on the Protocols, *Warrant for Genocide*, asserts that the concept of a Jewish world-control plan was derived from a nineteenth century French political satire in which the plotters were not Jewish.

Following the Russian Revolution in 1917, supporters of the deposed Czar circulated the Protocols with the intention of discrediting the Bolsheviks by linking Communism to the Jewish plot for world domination. Ironically, the Protocols were used later by Soviet dictator Josef Stalin to assert that Jews at the center of Western capitalism were directing an anti-Soviet conspiracy. Although the Protocols were proven to be fake in 1920, the document was still presented as authentic by two pro-Communist British journalists, Robert Wilton of the *London Times* and Victor Marsden of the *Morning Post*. In an introduction to eighteen articles, Marsden cited his own translation of the Protocols in 1920 to declare that the Jews were carrying out the world-control plan "with steadfast purpose." They were "creating wars and revolutions" in order to "destroy the white Gentile race, that the Jews may seize the power during the resulting chaos and rule with their claimed superior intelligence over the remaining races of the world, as kings over slaves."

The following year, Arabs in Palestine and Syria used the Protocols to stir up resentment against Jewish settlers in Palestine, claiming that they were the spearhead of an "international Jewish conspiracy," led by Zionists to establish a Jewish state. The Protocols have continued to be used as a basis of Arab resistance to "the Zionist entity" (Israel). According to the Jewish Anti-Defamation League, scores of books on political subjects published in Arabic "were either based on the Protocols or quoted in them." As evidence of the acceptance of the Protocols in the Muslim world as genuine, the ADL noted that they were treated as legitimate in a speech by a Jordanian delegate to the United Nations in 1980, and that in 1987 an Iranian embassy official in Brazil circulated the Protocols and said that it "belongs to the history of the world."

In the United States, the Protocols have been cited by anti-Semitic groups, including the Ku Klux Klan, neo-Nazi organizations, white supremacists, and Black Muslims. In 1920, automaker Henry Ford's anti-Semitic publication, *The Dearborn Independent*, presented a series of articles based on the Protocols titled "The International Jew: the World's Foremost Problem." During the rise of the Nazis in Germany, and throughout the reign of Hitler, the Protocols were an integral part of the anti-Jewish campaign that led to the "Final Solution" and Holocaust.

During the 1980s in the United States, the Protocols were sold as anti-Jewish propaganda by Muslim student associations at Wayne State University in Michigan and the University of California at Berkeley. They were also sold at an Islamic exhibition in Stockholm,

Sweden, and in London's Park Mosque, where recruiting was carried out on behalf of al Qaeda.

In a message of greeting to a world seminar on the centenary of the first publication of the Protocols, held in Venice, Italy, in December 2002, the director-general of UNESCO (the United Nations Educational, Social, and Cultural Organization), Koichiro Matsura, told the delegates, "It is a bitter lesson of history that still today, one hundred years after it was created by the Russian Czarist secret police and despite its being exposed over and over again as a forgery, the document known as The Protocols of the Elders of Zion continues to exercise its terrible power as an instrument of anti-Semitism. It is instructive because it demonstrates yet again that, given the necessary mind frame, people can be induced to believe what has been formally refuted, which can then be used to justify the most unspeakable atrocities."

100

THE MEN WHO REALLY
RUN THE WORLD

While history records that in every era of the human saga suspicions stirred and thrived among ordinary people that a small group of elite men met in secret to control world events and direct the future, no place on the globe has seen the birth of as many "conspiracy theories" as the United States in the years following World War II.

With the domination of the countries of eastern Europe by the Soviet Union's Red Army following the defeat of Nazi Germany and the beginning of the Cold War, investigations of "Communist subversion and infiltration" of the U.S. government and American industries, including motion pictures, created a sense that the United States had become obsessed with uncovering sinister people cooking up dastardly plots. Along with the Cold War came the formation of organizations for the purpose of containing the threat posed by "international Communism." But in the view of many Americans, these groups went far beyond stopping the spread of Communism.

They were seen as organizations whose purpose was the economic, political, and social domination of the world. According to believers in a scheme by powerful men to run the world, the organizations at the heart of these "conspiracies" are the Council on Foreign Relations (founded in 1921), the Trilateral Commission (1973), and the Bilderberg Group (1954).

Each has been accused of plotting to set up a "new world order" in which the United Nations, the World Court, World Trade Organization, and other international bodies have been established to abolish the sovereignty of nations and place the United States under the control of international corporations and world financial institutions. Membership of these groups consists of the "elites" of politics, industry, and commerce; leaders of the communications and news media; intellectuals; and the military. They have been described frequently as a "Great Right Wing Conspiracy."

People who believe in the existence of this new world order conspiracy offer as proof an annual gathering of America's "elites" at a 2,700-acre, redwood forest "camp" at Monte Rio, California, called Bohemian Grove. A private, all-male club founded in 1872, it has evolved into an association of the rich and powerful, including U.S. presidents, cabinet officials, directors and officers of corporations, bankers and financiers, military contractors, leaders of the oil industry and nuclear power companies, and journalists.

While those who attend Bohemian Grove conclaves dismiss such motions and assert that the two-week retreats involve nothing sinister and are simply a respite from the ardors of their demanding jobs, conspiracy seekers and alarmists fear that they are "an informational clearing house for the elite" and a threat to Democracy. An Internet website of the Bohemian Grove Action Network expressed a fear that has lurked in the minds of ordinary people throughout world history: "When powerful people work together, they become more powerful."

Sources

1. **Satan and Adam and Eve**. Holy Bible, Old Testament, Genesis 2: 2–3.

2. **The Greatest Conspiracy Ever Known**. Holy Bible, New Testament. Gospels of Matthew, Mark, Luke, and John.

3. **Declaration of Independence**. Ellis, Joseph J. *Founding Brothers: The Revolutionary Generation*. New York: Knopf, 2000.

4. **Japan's Sneak Attack on Pearl Harbor**. Hoyt, Edwin P. *Yamamoto: The Man Who Planned the Attack on Pearl Harbor*. New York: The Lyons Press, 2001.

5. **Al Qaeda**. Jenkins, Brian Michael, and Christopher Pike. *Countering Al Qaeda: An Appreciation of the Situation and Suggestions for Strategy*. Arlington, VA: The Rand Corporation, 2002.

6. **Lenin and the Bolsheviks**. Service, Robert. *Lenin: A Biography*. New York: Macmillan, 2000.

7. **Soviet Theft of the Atomic Bomb**. Roberts, Sam. *The Brother: The Untold Story of Atomic Spy David Greenglass and How He Sent His Sister, Ethel Rosenberg, to the Electric Chair*. New York: Random House, 2001.

8. **The "Final Solution" and the Holocaust**. Roseman, Mark. *The Wannsee Conference and the Final Solution: A Reconsideration*. New York: Metropolitan Books, 2002.

9. **Assassination of Abraham Lincoln**. Bishop, Jim. *The Day Lincoln Was Shot*. New York: Harper & Brothers, 1955.

10. **Soviet Missiles in Cuba**. Huchthausen, Peter. *October Fury*. New York: John Wiley & Sons, 2002.

11. **Assassination of John F. Kennedy**. Bishop, Jim. *The Day Kennedy Was Shot*. New York: Funk & Wagnalls, 1968.

12. **Assassination of Martin Luther King Jr.** Posner, Gerald. *Killing the Dream: James Earl Ray and the Assassination of Martin Luther King, Jr.* New York: Random House, 1998.

13. **Who Killed Bobby Kennedy?** Flaber, William, Philip H. Metausin, and Samuel Dash. *Shadow Play: The Murder of Robert F. Kennedy, the Trial of Sirhan Sirhan, and the Failure of American Justice.* New York: St. Martin's Press, 1997.

14. **Assassination of Archduke Ferdinand**. Gilfond, Henry L. *The Black Hand at Sarajevo.* New York: Macmillan Publishing Company, 1975.

15. **The Mafia**. Capeci, Jerry. *The Complete Idiot's Guide to the Mafia.* Indianapolis, IN: Alpha Books, 2001.

16. **The KGB**. Barron, John. *KGB Today: The Hidden Hand.* New York: Readers Digest Press, 1983.

17. **Death of Stalin**. Bortoli, Georges. *The Death of Stalin.* New York: Praeger Publishers, 1975.

18. **Capture of Adolph Eichmann**. Harel, Isser. *The House on Garibaldi Street.* New York: Viking Press, 1975.

19. **U-2 Spy Plane**. Beschloss, Michael R. *May-Day: Eisenhower, Khrushchev, and the U-2 Affair.* New York: Harper, 1986.

20. **Watergate**. Bernstein, Carl, and Bob Woodward. *All the President's Men.* New York: Simon & Schuster, 1974.

21. **Downfall of Nikita Khrushchev**. Taubman, William. *Khrushchev: The Man and His Era.* New York: W. W. Norton and Company, 2003.

22. **Iran-Contra**. Walsh, Lawrence E. *Firewall: The Iran-Contra Conspiracy and Cover-up.* New York: W. W. Norton and Company, 1998.

23. **Irish Republican Army**. Moloney, Ed. *The Secret History of the IRA.* New York: W. W. Norton and Company, 2002.

24. **The Hitler-Stalin Pact of 1939**. Read, Anthony, and David Fisher. *Deadly Embrace: Hitler, Stalin, and the Nazi-Soviet Pact, 1939–1941.* New York: W. W. Norton and Company, 1998.

25. **The Reichstag Fire**. Toland, John. *Adolf Hitler: The Definitive Biography.* New York: Anchor, 1992.

26. **The Plot to Kill Hitler**. Shirer, William L. *The Rise and Fall of the Third Reich.* New York: Crescent Books, 1994.

27. **Bodyguard of Lies**. Brown, Anthony Cave. *Bodyguard of Lies.* New York: The Lyons Press, 2002.

28. **Assassination of South Vietnamese President Diem**. Hammer, Ellen J. *A Death in November: America in 1963*. New York: E.P. Dutton, 1987.

29. **The Brink's Robbery**. Behn, Noel. *Big Stick-up at Brink's!* New York: Putnam Publishing Group, 1977.

30. **The Great Train Robbery**. Reid, Piers Paul, et al. *The Train Robbers*. New York: Avon Books, 1978.

31. **Assassination of Julius Caesar**. Parenti, Michael. *The Assassination of Julius Caesar: A People's History of Ancient Rome*. New York: New Press, 2003.

32. **Weatherman Underground**. Viorst, Milton. *Fire in the Streets: America in the 1960s*. New York: Simon & Schuster, 1981.

33. **Teapot Dome Scandal**. Noggle, Burl. *Teapot Dome: Oil and Politics in the 1920s*. New York: W.W. Norton and Company, 1995.

34. **Attack on Pope John Paul II**. Bernstein, Carl, and Marco Politi. *His Holiness: John Paul II and the Hidden History of Our Time*. New York: Penguin USA, 1997.

35. **Oklahoma City Federal Building Bombing**. Jones, Stephen and Peter Israel. *Others Unknown: The Oklahoma City Bombing Case and Conspiracy*. New York: Public Affairs, 2001.

36. **St. Valentine's Day Massacre**. Helmer, William J., and Arthur J. Bilek. *The St. Valentine's Day Massacre: The Untold Story of the Gangland Bloodbath That Brought Down Al Capone*. Nashville, TN: Cumberland House Publishing, 2003.

37. **Birmingham Church Bombing**. Eskew, Glenn T. *But For Birmingham: The Local and National Movements in the Civil Rights Struggle*. Chapel Hill: University of North Carolina Press, 1997.

38. **Ku Klux Klan**. Chalmers, David Mark. *Hooded Americanism: The History of the Ku Klux Klan*. Chapel Hill, N.C.: Duke University Press, 1987.

39. **The Manson Family**. Bugliosi, Vincent, and Curt Gentry. *Helter Skelter: The True Story of the Manson Murders*. New York: W. W. Norton & Company, 1994.

40. **Bombing of the King David Hotel**. Begin, Menachem. *The Revolt*. Jerusalem: Steimatzky's Agency Limited, 1952.

41. **Yasser Arafat and the Palestine Liberation Organization**. Rubin, Barry M. *The Transformation of Palestinian Politics: From Revolution to State Building*. Cambridge, MA: Harvard University Press, 1993.

42. ***Achille Lauro* Hijacking**. Cassese, Antonio. *Terrorism, Politics, and Law: The* Achille Lauro *Affairs*. Oxford, England: Blackwell Publishing, 1989.

43. **Nazi Submarine Spies**. Breuer, William B. *Hitler's Undercover War: The Nazi Espionage Invasion of the USA*. New York: St. Martin's Press, 1989.

44. **Murders of Three Civil Rights Workers in Mississippi**. Cagan, Seth, and Philip Dray. *We Are Not Afraid: The Story of Goodman, Schwerner, and Chaney and the Civil Rights Campaign for Mississippi*. New York: MacMillan Publishing Company, 1988.

45. **Attempts to Assassinate Charles de Gaulle**. Demaret, Pierre. *Target De Gaulle: The Thirty-one Attempts to Assassinate the General*. New York: The Dial Press, 1975.

46. **Death of Princess Diana**. Morton, Andrew. *Diana: Her True Story*. New York: Simon & Schuster, 1997.

47. **Jack the Ripper**. Rumbelow, Donald. *The Complete Jack the Ripper*. London: W. H. Allen & Co. Ltd., 1975.

48. **The Kim Philby Spy Ring**. Brown, Anthony Cave. *Treason in the Blood: H. St. John Philby, Kim Philby, and the Spy Case of the Century*. Boston: Houghton Mifflin, 1994.

49. **The OSS**. Moon, Tom. *The Grim and Savage Game: The OSS and U.S. Covert Operations in World War II*. New York: DaCapo Press, 2000.

50. **Bay of Pigs**. Wyden, Peter. *Bay of Pigs: The Untold Story*. New York: Vintage/Ebury, 1979.

51. **The Assassination of Egyptian President Anwar Sadat**. Heikal, Mohamed, and Muhammad Hasanayn Haykal. *Autumn of Fury: The Assassination of Sadat*. New York: Random House, 1983.

52. **The Benedict Arnold Plot**. Fritz, Jean. *Traitor: the Case of Benedict Arnold*. New York: G.P. Putnam's Sons, 1981

53. **Execution of Queen Anne Boleyn**. Warnicke, Retha M. *The Rise and Fall of Anne Boleyn: Family Politics at the Court of Henry VIII*. Cambridge, England: Cambridge University Press, 1991.

54. **Attempted Deposing of Queen Elizabeth I**. Weir, Alison. *Life of Elizabeth I.* New York: Ballantine Books, 1998.

55. **The Gunpowder Plot**. Fraser, Antonia. *The Story of the Gunpowder Plot.* New York: Doubleday, 1997.

56. **The Plot to Overthrow Mikhail Gorbachev**. Sheehy, Gail. *The Man Who Changed the World: Mikhail S. Gorbachev.* New York: Harper Collins, 1990.

57. **Richard III's Murder of the Two Princes**. Weir, Alison. *The Princes in the Tower.* New York: Ballantine Books, 1994.

58. **Freemasonry**. Ridley, Jasper. *The Freemasons.* New York: Arcade Books, 2002.

59. **The Aaron Burr Conspiracy**. Melton, Buckner F., Jr. *Aaron Burr: Conspiracy to Treason.* New York: John Wiley & Sons, 2001.

60. **Assassination of Huey Long**. Hair, William Ivy. *The Kingfish and His Realm: The Life and Times of Huey P. Long.* Baton Rouge, LA: Louisiana State University Press, 1991.

61. **Assassination of Emperor Caligula**. Barrett, A. *A. Caligula: The Corruption of Power.* New Haven, CT: Yale University Press, 1998.

62. **Assassination of Leon Trotsky**. Serge, Victor, and Natalia Ivanova Sedova Trotskaia. *The Life and Death of Leon Trotsky.* New York: Basic Books, 1975.

63. **CIA Overthrow of the Government of Iran**. Kinzer, Stephen. *All the Shah's Men: An American Coup and the Roots of Middle East Terrorism.* New York: John Wiley & Sons, 2003.

64. **The Lindbergh Baby Kidnapping**. Waller, George. *Kidnap: The Story of the Lindbergh Case.* New York: The Dial Press, 1961.

65. **The Barker Gang**. Winter, Robert. *Mean Men: The Sons of Ma Barker.* Danbury, CT. Rutledge Books, Inc., 2000.

66. **Burke and Hare**. Townsend, John. *Burke and Hare: The Bodysnatchers,* London: Nelson Thomas (Publishers) Ltd., 2002

67. **Murder, Inc.** Turkus, Burton, and Sid Feder. *Murder, Inc.: The Story of "The Syndicate."* New York: Farrar, Straus, and Young, 1951.

68. **The Night of the Long Knives**. Gallo, Max. *The Night of the Long Knives.* New York: Da Capo Press, 1997.

69. **Assassination of Lord Louis Mountbatten**. Ziegler, Philip. *Mountbatten: The Official Biography*. London: Phoenix Press, 2001.

70. **The Alger Hiss Case**. Weinstein, Allen. *Perjury: The Hiss-Chambers Case*. New York: Alfred A. Knopf, 1978.

71. **The Hollywood Ten**. Ceplair, Larry, and Steven Englund. *Inquisition in Hollywood: Politics in the Film Community: 1930–1960*. Champaign, Ill: University of Illinois Press, 2003.

72. **The Beltway Snipers**. Moose, Charles A., and Charles Fleming. *Three Weeks in October: The Manhunt for the Serial Sniper*. New York: E. P. Dutton, 2003.

73. **The Menendez Brothers**. Soble, Ron, and John Johnson. *Blood Brothers*. New York: Signet, 1994.

74. **Murder of Malcolm X**. Goldman, Peter. *Death and Life of Malcolm X*. Champaign, Ill: University of Illinois Press, 1984.

75. **Aliens Among Us**. Patton, Phil. *Dreamland: Travels Inside the Secret World of Roswell and Area 51*. New York: The Random House Publishing Group, 1999.

76. **The Death of Marilyn Monroe**. Guiles, Fred Lawrence. *Legend: The Life and Death of Marilyn Monroe*. Lanham, MD: Rowman & Littlefield Publishers, Inc., 1991.

77. **Symbionese Liberation Army**. Boulton, David. *The Making of Tania Hearst*. Bergenfield, NJ.: New American Library, 1975.

78. **Murder at the Mall**. Gribetz, Kenneth, and H. Paul Jeffers. *Murder Along the Way: A Prosecutor's Personal Account of Fighting Violent Crime in the Suburbs*. New York: Pharos Books, 1989.

79. **Walker Spy Ring**. Earley, Pete. *Family of Spies: Inside the John Walker Spy Ring*. New York: Bantam Books, 1988.

80. **Enron**. Watkins, Sherron, and Mimi Swartz. *Power Failure: The Inside Story of the Collapse of Enron*. New York: Doubleday, 2003.

81. **Rubout of Bugsy Siegel**. Jennings, Dean. *We Only Kill Each Other*. New York: Fawcett Crest Books, 1968.

82. **Leopold and Loeb**. Higdon, Hal. *Leopold & Loeb: The Crime of the Century*. Champagne, Ill: University of Illinois Press, 1999.

83. **Murder of Rasputin**. Moynahan, Brian. *Rasputin: The Saint Who Sinned*. New York: Random House, 1997.

84. **Murder of Thomas À Becket**. Winston, Richard. *Thomas Becket: The Life and Times of Thomas Becket*. New York: Alfred A. Knopf, 1967.

85. **American Hostages in Iran**. Christopher, Warren, Richard J. Davis, and Gary Sick. *American Hostages in Iran: The Conduct of a Crisis*. New Haven: Yale University Press, 1985.

86. **Assassination of Rafael Trujillo**. Espaillat, Arturo R. *Trujillo: The Last Caesar*. Chicago: Henry Regnery, 1963.

87. **The Black Hand**. Grice, Frederick. *The Black Hand Gang*. Oxford, England: Oxford University Press, 1970.

88. **Rubout of Paul Castellano**. O'Brien, Joseph F., and Andris Kurnis. *Boss of Bosses: The Fall of the Godfather: The FBI and Paul Castellano*. New York: Simon & Schuster, 1991.

89. **The James Brothers**. Love, Robertus. *The Life and Times of Jesse James*. New York: Blue Ribbon Books, 1940.

90. **The Falcon and the Snowman**. Lindsey, Robert. *The Falcon and the Snowman: A True Story of Friendship and Espionage*. New York: Simon & Schuster, 1980.

91. **Sacco and Vanzetti**. Ehrman, Herbert B. *The Case That Will Not Die*. Boston: Beacon Press, 1969.

92. **Ruth Snyder and Judd Gray**. Cook, Fred J. *The Girl in the Death Cell*. New York: Fawcett, 1953.

93. **The Purple Gang**. Kavieff, Paul. *The Purple Gang: Organized Crime in Detroit: 1910–1945*. New York: Barricade Books, 2000.

94. **The Tongs**. Asbury, Herbert. *The Gangs of New York*. Garden City, NY: Garden City Publishing Co., Inc., 1927.

95. **German-American Bund**. Canedy, Susan. *America's Nazis: A Democratic Dilemma: A History of the German-American Bund*. Menlo Park, CA: Markgraf Publications Group, 1990.

96. **Plot to Assassinate President Truman**. McCullough, David. *Truman*. New York: Simon & Schuster, 1992.

97. **The Billionaire Boys Club**. Horton, Sue. *The Billionaire Boys Club*. New York: St. Martin's Press, 1990.

98. **Fixing the 1919 World Series**. Asinof, Eliot. *Eight Men Out: The Black Sox and the 1919 World Series*. New York: Holt, Rinehart, and Winston, 1963.

99. **Protocols of the Elders of Zion**. Segel, Binjamin W., and Richard
     S. Levy. *A Lie and a Libel: The History of the Protocols of the Elders of
     Zion*. Lincoln, NE: University of Nebraska Press, 1996.

100. **The Men Who Really Run the World**. Ross, Robert Gaylon, Sr.
     *Who's Who of the Elite: Members of the Bilderbergs, Council on Foreign
     Relations, & Trilateral Commission*. Spicewood, TX: RIE, 1996.

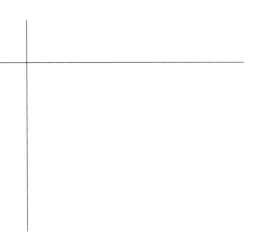

ABOUT THE AUTHOR

A broadcast journalist for more than three decades, H. Paul Jeffers has published more than fifty works of fiction and non-fiction. Before becoming a full-time author, he was a TV news producer and reporter in Boston, producer/writer/editor for the ABC and NBC radio networks, and is the only person to hold the position of news director at both of New York City's all-news radio stations. He has taught writing and journalism at New York University, the City College of New York, Syracuse University and California State University at Long Beach.

Among his non-fiction works are *Disaster by the Bay: The Great San Francisco Earthquake and Fire*; *The Good Cigar*; and *High Spirits* (The Lyons Press); *The 100 Greatest Heroes*, and biographies of Theodore Roosevelt, Grover Cleveland, Mayor Fiorello La Guardia, Diamond Jim Brady, Eddie Rickenbacker, and 1950s movie star Sal Mineo.

He lives in New York City.